Society and Psyche

Society and Psyche

Social Theory and the Unconscious Dimension of the Social

Kanakis Leledakis

BERG PUBLISHERS
Oxford • Washington, D.C.

First published in 1995 by
Berg Publishers Limited
Editorial offices:
150 Cowley Road, Oxford, OX4 1JJ, UK
13950 Park Center Road, Herndon, VA 22071, USA

Library of Congress Cataloging-in-Publication Data

A catalogue record for this book is available from the Library of Congress

British Library Cataloguing-in-Publication Data

A catalogue record for this book is available from the British Library

ISBN 1 85973 062 0 (Cloth)
1 85973 067 1 (Paper)

Printed in the United Kingdom by WBC Bookbinders, Bridgend,
Mid-Glamorgan

To the memory of my mother

Contents

Contents

Introduction

The present work is an essay on social theory. It argues for the existence of necessary and unavoidable elements of indeterminacy inherent in both the social and the individual, elements inhibiting any full determination and accounting for the open and thus potentially creative nature of human action and thought, of society and history.

In proclaiming the impossibility of any full determination, however, the study does not follow the manner of an *a priori*, essentialist or transcendental theorization, against which it specifically argues. The elements of indeterminacy are located within a detailed analysis of the ways the social influences the psyche and is reproduced through individual action and behaviour. Pivotal in the analysis is the recognition of the central role the unconscious, as a specific and irreducible level of psychical functioning, plays in this reproduction. Indeed, theorizing the existence of an 'unconscious dimension of the social' is crucial for establishing the openness and indeterminacy argued for.

The relevance of a specific interpretation of psychoanalytic theory for a theory of the social is thus highlighted. At the same time, a synthesis between approaches emphasizing the open nature of the social and those focussing on the reproduction of the social through the individual is effected. Moreover, the theorization advanced allows an alternative, and more satisfactory, way of addressing the central social theoretical questions of agency and historical change, while offering elements for a theory of practice.

The argument is presented in three steps. In part 1 different social theoretical approaches are analyzed and evaluated. Rejecting purely epistemological approaches, it is concluded that structural/objectivist models of the social, such as those outlined in the early work of Parsons or in a modified Althusserian scheme, avoid the pitfalls of both individualistic and teleological theories. They face, however, a major impasse. They cannot satisfactorily supply a theory of active agency and autonomy on the part of the social actor and they cannot theorize historical change, the reason being their conceptualization of the social as closed and fully determined structural entities. Overcoming these problems while retaining an overall structural orientation is a starting point for the remainder of the study.

In part 2 two distinct alternatives to structural/objectivist approaches are analyzed. It is argued that the move from 'structure' to 'structuration' – the production and reproduction of the social through social actors – exemplified by the work of Giddens and Bourdieu is necessary, but in itself it remains programmatic and insufficient. On the other hand we have a line of thought that presents social structural entities as open, identifiable as evolving from the general statements of Derrida to the specific theories of the social presented by Laclau and Mouffe and, in a more developed way, by Castoriadis. However, while this approach provides an alternative to a closed conceptualization of social structures, the level at which this 'openness' should be seen as operating remains unclarified. The danger of reintroducing a transcendental level behind the positivity of the social is present. To avoid this, a promising possibility presents itself: to locate the theorization of indeterminacy *within* the processes of the reproduction of the social through the individual, combining thus a theorization of the social as open with a theory of structuration.

Part 3 aims to provide such a synthesis. An extensive analysis of psychoanalytic theory in general and of Freud in particular allows the elaboration of a theory of social influences on the psyche and of social reproduction at its most elementary level, that of the individual. This reproduction occurs at the level of consciousness, but also at the level of the unconscious. We can affirm, moreover, the existence of an 'unconscious dimension of the social', meaningful and yet not reducible to either nature or consciousness. The specific mode of being of the unconscious implies that this dimension can never be fully determined or known and that points of indeterminacy are necessarily inherent in any reproduction through the unconscious. These points, combined with the indeterminacy stemming from the relative autonomy of the conscious, rational ego, ensure that the processes of social reproduction through the psyche are always open and indeterminate. Thus the social can be theorized as open without any reference to a transcendental level while the importance of the unconscious and of its specific mode of being for a theory of the social is highlighted.

The questions of agency and historical change can now be approached more satisfactorily. Because of the indeterminacy in the social determination of the individual, a deep, fundamental level of social determination can be asserted alongside levels of autonomy. The theorization of 'openness' advanced allows also the possibility of theorizing the emergence of the radically new in history as always inherent in social reproduction without resorting to teleological or combinatorial models. Moreover, since social practice is influenced directly by 'meaningful' unconscious elements, its specificity as a level with its own 'meaning', irreducible to conscious ideas guiding action, can be asserted. Finally, because of the existence of the 'unconscious dimension of the social', the impossibility of a full, objective knowledge of the social and the necessity of a radical hermeneutic approach can be claimed.

As is evident, the arguments advanced are gradually constructed out of elements located in the work of classical and modern theorists. Perhaps a more straightforward and less laborious way could have been followed. There are, however, compensations: they include an opportunity to appreciate the profound insights of the great theorists, sometimes in contradiction of their principal line of thought; a reminder that the thesis of the present work was prefigured and partially theorized long ago, without having been presented in its present form though; and, finally, an indication of the fruitfulness of dialogue between a variety of discourses and approaches.

The present study is question-oriented. It does not follow any specific paradigm and draws insights and elements from divergent approaches. This applies also to elements from discourses in – academically – distinct 'disciplines'. Advances in social theory – as in any field of scientific inquiry – necessitate starting from specific questions rather than from artificially-defined disciplinary areas. Even if these questions are formulated within a specific discourse, if they are followed sufficiently far disciplinary boundaries are bound to be transcended in the ever widening spiral of enquiry.

Having said that, certain approaches and certain authors have been more significant in the shaping of the present work. The relative weight particular authors carry in the overall synthesis will be evident. However, I would like to pay tribute to the work of C. Castoriadis, which has not only been pivotal in the context of the present study, but was also crucial in creating – long ago – the impetus and stimulus for such a study. Of course, any borrowing or any partial use of different approaches and theoretical works, always implies a certain violence towards them, involving interpretations, which can sometimes be controversial. The only criterion for the validity of such interpretations is the validity of the argument they are used to construct.

The aim of the present work is to provide explanatory mechanisms – theoretical principles upon which an alternative way of approaching certain central themes of social theory can be based. However, the relatively abstract level at which the analysis operates should not be seen as introducing *a priori* speculation divorced from concrete empirical material. Although such material is not directly used, it forms the background on which the theoretical elaborations proposed become meaningful. A division of labour sometimes makes necessary the separation of theoretical enquiry, in which greater rigour can be applied, from studies dealing with empirical material as such. Since what a high level of abstraction gains in generality it loses in detail and specificity and vice versa, research at different levels of abstraction is necessary if a more complete understanding is to be produced.

Although the argument of the study is presented in a seemingly atemporal manner, it bears, naturally, the imprint of a historical conjuncture. It marks a point in the gradual erosion of the belief in an ultimate (and absolute) rationality of society and history, a belief that, in one form or another, had been a dominant (if not *the* dominant) view of social thought over the past two centuries. The recognition and theorization of the limits of such rationality is a central guiding line of the present work. However, unlike a certain 'post-modernism', the indication of these limits is not seen as implying an all pervasive relativity. The relevance and significance of consciousness and rationality is retained, alongside the theorization of the elements that transcend and limit them.

An earlier version of the text was submitted as a doctoral thesis at the University of London. I want to thank Professors Paul Hirst and Nicos Mouzelis for their help and support. Given the general mistrust of theoretical work that characterizes British academia, they proved to be a refreshing exception. The help and encouragement of Professor Hirst, in particular, was instrumental in the completing of the thesis. The financial support of the Greek State Scholarship Foundation and of my parents made this work possible; Monica's love and patience made it bearable. It is dedicated to the memory of my mother who died while the final manuscript was being prepared. I hope she would have been proud of it.

London, December 1993
Athens, May 1995

Part I

Posing the Questions

–1–

Overture: A Return to Marx

Marx can be seen as a double landmark in the history of social thought. A landmark of the beginnings of this thought – creating moreover what Foucault has called an entire 'field of discursivity'[1] – and hence very much a representative of his epoch. And yet, paradoxically, in his contradictions and ambivalence, also a landmark of importance in today's crossroads. In a sense, therefore, a return to Marx is a paradigmatic way to pose certain themes of contemporary relevance while at the same time indicating which theoretical assumptions are to be discarded and which retained.

The German Ideology is the first, and in many ways the most consistent exposition of Marx and Engels' 'materialism'. This 'materialism' is proposed as an alternative to the idealism of the Young Hegelians who 'consider conceptions, thoughts, ideas, in fact all the products of consciousness, to which they attribute an independent existence, as the real chains of men'.[2] In contrast, Marx and Engels want to begin from the premise 'of real individuals, their activity and the material conditions under which they live, both those which they find already existing and those produced by their activity'[3] and they assert, in the famous passage, that 'the production of ideas, of conceptions, of consciousness, is at first directly interwoven with the material activity and the material intercourse of men, the language of real life. Conceiving, thinking, the mental intercourse of men, appear at this stage as the direct efflux of their material behaviour.'[4]

We have, therefore, 'the mental intercourse', 'mental production', 'consciousness', 'thinking', 'ideas', 'conceptions', in opposition to 'the material intercourse', 'the activity of real individuals', 'the

---

1. M. Foucault, 'What is an Author?' in P. Rabinow (ed.), *The Foucault Reader*, Harmondsworth, 1986, p. 114.
2. K. Marx and F. Engels, *The German Ideology* (1846), C.J. Arthur (ed.), London, 1974, p. 41.
3. Ibid., p. 42.
4. Ibid., p. 47.

material behaviour'. What is the nature of this opposition? Marx and Engels do not simply invert a causal chain, replacing the Young Hegelians' assertion that ideas determine people's 'real life' with the assertion that it is this 'real life' that determines ideas and consciousness, while retaining a sort of equivalence between the two levels. If thoughts, ideas, consciousness and the like reflect, more or less accurately, the 'materiality' of real life, the Young Hegelians' claim has simply to be completed: it is not enough to change what people think, to combat their unhappiness. People must also, and primarily, change their real life, their 'actual material intercourse'. However, as long as the two levels are seen as two sides of the same coin, it is not particularly relevant which of the two is considered as the determinant one. Since a change in material life implies a change of ideas, given an equivalence of the two, a change in ideas implies – and expresses, on the level of thought – a change in material life. The assertion that the real is reducible to the ideal is by no means affected by a reversal of the proposition while retaining an equivalential assertion.

Marx and Engels do not retain this equivalential assertion. The repudiation of the mental intercourse is made on the name of a material intercourse that is precisely not available to the participating individuals as an idea or consciousness. Marx and Engels' 'real life' is in disjuncture with the thoughts the very persons they live it have. The 'material intercourse' and 'real life' are reflected in thought, consciousness or ideas only in a distorted way (except in specific historical circumstances). Thus the determining character of the material level cannot be deciphered through an analysis of the ideal one. What people think and what they do represent two different modalities, the truth of which cannot be deciphered reciprocally.

What is then the 'truth' of the determinant level, the material one? What is the ontological status of the 'real life of men' as distinct from the 'mental' and what access do we have to the former? We can reconstruct Marx and Engels' answer in two consecutive steps: first, separating this 'material level' not only from 'ideas' but also from 'nature' and considering it as indicating what we may call a 'level' of the social. Second, presenting this social level as emanating from and reducible to the rationality of labour as a transhistorical human attribute reflected in the development of history.

Marx and Engels make immediately clear that the 'material intercourse', which is the 'language of real life', corresponds to 'production': '[Men] begin to distinguish themselves from animals as soon as they begin to produce their means of subsistence, a step which is conditioned by their physical organization.'[5] Yet the level of production is not seen as directly determined by this 'physical organization' within which production is carried out: 'By producing their means of subsistence men are *indirectly* producing their actual material life.'[6] Production is only indirectly reducible to the natural environment. Marx and Engels' analysis is focussed on production while the natural environment, as also the biological nature of man, remain on the background as limits rather than as the actual determinants of production, limits which are acknowledged but not discussed. While imposing 'definite conditions'[7] the material/natural environment is not determining, in a reductive way, the 'real essence of man'. The mode of production ('mode' referring simply to the form of production) is something more than a reflection of these natural limits: 'The mode of production must not be considered simply as being the production of the physical existence of the individuals. Rather it is a definite form of activity of these individuals, a definite form of expressing their life, a definite mode of life on their part. As individuals express their life, so they are.'[8]

Production as 'a definite mode of life', is precisely a characteristically human activity, not a reflection of nature. The counterposition of production, therefore, as 'material activity and material intercourse of men', to 'forms of consciousness', is not a distinction between nature and thought. The term 'matter' retains its traditional philosophical meaning, as the outside, the negation of thought, what is either opaque to it or only partially penetrable. However, the 'material' for Marx and Engels, while still the outside of thought, is not reducible to a closed, mute and determinant nature. It refers rather to a level of activity specifically human: production. Hence we have a threefold distinction:

nature -- production -- thought

a distinction in which a discontinuity is implied between each of the three terms. We could indicate as 'social' the level that production defines, while recognizing that 'thought' is also social but of a

5. Ibid., p. 42.
6. Ibid., emphasis added.
7. Ibid., p. 47.
8. Ibid., p. 42.
9. Traditional references to Marx and Engels' materialism tend to concentrate on the irreducibility of nature to thought, thus obscuring the specificity of the level of production that is the primary aim of Marx and Engels' discussion. Production, while differentiated from thought, is equally differentiated from nature. Such interpretations effect a naturalistic reduction of the level of production that is in no way present in Marx and Engels (an example is S. Timpanaro, *On Materialism*, London, 1975).

modality somehow 'different' from that of 'production'.[9]

In Marx's later writings the distinction between nature and production becomes more explicit and clear. Instead of the variations of the term 'intercourse'[10] which we have in *The German Ideology*, the term 'relations of production' is introduced in opposition to the 'forces of production', the latter referring to the actual natural/environmental/technological elements. In the famous words of the '1859 Preface':

> In the social production of their life, men enter into definite relations, that are indispensable and independent of their will, relations of production which correspond to a definite stage in the development of their material productive forces. The sum total of these relations of production constitutes the economic structure of society, the real foundation, on which rises a legal and political superstructure and to which correspond definite forms of social consciousness.[11]

This passage is revealing. It clearly dissociates the actual productive 'forces' from the 'relations' of production, the superstructure, and the latter from the 'forms of social consciousness'. Thus the three levels can be presented as:

```
                    forces of
                    production
nature (natural - - - - - - - - - - - - - relations - - - - - - - political - - - - - - - thoughts,
environment,                              of production      and legal              ideas
biological                                                  superstructure
human nature)

natural
level - - - - - - - - - - - - - - - - / - - - - - social level I - - - - - - - - - - / - - - social level II (level
                                                                                              of consciousness)
```

Figure 1

The forces of production are the mediating element between the level of nature and the relations of production. These relations, together with the 'political and legal superstructure' are in turn separate from the 'forms of consciousness'. It is this intermediate level that can be termed the 'social level I' as distinct from and not reducible

---

10. *Verkehr* was rendered as 'intercourse', *Verkehrsform* as form of intercourse, *Verkehrsweise* as mode of intercourse, and *Verkehrsverhältnisse* as relations or conditions of intercourse (see the editor's note in *The German Ideology*, p. 42).

11. K. Marx, preface to 'A contribution to a critique of political economy' (1859), usually referred to as the '1859 Preface'. The translation here is in K. Marx and F. Engels, *Selected Works*, 2 vols, London, 1953, vol. 1, p. 329.

to the – also social – level of consciousness (which can be designated as social level II).

Once a specificity is assigned to this 'first' level of the social, however, the question of how it is to be theorized arises. Since the mode of production is the determinant instance of this level, it is through an analysis of the modality of production that its modality has to be sought. We can see Marx's subsequent work as just such an attempt to define this modality of production.

Early on one possibility is ruled out: that of conceiving production as the result of interaction between individuals, in the manner, for example, of classical political economy. The repeated attacks of Marx against Robinsonades are well known:

> The solitary and isolated hunter or fisherman, who serves A. Smith and Ricardo as a starting point, is one of the unimaginative fantasies of the eighteenth century romances [. . .] No more is Rousseau's social contract, which by means of a contract establishes a relationship and connection between subjects that are by nature independent [. . .] The prophets of eighteenth century saw the individual not as a historical result but as the starting point of history; not as something evolving in the course of history but posited by nature.[12]

The historicity of the individual is continuously stressed. Not only do individuals not determine production through their interaction, but their very individuality is a historical product: 'Man is only individualised through the process of history.'[13]

Advancing on the rejection of individualism, Marx in his analysis of the capitalist relations of production in *Capital* specifically sees the individual as part of the greater structural whole of production.[14] Capitalist production is a structured whole that incorporates commodities, money and capital as well as capitalists and workers, all connected together in a circular relationship, and in a continuous flux. The elements of the system acquire their significance within the totality of the system (anticipating thus a relational definition of structure):

> In themselves money and commodities are no more capital than are the means of production and of subsistence. They want transforming into capital. But this transformation itself can only take place under certain

12. K. Marx, 'General introduction to Grundrisse' (1857), usually referred to as the '1857 Introduction'. The text here is in the appendix to Marx and Engels, *The German Ideology*, p. 124.
13. K. Marx, *Grundrisse* (1858), D. Mclellan (ed.), London, 1980, p. 96.
14. L. Althusser's important contribution was to emphasize the structural character of the analysis in *Capital*. The acceptance of this assertion, though, does not necessarily imply acceptance of Althusser's whole theoretical edifice.

circumstances that centre in this, viz., that two very different kinds of commodity-possessors must come face to face and into contact; on the one hand, the owners of money, means of production, means of subsistence, who are to increase the sum of values they possess, by buying other people's labour-power; on the other hand, free labourers, the sellers of their own labour-power, and therefore the sellers of labour.[15]

The agents of production, the capitalist and the worker, exist within the relations of production in exactly the same way as do commodities, money, or capital. As nodes in a network, determined in their specific function and with given relationships with the whole: 'The functions fulfilled by the capitalist are no more than the functions of capital executed continuously and willingly. The capitalist functions only as personified capital, capital as a person, just as the worker is no more than labour personified.'[16] Moreover, the nexus of relationships which determines individual persons is not presented as such to these individuals. Capitalists and workers are not consciously creating or reproducing the capitalist relations of production. The famous 'commodity fetishism' is a case of the misrecognition of the social relations that exist behind and determine commodities as such. Finally, the 'whole', the totality of capitalist relations of production, is not static. Rather it is in a continuous flux reproducing itself in an ever expanded form, in a 'progressive accumulation'.[17]

How can this structured whole operate 'behind people's backs' while these very people are parts of that whole? How can people 'produce materially', not only 'under definite material limits, presuppositions and conditions independent of their will', but also being in the dark about these limits and conditions that are inherent in their actions? What anthropological model can be used to conceive such a disjuncture? Moreover, in what sense can we conceive of this whole as following 'laws' in an abstract way, laws independent from persons' volition? What, in other words, is the ontological status of the 'material' – i.e. social – level of production?

Marx's answer is not direct, but is implied in his further analysis of capitalism. We can trace it in the basic assumptions underlying the analysis in *Capital*. The same assumptions, though, are present in Marx's earlier work.

---

15. K. Marx, *Capital* (1867), 3 vols. Reference here is to the edition published by Lawrence and Wishart, London, 1954, vol. 1, p. 668.
16. From the chapter of *Capital* not published in the original; see the Penguin edition, vol. 1, Harmondsworth, 1976, p. 989.
17. Marx, *Capital*, vol. 1, p. 555.

Establishing that capitalist relations of production form a structured whole in flux is only the first step. The second, and pivotal one, is the definition of value. Marx defines value as corresponding to 'simple average labour' by postulating a measure of value invariable within the context of analysis. This measure of value, in conjunction with the acceptance of a 'necessary labour' for the worker to survive – also seen as a given – allow the definition of 'surplus value'. Capital can thus be seen as nothing more than accumulated surplus value and the primary law of capital accumulation as reflecting the accumulation of surplus value: 'It should never be forgotten that the production of this surplus value is the immediate purpose and the determining motive of capitalist production.'[18] What the labour definition of value does is to effect a connection between the structured whole of the capitalist mode of production and a fundamental human activity, labour. The law of accumulation, the guiding force of capitalist production appears thus as a form of surplus value accumulation, i.e. as the exploitation of this labour. Thus capitalist relations may be 'fetishized' and people may not recognize their role either as exploited or as exploiters, but the moving force behind all, the thread that holds all the elements of the mode of production together, is nothing more – or less – than the fundamental human activity of labour.

The labour definition of value requires the possibility of defining a constant and given measure of 'simple average labour'. Marx considers 'simple average labour' to vary in different countries and at different times, but in a particular society to be given.[19] Closer examination, however, reveals that only in single commodity production with no technological change can we indeed have such a constant measure.[20] But capitalism, in Marx's own account, is obviously not such a case. Moreover, the labour theory of value cannot provide Marx – or classical economics in general – with a measure of value independent of prices and wages. Marginalist economists have rightly stressed this point:

> On a strictly analytical ground, there is no justification whatever for giving any sort of logical priority to either 'values' over prices or to prices over 'values'. Each of them can be derived from the other; and both of them

---

18. Marx, *Capital*, vol. 3, p. 352.
19. Marx, *Capital*, vol. 1, p. 51.
20. See the detailed analysis in A. Cutler, B. Hindess, P. Hirst and A. Hussain, *Marx's Capital and Capitalism Today*, 2 vols, London, 1977, vol. 1, pp. 30–7. Also the analysis of C. Castoriadis in 'Value, Equality, Justice, Politics: From Marx to Aristotle and from Aristotle to Ourselves' (1975), in *Crossroads in the Labyrinth*, Brighton, 1984, pp. 266–73.

can be obtained from the interindustry relations expressed in terms of physical quantities of commodities . . . [However] the only system of exchange ratios which can be observed empirically is the system of prices. The 'value' system therefore [. . .] has no empirical correlate.[21]

The assumption implicit in Marx's next step, the calculation of surplus value is equally debatable. The 'necessary labour' as a bare minimum of survival is by no means historically constant, even within a given mode of production, and especially so within capitalism.

Thus in both the definition of value and that of surplus value, labour appears as a constant, axiomatically endowed with an immutability not justified by the rest of Marx's analysis. Indeed labour is seen, as Castoriadis notes, as 'a substance/essence, which can appear under a given form or take a given expression, but which, in itself, does not modify itself, does not alter, and subsists as the immutable foundation of changing attributes and determinations'.[22] The basis of *Capital* is, therefore, of an essentialist nature. The postulation of labour as the missing link between the mode of production with its abstract laws and the people that participate in it, rests on an ultimate rationality of the mode of production, a rationality expressed through the fundamental 'essence' of labour.

If we can identify such an – implicit – essentialism in *Capital*, it is all the more explicit in Marx's earlier work. The very centrality attributed to production, requires an assumption of labour as a transhistorical essence. Marx and Engels do not introduce production as the mirror of nature but as a social category, i.e. as a level distinct from both nature and thought. Yet they consider production as determining the social as a whole. This determinacy seems to be based on a convincing argument: since production is necessary for the existence and continuity of any social formation, the 'organization of production' – the relations of production, the mode of production, the economy – is also necessary and therefore determinant. However, there is here a logical gap: the necessity of the function of production does not imply, ipso facto, that the mode of production will be a determinant social instance. Precisely because production for Marx is a social and not a natural instance, the necessity of production by itself only poses a barrier, a natural given, a limit to what is at any moment possible. But this necessity does not imply anything at all about a possible determinant role of production within society. To argue for such a determinacy a further assumption is necessary. And

21. L. Passineti presenting the argument of the marginalists in *Lectures on the Theory of Production*, London, 1977, p. 149.
22. Castoriadis, 'Value, Equality', p. 274.

this assumption is made by Marx and Engels, though implicitly: it is the assumption that man is primarily *Homo faber* and that labour is the underlying essence of man.

This assumption traverses the whole of Marx's work. In the *1844 Manuscripts* it is claimed that 'productive life is the life of the species'.[23] Similarly in *The German Ideology* we read: 'Men begin to distinguish themselves from animals as soon as they begin to produce their means of subsistence [. . .] As men express their life so they are. What they are, therefore, coincides with their production.'[24] Quite revealing: production is the dividing line between men and animals; it is the primary human attribute. Hence the second part of the assertion ('what they are . . .') follows naturally. Men's life does not coincide with their production because the latter is necessary, but because it is the attribute *par excellence* of man. Man does not simply have to produce. Man is man in so far as he produces, in so far as he is *Homo laborans*.

In a similar vein, in the '1859 Preface' the forces of production are not, in their determinant role, a chance residue of the successive modes of production but the reflection of the most important attainment of man: the gradual increase in – technological – mastery over nature, the continuously ascending curve of technology, a mastery that is the effect of man as *Homo laborans* over history. In this way to the assumption of labour as the predominant human activity, a notion of historical progress is added: the rationality that, by definition, characterizes production, can only be reflected in a continuous development of the productive forces. The weight of this development transcends the inertia of any particular mode and forms the visible side of the invisible motor of history: the increasing rationality, that through a period of alienation of man from his work, leads him, but in an immensely advanced form, back to his beginning: in the mastery and self-consciousness of production. From primitive communism to communism via the different historical modes of production, the human essence realizes itself in a series of dialectical turns. The argument of the '1859 Preface', therefore, is not so much based on an autonomous development of the productive forces as on human labour as the characteristically human activity. Productive forces are the residue of this activity. They represent the accumulation, over history, of man's labour. Thus their determinant role is another way of expressing the ultimately rational character of this labour, a

23. *Economic and Philosophic Manuscripts of 1844*, in K. Marx and F. Engels, *Collected Works*, vol. 3, London, 1975, p. 276.
24. Marx and Engels, *The German Ideology*, p. 42.

rationality that is reflected in their unidimensional, evolutionary, path.[25]

In Marx's analysis of capitalism, the transhistorical constant of labour becomes, for the first time of history, the moving force of the totality of production. In precapitalist societies the (economic) surplus was appropriated by non-economic means, but in capitalist production it appears for what it really is: pure economic exploitation. By appearing as such, by realizing itself in the principle of the whole, the exploitation of labour opens also, for the first time, the possibility of its transcendence in what Lukacs called 'the objective possibility of class consciousness',[26] i.e. the possibility of the proletariat to assert itself by abolishing, at the same time, exploitation in general. The (pre)history of mankind, based upon exploitation, can thus be ended, and a new chapter can begin in which production is socially and consciously controlled. One can only marvel at this magisterial synthesis that combines a philosophy of history, an analysis of capitalism and a political/social ideal in a most fascinating way. It is precisely the grandeur of this synthesis that still appeals. However, the underlying foundation of this synthesis remains the assumption that labour is an essential, and historically unchangeable, attribute of man.

Thus the second step of Marx's – and Engels' – analysis of the social level introduced as 'material' in *The German Ideology* and identified with production is completed: the specificity of production, discernible from both nature and thought in its materiality and, as a consequence, the specificity of the whole of the social that production determines, rests on the assumption of a transhistorical human essence.

In the very core of his thought, therefore, Marx remains a Hegelian. It may not be 'thinking' that 'causes its own synthesis, its own deepening and its own movement',[27] of which Marx accuses Hegel of

---

25. This is clearly recognized by G.A. Cohen in his 'defence' of the '1859 Preface' argument. The underlying assumption about human nature is, for Cohen, that:
   - Men are, in a respect to be specified, somewhat rational
   - The historical situation of men is one of scarcity
   - Men possess intelligence of a kind and degree which enables them to improve their situation (G.A. Cohen, *K. Marx's Theory of History: a Defence*, Oxford, 1978, p. 152).
   Cohen simply makes explicit a version of the essentialism that necessarily has to be assumed alongside any argument about the primacy of the productive forces.
26. G. Lukacs, 'Class Consciousness' (1920), in *History and Class Consciousness*, London, 1971, p. 79.
27. Marx, '1857 Introduction', p. 141.

asserting, but it is human labour and production that does. Marx's scheme provides a most elaborate and subtle illustration of Hegelian thought. The transgression of exploitation becomes possible because of its – unique in history – appearance as such in the very driving principle of the capitalist mode. Society may not be a reflection of nature or the product of people's thoughts, but it remains, in its historical unfolding, the development of an essence through a series of reductions: man as *homo laborans* – development of production – history as the realization of this essence.[28]

This Hegelianism provides Marx also with a theory of his own discourse. The distinction between the 'truth' of Marx's analyses in *Capital* and the 'errors of bourgeois economists', is based on the possibility of the moving force of history, the exploitation of labour, becoming self-transparent to thought at a particular historical juncture and for a particular historical agent. Through the historically unique feature of capitalist relations of production, positing the extraction and accumulation of surplus value as the motor of the mode of production, this process can indeed be conceived for what it really is, i.e. exploitation, from the part of the agent that is exploited: the proletariat. The proletariat is thus a privileged agent that becomes, by virtue of its position, capable of touching the true kernel of man's historical existence. In this way Marx and Engels can present a theory of their own discourse consistent with their denunciation of thought and 'forms of consciousness' as mere epiphenomena. The social – as production – determines thought, but since the social is the expression of a human essence, and hence ultimately rational, at the appropriate moment in the movement of history this rationality can reveal itself directly to thought.

28. Thus a 'Hegelian' interpretation of Marx, such as Cohen's, is perfectly legitimate. Moreover, it can be claimed not only for the '1859 Preface' but for the whole of Marx's work. The same cannot be said, however, for attempts to provide a 'rational choice' model of action as the appropriate foundation for Marx's more substantive assertions and analyses. Writers such as J. Elster, J. Roemer, and others (see, for example, J. Elster, *Making Sense of Marx*, Cambridge, 1985; J. Roemer, *A General Theory of Exploitation and Class*, Cambridge, 1982) disregard not only Marx's explicit anti-individualism but also the subtle – 'Hegelian' – way in which he retains a certain essentialism that cannot be captured by crude rational choice models. These authors are absolutely blind to whatever differentiates Marx from, say, J.S. Mill. It is therefore misleading to consider Cohen as arguing the same as Elster or Roemer under the label of 'Analytical Marxism', as in J. Roemer (ed.), *Analytical Marxism*, Cambridge, 1986.

Marx's implicit theoretical assumptions have important consequences for his political project. This project of emancipation, closely connected with his theoretical work, draws from the Enlightenment's ideas and has the French Revolution as a reference point. Marx accepts the advantages of the modern polity as opposed to the monarchy it replaces and applauds the sovereignty it allows the citizen. The possibility to determine the affairs of the state allows an autonomy compared with the heteronomy of earlier times. But this autonomy is not enough for Marx. It does not affect men's life outside the sphere of the citizen. In order to be really able to speak about autonomy, 'civil society, the world of needs, labour, private interest, civil law',[29] has also to come under the sovereignty of man. It is social existence as a whole that has to become autonomous and not only the 'political' sphere: 'Political emancipation itself is not human emancipation [. . .] only when man has recognized and organized his *forces propres* as *social* forces, and consequently no longer separates social power from himself in the shape of *political* power, only then will human emancipation have been accomplished.'[30]

Since social existence is determined for Marx by production, these *forces propres* refer primarily to the production sphere. Only through controlling the 'multiplied productive force', i.e. by establishing the sovereignty of man on the field of production, can the 'social being' of man become really autonomous. As with political autonomy, however, personal emancipation is possible only through the establishment of an autonomous community. The possibility of such a community comes about with the individuation associated with the rise of the bourgeoisie and the separation of man from his labour entailed by capitalist relations of production. While, however, this individuation is, in itself, a positive step, as long as production relations remain beyond man's social control, a 'real' community is impossible. Thus Marx, while accepting the political ideals of Enlightenment thought and the importance of democracy, goes beyond these ideals. He wants to widen the field of autonomy to include the whole of man's social life. Marx's intervention constitutes a broadening of the political ideal of the century, bringing in a conception of the social as something more than the political and a historization of the whole possibility of emancipation.

29. K. Marx, 'On the Jewish Question' (1843), in Marx and Engels, *Collected Works*, vol. 3, p. 168.
30. Ibid., pp. 160, 168.

However, the whole political project rests on the assumption of the existence of the possibility of actual political action. The very reference to a political project implies that a social class – and, correspondingly, the individual – can never be fully determined by the relations of production. In particular it implies that the proletariat has – at least potentially – the ability to conceive its 'objective possibilities' and to fight for their realization. Therefore something 'more' than what a full determinacy allows has to exist. However, this 'more' is not theorized by Marx. His account of the individual as a product of the social and as simply an element in the structural whole of the capitalist production does not allow the possibility of autonomy. As for classes, their autonomy seems minimal, appearing as they do as passive bearers of the historical process. Thus a contradiction is revealed: Marx's theoretical framework is supposed to provide a political tool, the means for a political project. Yet within this framework, the – individual or collective – autonomy necessary for the very existence of a political project cannot be theorized. The broadening of the Enlightenment's political project, therefore, is limited to the programmatic statements of Marx's political project. The theory that would support the existence of such a project is lacking.

Moreover, if labour is the historical 'essence' of man, the control of the economic activity is not simply a broadening of the political project. It is the 'liberation' of man's ultimate essence, a liberation which can only lead to a full self-transparency of society in an almost automatic way. Marx's ideal society is a society transparent to itself. Since man's *forces propres* are to be consciously controlled and since these forces represent the innermost kernel of man, their social control implies a self-transparency of each individual *vis-à-vis* himself and of the social *vis-à-vis* each of its members, a transparency inconceivable within the framework of the public/private dichotomy. In addition, since production determines the whole of social life, the establishment of social control of production necessarily implies the autonomy of the whole of society, including the political sphere. The fact that Marx did not deal in particular with the political forms of a communist society, with the implications of the 'withering away of the state', indicates that he considered these forms as necessarily following the social control of production. Social change in general is seen as mechanically following changes on the level of production and as unavoidably leading to a self-transparent society. While a mechanistic view of history and an ideal of personal and social self-transparency are not, in the context of nineteenth century thought, limited to Marx, the – disastrous – political implications of accepting such views have become particularly clear in the course of our century.[31]

To conclude: Marx, in his theoretical account of the social, is definitely arguing for:

1. The existence of a social level irreducible to both nature and 'consciousness' which, moreover, determines thought.
2. The denial of any transhistorical human nature as a founding moment for this level.
3. An analysis of the level of production as non reducible to individual interaction but rather as a structured whole determining its elements, including persons.
4. The possibility of active political action in a broad sense aiming at the conscious social control of society at large and not only of the political.

However, when Marx is to provide a foundation for the specificity of a social level he argues for, it is to labour (and hence production) as a transhistorical essence of man that he resorts. Production is seen as the determinant instance of the social in all historical periods while the development of production provides an evolutionary theory of history. The analysis of capitalist production is similarly founded on a measure of 'pure' labour reflecting this 'essence' and the passage to the highest stage of development, a communist society, depends precisely on the appearance of the guiding force of history, the exploitation of labour, as such for the first time in history.

The assumption of transhistorically constant elements of human nature is not necessarily to be rejected. It can be seen in a positive light and espoused either as a theoretical principle or as an empirical generalization or as both.[32] However:

1. It evidently contradicts Marx's own denial of transhistorical human attributes.
2. It neutralizes Marx's critique of philosophy since it affirms that the social/material level presented as the outside and determinant of consciousness and thought is itself ultimately rational – reducible to a rational essence.

31. For the close connection between the ideal of self-transparency and totalitarianism, see C. Lefort, 'The Logic of Totalitarianism' (1980), in *The Political Forms of Modern Society*, Cambridge, 1986.
32. A recent example is G.A. Cohen's 'defence' of Marx's theory of history as it is presented primarily in the '1859 Preface'.

3. It is not theoretically defensible as a foundation of Marx's own analysis of the capitalist mode of production in *Capital*, as argued above.

4. In so far as it supports a theory of history, as in the '1859 Preface', it presents a view of historical evolution based on a necessary and unidimensional development of productive forces that cannot be sustained in the light of empirical material.[33]

5. In so far as it implies a transhistorical determinacy of production as a specific social instance it simply projects to the past a situation valid only for capitalism.[34]

6. Finally, it has consequences for the political project Marx advances, making impossible to theorize any real autonomy from the part of political actors and introducing the fiction of a self-transparent society.

For all the above reasons we have to reject the 'essentialist' elements in Marx's thought. Indeed it is easy to see this essentialism as reflecting dominant philosophico-anthropological assumptions of the nineteenth century regarding the attitude of man towards nature, the ultimate rationality of history, the positive role of technology, etc. As J. Baudrillard remarks, 'Radical in its logical analysis of capital, Marxist theory nonetheless is sustained by an anthropological consensus with the options of Western rationalism, in the definite form it acquired in eighteenth century bourgeois thought.'[35]

We cannot, however, simply reject the 'essentialist' elements in Marx's thought and 'take out', as it were, the elements that break with this essentialism. Because of the fundamental role of the former, the latter – the elements that break with nineteenth century rationalism –

---

33. One has to distinguish between a certain development of productive forces throughout history and the necessary and unidimensional nature of this development Marx's argument requires. For comments see D. Dickson, *Alternative Technology and the Politics of Technical Change*, London, 1974. Also C. Castoriadis, 'Marxism and Revolutionary Theory' (1965), in *The Imaginary Institution of Society*, Cambridge, 1987, pp. 18–20.

34. The importance of production could be saved if we see it as a function operating within diverse institutional forms, intermingled with political or ideological operations. This is the argument of M. Godelier who presents it as an empirically testable hypothesis (M. Godelier, *The Mental and the Material* (1984), London, 1986). In this formulation, however, the significance that Marx attributes to production disappears and the affirmation of its determinacy becomes indifferent.

Points (4) and (5), not argued for in the context of the preceding analysis, are noted here simply to present a more comprehensive list of the problems Marx's 'essentialism' encounters.

35. J. Baudrillard, *The Mirror of Production* (1968), St. Luis, 1975, p. 32.

cannot stand alone without their supporting framework.[36] If certain elements of Marx's theoretical edifice are to be retained, while a stand is taken against their essentialist foundation, an alternative theoretical grounding for the former has to be provided. Only thus can they acquire a theoretical significance.[37]

We can consider as the starting point of the present enquiry, the examination of such alternative frameworks around the central questions Marx's work poses: how can we provide a theorization of the specificity Marx assigns to a level of the social as distinct from both 'nature' and 'forms of consciousness' without seeing this specificity as the reflection of a transhistorical essence of man developing throughout history and therefore without assigning any privileged role to production?

Would such a theorization offer any insights helpful to reconcile a structural determination of the individual with the necessary autonomy a political project requires? Would it offer, moreover, a way to escape from an evolutionist, or – more generally – any deterministic, theory of history?

These are the questions from which we start.

36. The example of Althusser's interpretation of Marx is instructive in this respect. Althusser explicitly wants to reject all the historicist and essentialist elements in Marx and to retain, at the same time, the transhistorical determinacy of economy and production. This proves to be, however, an impossible project, as will be argued in the next chapter.

37. The above critique of Marx concerns his general theorization of the social. The rejection of central elements of this theorization does not, however, necessarily invalidate Marx's more substantive analyses, for example parts of his analysis of capitalism, class struggle, etc. These theses have to be separately addressed and evaluated.

–2–

Positivism and Hermeneutics

We can attempt now to situate our enquiry more broadly, with respect to different social theoretical approaches, approaches seeking to account for that novel object of study, the 'social' and 'society' in the specific meaning these terms acquire at the beginning of the nineteenth century. By necessity such an attempt will be quite superficial regarding the discussion of the authors mentioned: its object is rather to delineate the broad lines of different approaches than to discuss in depth these authors, the wealth, diversity or contradictions within their work. It is a sketch rather than a detailed map, providing simple bearings in a landscape of extreme variety and complexity.

The Modern Conception of the Social

The conception of the social – of 'society' – upon which the social sciences are based, is a relatively recent one. Up to the eighteenth century, the social was seen as transparent and self-evident: it is relations between men, men in the given positions they occupy by birth and which are little expected to change in the course of their life. The serf is the serf and the lord the lord. Their relationship, in its asymmetry, its distribution of power and exploitation is known to both and accepted as natural. The social is nothing more (or less) than what people do in their everyday action: exchange, fight, worship, etc. The actors' positions are fixed and so is the stage. As for historical time it is the circular time of the same, homocentric cycles around a fixed centre.

The etymology of the Latin *societas*, corresponding to the Greek *koinonia*, is revealing in this respect. The Greek *koino(s)* and its Latin translation *socius* denote the fellow, the sharer, the partner, the comrade, the companion, the associate, a person in short that shares a common element or project. Correspondingly the nouns *koinonia* and *societas* denote a fellowship, an association, a union, a community, a 'society' implying union for a common purpose.[1] The meaning of these terms begins to gradually change only around the end of the

1. See for example Lewis and Short, *A Latin Dictionary*, Oxford, 1945.

seventeenth century.

The Enlightenment subverts not the transparency of social relations, but the naturality that legitimized them. This subversion operates on the level of the individual, which is portrayed not any more as a function of the social position he occupies, but as a transhistorical, immutable essence, a human nature upon which the different social positions are engraved. All persons partake of this nature, hence all persons are primarily the same. It is only as a result of differential social conditions that we have serfs and lords.

Thus for the eighteenth century the question of the social circles around the problem of order: since the individuals can exist as isolated, autonomous monads, the question of how and why their coexistence in society is possible arises. The two ends of the spectrum were to consider this coexistence as necessary for the protection of all (Hobbes, Locke) or as a burden that prevents the happiness inherent in men's natural condition (Rousseau). For Rousseau the whole of 'society' is a burden to man, introducing inequality, divisions and unhappiness to a natural state of much greater freedom and happiness. It is therefore through the restriction of power to the general will manifested in the 'social contract' and through the development of men's own inherent nature that the prevailing social institutions suffocate, that the inequalities of civilization can be tackled.[2]

The Enlightenment thus reactivates the Christian dogma of an equality of all men at birth – a dogma that has been neutralized by the role assigned to the Church in medieval times – secularizes it and combines it with a political philosophy drawn from classical Athens. An ontological position – that of the Christian dogma – is added to a theory of politics that did not presuppose it (Aristotle's *Politics*, for example, nowhere evokes a natural equality of men). Thus the political project is reinforced and the personal ethics of Christianity (also going back to the Stoics) are broadened to political ones. The individual assumes in this way a fundamental position: he becomes, as the embodiment of a transhistorical, unitary, autonomous and self-sufficient human nature, the foundation of the social relations in which he partakes. In addition, for the critical approach exemplified by Rousseau, since these relations are unequal – in contrast with the equality of 'the state of nature' – this human nature becomes the basis of a critique of society.

The legacy of the Enlightenment is still with us, in both its

2. Cf. J.-J. Rousseau, 'Discourse on the Origin of Inequality' (1755), and 'Social Contract' (1762), both in *The Social Contract*, London, 1973. See also his *Emile: or, On Education*, New York, 1979.

ontological assumptions and its critical function. But what mediates it is the emergence of a conceptualization of the social that departs from the assumption of transparency of social relations that Enlightenment thought continues to accept.[3]

As with Enlightenment thought which was closely linked with the ascendance of the bourgeoisie, the emergence of the modern notion of the social was closely linked with the gradual but obvious increase in national wealth (linked to what was to be later termed the capitalist mode of production).[4] Already from the middle of the eighteenth century an 'inquiry into the causes of the wealth of nations' became necessary since this wealth appeared as visibly accumulating.[5] The crucial point was, however, that this accumulation was not an expected consequence of planned actions. It appeared as an unexpected result of actions seemingly unrelated and definitely having personal gain rather than any aggregate increase of wealth as their immediate aim. In contrast to the transparency of social relations up to that point, a new phenomenon, obviously a social product but equally obviously not an anticipated one, appeared.[6]

To theorize this phenomenon, Adam Smith, breaking with the physiocrats, inaugurates classical economics. He sees the increase in productivity as the result of the division of labour, in turn correlating to the expansion of the market. The resulting accumulation of capital is seen as the reason for the wealth of England and other states of Europe. Instead of exchange between classes, exchanges visible and known (in the physiocrats) comes into being an internally coherent

3. There are approaches in social science and philosophy that go directly back to the Enlightenment's notion of the individual. Ethical and political philosophy is often so. In Rawls's *A Theory of Justice*, for example, he remarks, 'I have attempted to carry to a higher order of abstraction the traditional theory of the social contact as represented by Locke, Rousseau and Kant' (J. Rawls, *A Theory of Justice*, Oxford, 1972, p. viii). These approaches disregard the modern conception of the social and the body of thought it has given rise to. Whether such neglect is permissible is highly doubtful.

4. The linkage with changes in the sphere of the economy, forcefully argued by Marx, is not the only one. There are relevant changes also in the political field with the emergence of the modern nation–state as an entity founded on itself and not on some 'external' source of legitimation as the medieval and Renaissance kingdoms were. Undoubtedly changes of a related nature can be located on other levels of social life as well. Our intention here is simply to establish the change in the conception of the social and such linkages do not concern us directly. Even less can the formidable problem of directions of determinacy within these linkages be addressed.

5. A. Smith, *An Inquiry into the Nature and Causes of the Wealth of Nations* (1784), Indianapolis, 1976.

6. This is evident also in the meaning of the term 'society'. By the eighteenth century, the previous primary meaning of companionship or fellowship gives its place to a more general and abstract sense (R. Williams, *Keywords*, London, 1988, p. 293).

system which emerges without planning, functions without the participants having a knowledge of the whole, and, moreover, contributes to an increasingly accumulating wealth. Two of the central underlying assumptions of earlier thought are thus undermined: the transparency of social relations, and the circularity of time. In their place a systemic whole guided by an invisible hand and history as a cumulative development and progress emerge. As M. Foucault remarks: 'From Smith onward, the time of economics [. . .] was to be the interior time of an organic structure which grows in accordance with its own necessity and develops in accordance with autochthonous laws – the time of capital and production.'[7]

Adam Smith refers only to the economy and indeed it is the analysis of the economy that constitutes, for the better part of the nineteenth century – at least until Walras and the marginalists – the most developed area of theorization of the social (Ricardo and Marx being the primary examples). Soon however, the modality of 'systemness' and internal dynamic attributed to the economy, as well as its relative opacity in relation to the participants, were to be transported to a greater system, 'society', of which economy was merely a subsystem. Thus a certain rupture with both pre-Enlightenment and Enlightenment thought is introduced. Society, unlike pre-Enlightenment conceptions, is not the visible and natural association of men in their different functions, but displays a certain opacity as well as a systemness and internal dynamic. At the same time, unlike Enlightenment thought, society appears as something not directly based on the individual as a fundamental autonomous entity predating it.

We can consider that the above constitute the two central assumptions marking the semantic borders of a 'novel' object of study, covering phenomena which are either equally 'novel' or hitherto went unnoticed, society in its modern meaning. These assumptions can be expressed as: (i) 'society' as a structured whole is assumed to have an internal coherence and dynamic, and (ii) this whole is seen as – at least partly – independent of what people consciously intend and thus

7. M. Foucault, *The Order of Things*, (1966), London, 1974, p. 226. Foucault sees the change in this conception of time as representing a general paradigmatic shift in the whole field of the Western conception of the world, a shift that replaced the taxonomic mode of conceiving of the classical era with a 'modern' one. This 'modern' structuring of knowledge is characterized by the postulation of autonomous entities with an internal time and dynamic: the time of capital in the economy, the concept of life in biology, the concept of language as a system. Our presentation of the modern notion of the social owes much to Foucault. However we refer to the 'social' in a more general sense, encompassing for example both 'economics' and the study of language. Moreover, Foucault's strange taxonomy of the 'human sciences' (ibid., pp. 344ff.) is not followed.

a certain opacity of society exists towards its participating actors.

Evidently such a strange 'object', 'society' or the 'social' as the semantic area delimited by these two assumptions, created questions regarding the theoretical foundation of its specificity. The questions concerned both the scientific status of such a study and the theoretical model that would account for the 'modality' of this social.

Broadly speaking, epistemological claims, following already established currents of Western thought, alternated between an alliance with the methodology of (positive) natural science and an idealist tradition. Later, a hermeneutic approach was added while a rationalism/objectivism replaced the early idealist approaches. At the same time, accounts of what the social 'is', primarily in relation to the individual (the concept of the person as an autonomous and individual entity being a central and fundamental one in the up to then Western thought), took two main lines of differentiation: on the one hand different variants of individualism saw the social as produced by individuals; on the other, 'holistic' approaches asserted that the social was a *sui-generis* and irreducible entity. In fact, epistemological and ontological claims were usually inextricably intermeshed, each seeking to reinforce the other. Nevertheless the distinction can be seen as providing a convenient system of co-ordinates along which we can attempt to situate some of the main thinkers of the social.

Positivism

Positivism in general seeks to imitate the methods and form of the already established natural sciences as a guarantee of scientificity. Within this general framework, two distinct paths were followed. The first, drawing upon the Enlightenment's assumptions in a diluted form, presented society as a kind of emergent property of autonomous individuals put together and can be termed individualistic positivism. The second, a 'holistic' positivism, posited society as a *sui generis* reality, irreducible to individuals, which can be studied in a manner similar to natural science.

One of the earliest and yet most consistent and lucid exponents of individualistic positivism is J.S. Mill. For Mill, there are certain given unalterable 'laws of mind, whether ultimate or derivative, according to which one mental state succeeds another'.[8] These general laws, which he considered to be constant, independent of society and operating in different external circumstances, produce through

8. J.S. Mill, *A System of Logic* (1843), London, 1967, p. 557.

'character formation' different individuals. (And 'ethology' is the science that examines this character formation.) Given these laws and the conditions that an individual faces in his/her development, we can deduce the character of persons. The aggregate of these results would give the laws of social phenomena:

> Society is [. . .] the actions of collective masses of mankind. [. . .] All phenomena of society are phenomena of human nature, generated by the action of outward circumstances upon masses of human beings: and if therefore, the phenomena of human thought, feeling, and action, are subject to given laws, the phenomena of society cannot but conform to fixed laws, the consequence of the preceding.[9]

However, given the enormous quantity of data necessary to make accurate predictions, it is impossible to expect from these laws the accuracy possible in natural sciences. Mill draws the analogy between the sciences of society and 'inexact' sciences such as meteorology. Indeed, statistical mechanics and the kinetic theory of gases, which were developed at around the same time, provide a pertinent example: though the molecules of a gas have determinate qualities and follow fixed and known laws, it is only in a statistical way that we can describe the behaviour of the gas as a whole.

There are two central assumptions around which Mill's theoretical scheme is constructed. First, that there are 'laws of the mind' which have the modality of natural laws, i.e. they are constant and, given the same conditions, produce the same results. These laws are part of a human nature outside any 'social' influence. Second, from the 'laws of the mind' we can infer, in a suitable manner, laws for the whole of society. However, the number of facts and conditions makes any accurate prediction, in the manner of natural sciences, impossible.

The internal coherence of the 'laws of the mind' would account for the coherence of the social. And their non-evident nature, plus the number of facts needed to infer any result, would account for the individuals' ignorance of the effects of their own actions on a societal level, i.e. for the opacity of the social. Thus the social can exhibit both an internal dynamic and opacity *vis-à-vis* the individual actors comprising it while at the same time being ultimately reducible to these individuals. Mill attempts to retain the individual as the foundation but, unlike Rousseau, Hobbes or Locke, also to account for the features of the novel notion of the social (while also drawing from the methodology of the natural sciences). He presents a well thought out and plausible thesis. However, he provides neither any

9. Ibid., p. 572.

real 'laws of the mind', except some vague examples, nor, more importantly, any connection between such laws and societal laws. In so far as he proposes any of the latter, he more or less accepts Comte's scheme as self-evident.[10]

More than a century later, the two central assumptions on which Mill's theoretical scheme is based have not been reinforced. Proponents of individualism have either regressed to a 'methodological individualism',[11] which is in fact an impoverished version of Mill's position and subject to the same criticism, or they have turned to a kind of 'interpretive individualism' which departs from Mill's positivistic assumptions (which we shall discuss together with other hermeneutic approaches below), or, finally, they have put emphasis on the epistemological argument rather than on the explanatory one.

In this last category belong behaviourism and 'experimental' methods in psychology, rational choice theories, game theory and marginalist – neoclassical – economics. All appeal to a positivist epistemology for their justification. They claim an absolute similarity of method with that of natural sciences (having in mind classical mechanics rather than quantum physics). Thus they present their assumptions as hypothetical, not having any explanatory value as such, but leading to results that are empirical regularities in the manner of physical laws, to correlations between facts, and possibly even to predictions. It is because of these results that a wider validity of the approach is claimed.

Marginalist economics can be considered as the paradigmatic form of this kind of approach. Starting with Walras, Wicksell and Bohm-Bawerk, marginalist economists abandon any inquiry into an ultimate measure of value, which has occupied classical economists, and any enquiry into the causes of wealth. They concentrate on short-term analysis, mathematization and the definition of conditions of equilibrium and consciously reject any 'metaphysical' enquiry such as the question of value that occupied their predecessors. In this way they limit the scope of economics to providing management tools[12] for an economy whose emergence, long-term prospects, and internal dynamic are taken for granted. Given the specific nature of the capitalist economy, a certain degree of success in describing microeconomic behaviour, making short-term predictions and an overall

10. Ibid., p. 603.
11. See for example J. Watkins, 'Ideal Types and Historical Explanation' (1952), 'Historical Explanation in the Social Sciences' (1957), and 'Methodological Individualism: a Reply' (1955), in J. O'Neil (ed.), *Modes of Individualism and Collectivism*, London, 1973.
12. As S. Amin remarks in *Accumulation on a World Scale*, Sussex, 1974, p. 10.

management of the economy was generally possible. Hence marginalist economics came to be considered as economics *tout court* and any deeper enquiry as irrelevant. Similarly, models based on game theory or rational choice could also claim a certain strength at describing specific – and limited – social and political phenomena.[13]

However, the relative success of these approaches is possible only in bounded and highly systematized systems such as the economy of advanced capitalist countries and even in such cases only for short periods in which there is relatively little structural change. Results are not obtainable in long-term predictions or in broader systems and no 'laws' of any kind have been established. Hence such approaches cannot be considered as providing an alternative to the study of the social in general as they claim.

While individualistic positivism proved unsatisfactory, the possibility of a holistic study of society still within a positivist framework offered an alternative. V. Pareto and E. Durkheim typify this kind of approach.

Pareto accepts the validity of a 'logico-experimental method' for the study of society, a method which is subject to 'proof or disproof from the facts'. He considers that 'economic and social laws as well as the laws of the other sciences never suffer any genuine exception',[14] thus postulating identity in the method of enquiry of the natural and the social sciences. Unlike Mill, though, he does not attribute these 'laws' to the individual in order to reconstruct society out of them.

For Pareto, leaving aside external elements (such as soil, climate, as well as other societies), a study of society is to be based chiefly on 'residues', which are 'manifestations of sentiments or instincts'. What people think – what Pareto calls 'derivations' – is only secondary, since 'human beings are persuaded in the main by sentiments (residues)'. The residues, however, are not individual characteristics. They are rather broad social orientations of action which are relevant and intelligible only at the level of society. They are propensities to act in a certain way only manifested in social settings. Thus they are not autonomously observable, but have to be derived, *ex post facto*, from such settings. Pareto tries to establish uniformities or laws that would provide a theory of the social on the level of residues. But as the residues are intelligible only on the level of society, Pareto's 'laws' have to appear directly on the social level.

13. The work of J. Elster is a prime example of rational choice approach. For example, J. Elster, *Nuts and Bolts for the Social Sciences*, Cambridge, 1989. See also note 28, p.17 of the previous chapter on 'rational choice' Marxism.

14. V. Pareto, *The Mind and Society: A Treatise on General Sociology* (1916), 2 vols, New York, 1963, vol. 1, p. 101.

Pazeto categorizes the residues into five classes, concentrating mainly on the first two. Class I refers to 'instincts for combinations' and includes the ability for knowledge. Class II refers to 'group persistence' and covers mainly relations between people. Historical development is presented as the growing or diminishing importance of each of these two classes. Pareto does not adopt an evolutionary or even a developmental view, rather a circular one. For example, he takes account of modernity by affirming that 'class I residues and the conclusions of logico-experimental science have enlarged the field of their dominion', but he never implies any necessity or even irreversibility in this.

Pareto's classification and account of history do not establish any 'uniformities of social facts', let alone 'laws' in the manner of natural sciences. His own methodological aim – the establishment of social laws – is not fulfilled. A method claiming a methodological identity with natural science can thus be considered as inadequate for the social domain in the context of a holistic approach, just as in the context of an individualist one. What remains is Pareto's account of 'residues' as being the primary 'social' level, distinct from thought and yet influencing (individual) behaviour. But what is the modality of these residues? How can this level be approached if not through the establishment of laws as Pareto had hoped?

The questions were left unanswered by Pareto, to be taken up in a different form but in a similar vein by Durkheim. Durkheim also wants to adhere to the maxims of positive natural science while approaching the social as an irreducible whole. He considers what he calls the 'comparative method' and particularly its form of 'concomitant variations' to be the most suitable for the study of social phenomena and a kind of 'indirect experimentation'.[15] Moreover, he claims that, as far as social phenomena are concerned, 'to the same effect there always corresponds the same cause', and thus a strict line of causality can always be established. However, he is forced to concede that even the method of concomitant variations gives results that always have to be interpreted, for example to establish whether two phenomena that correlate to each other are both caused by a third or whether one of them causes the other. Thus Durkheim abandons the claim that establishing fixed laws or uniformities in the social sciences is possible. His positive method rests content with the possibility of simple inferences from correlative phenomena. At the same time, he strongly stresses – much more than Pareto – the *sui generis* character

15. E. Durkheim, *The Rules of Sociological Method* (1901), London, 1982, pp. 147ff.

of the social, its irreducibility, its exteriority to the individual which it confronts as coercive. Indeed, Durkheim's whole work can be seen as first and foremost an attempt to establish this irreducibility. He knows, however, that to achieve this aim his 'positive' method is not enough, providing as it does a loose methodology. He attempts, therefore, to provide a theorization of the social specific to its irreducibility.

The moral dimension of society having always been a point of departure for Durkheim, his first attempt for such a theorization is to see society as the *conscience collective*.[16] The *conscience collective* is 'the totality of beliefs and sentiments common to the average members of a society that forms a determinate system of life of its own'.[17] In later work, instead of this 'conscience', the term *representations collectives* is employed and a distinction between 'individual' and 'collective' representations is established, in a manner similar to the distinction between 'mind' and 'body'.[18] As with the 'conscience' which refers not only to beliefs but also to sentiments, the 'representations' are not seen as necessarily conscious or ideal. Their collective character refers to the fact that they are 'produced by the action and reaction between individual minds that form the society, though they do not derive directly from the latter and consequently surpass them'.[19]

Durkheim does not deny the specificity of the individual – either as 'conscience' or as 'representations' – nor does he attempt to subsume the individual to 'society'. But he considers that there is a region of phenomena, both 'conscious' and 'unconscious', both 'beliefs' and 'emotions', that are the product of a 'collective' level and are intelligible only on that level. The individual mind remains Durkheim's model for society, which he sees as a kind of collective mind, a 'psychological type' similar to but distinct from the individual one.[20] Society emerges as a supra-individual entity, sharing broadly the modality of individual minds but existing at a superior level.

16. On the translation of the terms as 'conscience' rather than as 'consciousness', see Parsons's remark, in T. Parsons, *The Structure of Social Action* (1937), New York, 1968, p. 309.
17. E. Durkheim, *The Division of Labour in Society* (1893), London, 1984, p. 39.
18. E. Durkheim, 'Individual and Collective Representations' (1898), in E. Durkheim, *Sociology and Philosophy*, London, 1953.
19. Ibid., p. 24.
20. At certain points Durkheim considers that there is also a qualitative difference between individual and collective: 'the states of the "conscience collective" are of a different nature from the status of the "conscience individuelle"' (Preface to *The Rules of Sociological Method*, 2nd edition, p. 40). In general, however, he does not amplify on any difference of this kind.

Society is neither a reflection of nature, nor the product of individuals, but a kind of human mind writ large.

In his last major work,[21] Durkheim further clarifies the modality he attributes to society. He establishes a distinction between concepts and categories of thought and the level of society. Concepts and categories are generated by society, by social 'things' (*'choses sociales'*) and they express them on the level of thought. Ideas have a social origin, they are 'a natural product of social life'. At the same time, social practice – as for example religious rites – is seen as embodying 'meaning', a 'meaning' that can be later transferred to explicit 'ideas' and 'categories'. 'Social life' appears as something meaningful and yet as not reducible to ideas, concepts, categories, which it generates (and also as irreducible to nature). Social phenomena are both expressible on the level of ideas, as categories socially produced, and at the same time determine this level. The similarity to Pareto's 'residues' is, at this stage, evident. A certain parallel with Marx can also be drawn: part of the social is neither nature nor ideas; it determines categories of the mind and yet it is not reducible to 'nature'. Durkheim does not proceed further, like Marx, to reduce this specificity of the social to a transhistorical essence, nor does he develop further his theorization. Marx has recourse, in the final moment, to a Hegelian essentialism to provide a foundation for both his object of study – production, economy and the whole of the social – and for his methodology. In contrast, Durkheim, advocating a positive study, rejects any founding essence. Since, however, no strict regularities or laws can be established (as Pareto had hoped but as Durkheim himself had ruled out), the scientific approach depends on further elucidation of the modality of the object of study. But how can 'social life' be neither 'ideas' nor 'nature'? What is the mode of knowledge appropriate to this 'social life'? We face the same kind of questions that we encountered in Pareto.

Pareto and Durkheim are unable to fulfil their promise of a positive study of society as a *sui generis* reality based on methodological grounds alone, because none of the robust methods of the natural sciences seem to be applicable on the social field (uniformities, laws, strict causal inferences, etc.). They indicate, therefore, by default, that such a positive study has, necessarily, to proceed, to clarify both its specific methodology – which cannot be identical with that of the natural sciences – *as well as* the specificity of its object – society – as a separate object of study. Far from being 'metaphysical', such an (ontological) theorization is necessary if the possibility of any positive

21. E. Durkheim, *Elementary Forms of Religious Life* (1912), London, 1961.

study is to be established. Both Durkheim and Pareto offer a number of elements for such a theorization, which, however, remain tentative and incomplete.

Early Idealism

The positivist attempts to provide a foundation for the study of the social in either their individualist or holist variants have been conceived always as an answer to the implicit alternative, that which followed the idealist current of Western thought. This current saw the social not as the domain of regularities or laws but rather as the domain of manifestation of a (hidden) transhistorical essence or essences. Man as the embodiment of such an essence, man as a necessary 'becoming' towards the realization of this essence, is a common element from the Stoics to the Christian view of the person. It is to such a – natural – essence of man that Enlightenment based its critique of the social relations impeding and hindering (or, for some, advancing) its development.

The end of the eighteenth and the nineteenth centuries saw the emergence of a notion of progressive historical development. The circular notion of time of the Middle Ages, which still survived in the Renaissance, fades away, giving way to a view of history as developing in a unidimensional line, history as irrevocable progress. Such a notion of history required a subject that could no longer be the individual. The emergence of the concept of society, in its modern meaning, provided precisely that: society became the subject of history, developing itself trough historical time in a line of progress (the approaches to the social that operate within this tradition are thus necessarily holistic rather than individualistic). To the two central assumptions marking the modern conception of the social, its internal coherence and dynamic and its independence of what individuals consciously aim, a third one is added: history as progressive development and society as the subject of history.

All the early accounts of society share this view of history. Even before the modern notion of society emerged in Adam Smith's theorization of the economy, Vico based his 'science of history' on such a developmental scheme (the age of the Gods, the age of heroes and the age of men successively).[22] Comte's three stages of human mind (theological–metaphysical–positive) and the corresponding

---

22. G. Vico, *The New Science* (1744), Ithaca, 1948.

types of society (theological–military–industrial)[23] is a similar case, as is Spencer's principles of evolution.[24]

What is not immediately apparent is that a notion of history as progress necessarily implies a homogeneous plane upon which this progress can be charted, a plane in itself before and after history. A transhistorical constant is necessary to account for historical development, a constant that can be nothing other than a hidden essence providing the *arche* and/or the *telos* of history. Thus Vico's, Comte's and Spencer's projects necessarily require such a constant. It is the fixed laws of development of the human mind (and correspondingly of society) that provide such a constant for Vico and Comte and it is the necessary attributes of evolutionary development that provide it for Spencer. These constants are not deduced from any facts, but they are posited *a priori*, even when, as in Comte, a 'positivism' is advocated. They bear therefore the imprint of the idealist tradition.

It is with Hegel, however, that the full philosophical implications of a move from the Kantian transcendental subject to society as the subject of history are revealed. Becoming, the realization of man's inner essence is seen as operating simultaneously on the domain of the individual and on that of history. A name is given to this essence: Universal Spirit. The process of historical development is seen as dialectical; and the end of history is explicitly posed as the self-realization of this essence: Absolute Knowledge, the Spirit reunited with itself. With Hegel the fundamental assumption of idealism is explicitly presented: the invariable presence that has to support any evolutionary trajectory appears in the form of ideal entities, as pure form or idea. Knowledge can discover this essence since it has the modality of man's own mind, it is a reflection of the same forms reason has.

Marx powerfully transfers the Hegelian approach to the study of society. Despite his denunciation of Hegel he remains, at the core of his theoretical enterprise, a Hegelian. For Marx, society is determined by the economy within which the instance of production is dominant. At the same time historical development is based on the accumulation of the results of man's productive labour (the forces of production). It is man's fundamental essence, therefore, man as a producer, that is both realized in history and determines society, the subject of this

23. A. Comte, *Physique sociale* (lessons 46–60 of *Cours de philosophie positive* [1830–42]), Paris, 1975.
24. Cf. H. Spencer, *First Principles* (1862), in *Structure, Function and Evolution*, S. Adreski (ed.), London, 1971; idem, *Principles of Sociology*, vol. 1 (1876), S. Adreski (ed.), London, 1969.

history. In addition, this determinant instance is a rational one since production is – for Marx – the rational activity of man par excellence. The apparent denial of the individual, therefore, in favour of a 'whole' that is the social, conceals nothing more than the rediscovery of the human essence of 'production' – individual as well as collective – as the founding moment of this 'whole' and as the driving force of its (historical) development. Of course, Marx is by no means only a Hegelian. He marks precisely an attempt to break with Hegel. But in so far as he proposes a coherent scheme, it is along the above lines that it can function.

In general, the central assumption of the idealist tradition, that of an invariable essence behind the multiplicity of phenomena, guiding their development, being the end and/or the beginning (the *arche* or the *telos*) of this development, sharing the modality of ideas and thus accessible to the rational mind, found fertile ground in the sciences of the social. This was reinforced by the fact that the 'positivist' method, which was conceived precisely as an answer to idealism, was unable, in both its holistic and individualistic variants, to offer an alternative sufficiently solid to counteract it. However, the earlier, most historicist forms of this tradition were to give way to less extreme ones in which the overall evolutionary pattern of historical development became a less pronounced feature. We shall return to these approaches after an examination of the other major epistemological paradigm for the human sciences, that of hermeneutics.

The Hermeneutic Approach

Dilthey is the principal pioneer of an attempt to establish the basis of a possible social study different from both positivism and the idealist tradition. Dilthey seeks an alternative to Mill's positivism and individualism, while at the same time taking his distance from Hegel and idealism ('Hegel constructs metaphysically. We analyse the given.')[25].

Dilthey's approach is based on the 'objectifications of life'. 'Life' is not a realization of spirit as in Hegel, but the primary and irreducible

25. W. Dilthey, *Selected Writings*, H. Rickman (ed.), Cambridge, 1976, p. 194. Dilthey's account of his 'hermeneutic' approach to the sciences of the mind – *Geisteswissenschaften* – has to be reconstructed from his many works and fragments. More suggestive are the fragments collected in volume seven of his collected works, partly translated in English. Not being a systematic whole, they contain contradictions and unfinished arguments. They indicate, however, sufficiently clearly, an overall direction.

creative reality that replaces the notion of spirit: 'Life contains the sum of all mental activities.' The objectifications of life, which are the 'subject-matter of human studies', range 'from the distribution of trees in a park, the arrangement of houses in a street, the functional tool of the artisan, to the sentence pronounced in the courtroom[26] [. . .] The objective mind embraces language, custom and every form or style of life, as well as the family, society, the state and the law.'[27]

All these 'objectifications of life' have a structural form which has to be constructed from the given historical reality in the process of 'understanding': 'We cannot understand the objective mind through reason, but must go to the structural connections of persons, and by extension, of communities.'[28] The understanding of these 'structural connections' is coextensive with the attribution of their 'meaning': 'The totality of a life, or any section of the life of mankind can only be grasped in terms of the category of the meaning which the individual parts have for the understanding of the whole [. . .] The category of meaning designates the relationship inherent in life, of parts of a life to the whole.'[29] An individual life, a cultural system, a community, are all to be seen, for Dilthey, as structural wholes through the assignment of meaning to their constituent parts, a meaning that connects them and fuses them into a whole. The process of 'understanding', that assigns this meaning, is the distinguishing element of a hermeneutic approach. Thus Dilthey distances himself also from the tradition of Romantic hermeneutics that had been primarily subjectivistic. As far as the social is concerned it is a structural hermeneutics that he advocates.[30]

However, while the hermeneutic procedure seems to imply an inescapable relativity, in fact Dilthey claims the possibility of a final objectivity. The final aim of hermeneutics remains the objective and absolute knowledge of history: 'Our task today is to recognize the actual historical expression as the true foundation of historical knowledge and to find a method of answering the question how universally valid knowledge of the historical world can be based on what is thus given.'[31] 'Life' is seen as 'ordered towards reflection' and

---

26. Ibid., p. 192.
27. Ibid., p. 194.
28. Ibid.
29. Ibid., p. 235.
30. It has to be noted that despite his overall structural orientation, the model for understanding remains for Dilthey the understanding of our own life, i.e. autobiography: 'The reflection of a person about himself remains the standard and basis for understanding history' (Dilthey, *Selected Writings*, p. 218).
31. Ibid., p. 195.

its objectifications as fully analysable by reason. The only residue of uncertainty in the understanding of history comes not from the modality of the 'objectifications of life' but from the incompleteness of history. Just as 'one has to wait for the end of a life', equally one would have to wait until 'the end of history to have all the material necessary to determine its meaning'.[32] The goal of objective and valid knowledge remains always relatively incomplete, but in principle attainable. Thus, although he recognizes a difference in the mode of knowledge of human sciences from the natural sciences, Dilthey still holds a belief in an aim common to the two in the possibility of certainty, objectivity and universality. As Gadamer remarks, for Dilthey 'historical consciousness was supposed to rise above its own relativity in a way that made objectivity in the human sciences possible'.[33] Although Dilthey rejects Hegel's 'a-prioristic' metaphysics, society and history continue to be seen as primarily rational, not as the expression of an essence but as – ultimately – fully accessible and analysable by reason.

Dilthey's intended break with both positivism and Hegelianism remains, therefore, partial. However, his initial exposition of the 'objectifications of life', as structural wholes constructed in the process of understanding, implies a constant relativity in this 'construction', rather than a final 'objectivity'. Such a relativity, implying in turn a radical historicity, would require the social to be seen as always amenable to such constructions, i.e. as a 'field' embodying meaning, and yet as never fully reducible to it, as not being of the same order as rational thought. Dilthey can thus be seen as opening a novel path which, however, he does not follow sufficiently far.

To further explore this path, we turn to the work of E. Husserl and A. Schutz. Although Husserl did not explicitly concern himself with the problems of social science, nor did he seek to provide a foundation for the study of the social, his work is of importance within the context of our enquiry both directly and as interpreted by Schutz.

Husserl wants to transcend both empiricism and idealistic objectivism as a foundation for the possibility of scientific knowledge. To that aim, he posits an '*ego cogito*' as the 'ultimate and apodictically certain basis for judgements, the basis on which any radical philosophy must be grounded'.[34] This *ego cogito*, this primary consciousness, however, does not imply a return to subjectivism and psychologism.

32. Ibid, p. 236.
33. H.G. Gadamer, *Truth and Method*, London, 1979, p. 207.
34. E. Husserl, *Cartesian Meditations* (1931), Dordrecht, 1960, p. 18.

It refers to a transcendental ego and to a primary level of intentionality which forms experience instead of being a residue of experience. What Husserl posits is a level that is prior to experiences, a level of intentionality that gives form and meaning to experiences and that can be used as the ultimate basis for a philosophy of knowledge. This level appears to have a modality similar to that of concepts and ideas, to which it gives birth and for which it forms the supporting substratum. It is, nevertheless, distinct from them, referring to a 'meaning' of some sort, but not necessarily to the explicit meaning of *logos*.

Initially this level of intentionality is considered to be generated in each individual, though in a transcendental way. Gradually, however, this assertion is abandoned. In the fifth 'Cartesian Meditation' the notion of 'transcendental intersubjectivity' is introduced, to give way in turn, in Husserl's later work, to the notion of 'lifeworld' (*Lebenswelt*). Thus Husserl moves from 'consciousness' and 'subjectivity' to 'life' as the foundation of his phenomenology. It is the lifeworld that becomes the 'grounding soil of the scientifically true world'. The lifeworld exists as the 'horizon of all actual and possible praxis', as the pregiven and necessary 'universal field'.[35]

At this point Husserl's possible relevance to a theorization of the social becomes obvious: the lifeworld, as a level of intentionality and meaning, can be regarded not as transcendental but as referring to a primary level of the social, a level that transcends individual consciousness and action and yet is the origin of both. The lifeworld could be theorized thus as a social level with its own specificity, irreducible to concepts and ideas and yet at their origin, irreducible to individuals and yet allowing their existence as individual beings.

This way of situating Husserl within a social theoretical context, runs counter to A. Schutz's interpretation, the most elaborate attempt to use Husserl's phenomenology in order to construct a theory of the social. Schutz distinguishes a primary, unmediated experience (which he calls 'prephenomenal') from 'phenomenal' experience. The latter results when meaning is endowed upon 'prephenomenal' experience through a retrospective glance. For Schutz, 'meaning is the way in

---

35. E. Husserl, *The Crisis of European Sciences and Transcendental Phenomenology* (1954), Evanston, 1970, p. 142. Husserl does not explicitly incorporate into the concept of lifeworld the totality of attributes of intentionality and primary 'meaning' he earlier attributed to the transcendental ego. The lifeworld appears as a rather unspecified substratum out of which knowledge springs. There are, however, all the indications that it can be seen as the origin of this meaning and intentionality as they are manifested in particular egos.

which the ego regards its experience'.[36] To construct a theory of the social, Schutz takes only the level of 'phenomenal' experience to be relevant and employs Weber's typology of social behaviour, social action and social relationships. The 'meaning' of action is accessible to the actor himself. In order, however, for social science to exist, the other's behaviour has also to be understood. This can be done by postulating 'ideal types' as the 'existence of a person whose actual living motive could be the objective content of meaning already chosen to define a typical action'.[37] Since these 'ideal types' are never identical to the actor's 'actual motive' a certain opacity is introduced, an opacity with respect not to the actor himself, but to the social scientist trying to account for the actor's actions. Thus while the person's understanding of his own social actions – as intentional conscious experiences – is full and unproblematic, the understanding of the other is necessarily limited.

Schutz advocates therefore, at this stage, a kind of hermeneutic individualism. In doing so, however, he inevitably faces the traditional problem of individualism, the question of order. The very existence of the social comes into question because there is no explanation of why seemingly unconnected behaviour simply oriented towards the other would produce any structured society at all. As we will see, for Weber reason and rational action serve as a vehicle to reintroduce society to his initially similar scheme. Schutz is not willing to follow the same path, and is left with no possibility of connecting individual action to a structured outcome.

Perhaps as a response to this problem, Schutz introduces in his later work the notion of 'lifeworld' which he elaborates quite independently of Husserl.[38] 'Lifeworld' for Schutz represents 'the natural attitude in which we, as human beings among fellow beings experience culture and society, take a stand with regard to their objects, are influenced by them and act upon them'.[39] The 'lifeworld' is thus a first level, a 'common sense' interpretation of human action.[40] It refers to a primary knowledge of the social world, necessarily existing in everyday action. This knowledge conditions the 'subjective stock of knowledge' and

36. A. Shutz, *The Phenomenology of the Social World* (1932), London, 1972, p. 69. Thus Husserl's primary level of intentionality and meaning is seen as referring to this level of individual experience.

37. Ibid., p. 189.

38. Husserl's definition became known only after the posthumous publication of the *Crisis of European Sciences and Transcendental Phenomenology*.

39. A. Schutz, 'Some Structures of the Life-World', in *Collected Papers III*, The Hague, 1970, p. 116.

40. As is evident in A. Schutz, 'Common-Sense and Scientific Interpretation of Human Action' (1953), in *Collected Papers I*, The Hague, 1962.

determines, to a degree, the orientation of individual social action. Thus the social is no longer theorized as the creation of individual action through isolated 'intentional conscious experiences', but as already there, endowed with a cohesiveness and wholeness in the form of 'lifeworld', which guides this individual action. The social is still seen, however, as pertaining to intentional and conscious experiences of individuals, themselves existing independently of the lifeworld which they 'employ', as a system of concepts, only at the moment of action.

At this point Schutz faces a dilemma: since he considers the primary lifeworld to be a 'stock of knowledge' and hence a system of concepts and ideal elements guiding action – however imperfectly conceived by the actor – the social scientific knowledge can claim the possibility of 'objectivity'. It can aim at 'discovering' the central elements of this stock of knowledge in a total and unbiased manner, without being constrained by the creation of 'ideal types' based on typifications of individual experiences. If so, however, any 'interpretive' claim, other than the always incomplete knowledge of the lifeworld due to its complexity, has to be abandoned and Schutz's scheme becomes very similar to Parsons's in *The Structure of Social Action*. The lifeworld closely resembles the 'systems of norms', while the actor is seen by both writers as independent and outside these systems.[41] If Schutz is to escape this objectivism and to retain relativity in social knowledge – and hence a necessarily hermeneutic position – which was his original project and which both his reservations for Parsons's unconditional objectivism[42] and his few late comments on social scientific knowledge indicate,[43] he has no other route than to return to his initial position outlined in *The Phenomenology of the Social World*. But this in turn implies abandoning any pre-existing structurality of the social world and facing the problem of order.

Schutz's dilemma indicates that if an interpretive approach is to be developed starting from 'conscious, meaningful action', then the only way to retain its hermeneutic character is to remain within a – problematic – individualism. If this individualism is abandoned, as in the case of Schutz's concept of lifeworld, the cognitive level of action involved necessarily leads to objectivism, however qualified. However, if we return to Husserl's definition of lifeworld, Schutz's dilemma disappears. For Husserl the lifeworld refers to a level of

41. The few letters exchanged between Schutz and Parsons indicate that Schutz was aware of this similarity. See A. Schutz and T. Parsons, *The Correspondence of A. Schutz and T. Parsons*, R.H. Grathoff (ed.), Bloomington, 1978.
42. Ibid.
43. Schutz, 'Common-Sense', pp. 34ff.

intentionality and primary 'meaning' not necessarily corresponding to 'intentional, conscious action', a level not coextensive with ideas, norms, or concepts. Placing this concept of lifeworld in the field of the social we could retain and expand a difference between such a primary level of meaning and the level of thought and ideas, rather than dissolve it in an sequential 'order of concepts' as Schutz's theory does. Thus both the problem of order could be avoided and the necessity of a hermeneutic procedure be asserted.

This line of thought is reinforced from a reading of G.H Mead's work, even though he starts from a different tradition, that of pragmatism. Mead wants to retain the epistemological strictness of behaviourism while taking into account the peculiarity of the human world. To that aim he considers it necessary to theorize the level of consciousness and meaning. The category of meaning has for Mead connotations similar to Husserl's original references. 'Meaning' is the ground of language and ideas but not coextensive with them:

> Meaning is a development of something objectively there as a relation between certain phases of the social act; it is not a physical addition to that act and it is not an 'idea' as traditionally conceived [. . .] The mechanism of meaning is present in the social act before the emergence of consciousness or awareness of meaning occurs.[44]
> Meaning is not to be conceived fundamentally as a state of consciousness, or as a set of organized relations existing or subsisting mentally outside the field of experience into which they enter.[45]
> Meaning can be described, accounted for or stated in terms of symbols or language at its highest and most complex stage of development (the stage it reaches in human experience), but language simply lifts out of the social process a situation which is logically or implicitly there already.[46]

Out of this field of meaning in social experience arises the 'self' as distinct from the biological organism: 'The self is essentially a social structure, and it arises in social experience [. . .] There are all sorts of different selves answering to all sorts of different social reactions.'[47] The self, however, cannot be reduced to the social reaction in which he originates but has a certain autonomy, which for Mead is encapsulated in the concept of the 'I' (as opposed to the 'Me' representing the 'generalized social other'). The self interprets situations in which he

44. G.H. Mead, *Mind, Self and Society*, C. Morris (ed.), Chicago, 1962, p. 77.
45. Ibid., p. 78.
46. Ibid., p. 79.
47. Ibid., pp. 140, 142.

exists and acts accordingly. Hence individual action cannot be reduced to mechanical models of causality.

However, when Mead addresses the question of the social, he locates the social not on the whole of this 'field of meaning' in which selves originate, but in its higher echelons – language and conscious communication between selves, seen as autonomous and independent actors. In this way he produces a scheme similar to early Schutz and he faces necessarily the same problem, that of accounting for the structurality of the social. Mead implicitly recognizes the problem and, in his brief statements on society at large, he introduces the existence of certain fundamental 'socio-physiological impulses', such as the 'reproductive, the parental, the impulse of neighbourliness'.[48] These provide a basis for society which is consequently seen as exhibiting certain 'universals', such as religion and economy.[49] The 'impulses' and the 'universals' are presented not so much as connected to 'conscious communication' but as pre-ordaining the lines of this communication. Implicitly Mead recognizes, therefore, the insufficiency of 'conscious communication' as a foundation of the social.

However, Mead's own formulations of meaning and the self offer an alternative. They point towards a field of meaning that precedes conscious communication and even language, a field that participates in the formation of the 'self' and yet is not necessarily conscious, a field that necessarily exists in every (social) interaction, in the same direction that Husserl's notion of lifeworld indicates. Once again, though, this alternative remains undeveloped.

At this point we can discuss a kind of individualistic hermeneutics that is implied by certain micro-sociologies of interaction. As the case of early Schutz and Mead indicates, if the social is seen as the product of conscious, intentional, meaningful action and the hermeneutic element located on intersubjective understanding, no account of the structurality of the social out of individual, independent actions can be advanced. The classical problem of order reappears. Moreover, the relative opacity of the social in relation to participating individuals, which we identified as a constituent element of the modern notion of the social cannot be taken into account at all. However, if interaction between individuals is emphasized instead of individual action, then 'macro events can be seen as made up of aggregations and repetitions

48. Ibid., p. 228.
49. Ibid., p. 258.

of many similar micro events'[50] and social structure as 'nothing other than large numbers of micro encounters repeated over time and actors' space'.[51] If so, we have a plausible individualistic approach based on a subjectivist hermeneutics. The individuals appear as relatively autonomous and self-supporting entities interacting in an interpretive way with others. The social at large is produced out of these processes of interaction. As for the (social scientific) knowledge of these processes, it has to be hermeneutic, necessitating the deciphering of individual interpretations. Thus the problem of order is overcome. The opacity of the social can also be accommodated within this account since the 'emergent properties of interaction' are not immediately apparent to actors. This is a theoretical interpretation of a substantial body of primarily empirically oriented work, within the broad labels of 'symbolic interactionism', 'phenomenology' and 'ethnomethodology', which includes the work of such leading figures as E. Goffman and H. Garfinkel.[52]

However, this approach is unable to account successfully for the emergence of 'macro' structures from 'micro' interaction. This deficiency points, in fact, to the weak link in the chain of the claims above: the theoretical argument is based on a non-legitimate generalization. While it is true that the 'micro' studies referred to indicate that certain micro situations can be successfully analysed through the assumptions of autonomous and actively functioning individuals in interaction, it is a false claim that *all* micro situations can be so analysed. The types of 'micro' situations on which these empirical studies focus are primarily separated from institutional restraints and concern action having no bearing on 'macro' issues. But many 'micro' events cannot be analysed through these assumptions at all. As Mouzelis remarks, 'face-to-face interactions by or with actors who have privileged access to the means of economic, political or cultural production may have intended or unintended consequences affecting a large number of people [. . .] Such encounters, even if they

50. R. Collins, 'On the Micro-foundations of Macro-sociology', *American Journal of Sociology*, vol. 86, 1981, p. 988.

51. R. Collins, 'Interaction Ritual Chains, Power and Property: the Micro-Macro Connection as an Empirically Based Theoretical Problem', in J. Alexander (ed.), *The Micro-Macro Link*, Berkeley, 1987.

52. To cite just a few texts: H. Blumer, 'Society as Symbolic Interaction', in A.M. Rose (ed.), *Human Behaviour and Social Processes*, London, 1962; H. Garfinkel, 'What Is Ethnomethodology?' (1967), in *Studies in Ethnomethodology* (1968), Cambridge, 1984; E. Goffman, *The Presentation of Self in Everyday Life*, New York, 1959.

involve two persons only, are clearly macro-encounters.'[53] Such 'micro' events, to be satisfactorily analysed, necessitate the introduction of 'stocks of knowledge', of 'lifeworld', or of some sort of 'norms' guiding the individuals' behaviour, of a level, that is, beyond the immediate consciousness of the individuals and directly connected to greater ('macro') structural wholes. Even micro situations which can be successfully analysed through the assumptions of interacting autonomous individuals, always operate within greater structural constraints which have to be taken into account before any theorization of society in general is attempted. But the type of questions asked by the researcher is such that only elements of interaction not immediately related to 'macro' structures are revealed.

Therefore, despite a certain limited applicability, the social at large cannot be explained through the 'interactional' individualism that 'micro' approaches advocate. Consequently, the subjectivist hermeneutics that goes with them offers no viable epistemological foundation for the study of the social. Even the appropriation of the term 'micro' by these approaches is not justified because they are not the only attempts to account for 'micro' phenomena.

Hermeneutics, from Dilthey onwards, have been advanced as a mainly epistemological alternative to both positivism and idealism for the theorization of the social. However, in their subjectivist variant, when the hermeneutic element is located in intersubjective understanding, the problem that individualism has traditionally faced reappears: the social in general cannot be seen as produced out of the action of autonomous individuals and this is not altered by a change of emphasis from 'action' to 'interaction'. The only way to avoid this problem is to introduce a system of social 'knowledge' as 'norms' guiding individual action, as Schutz does with the concept of 'lifeworld'. But then the hermeneutic element also disappears, as this system of norms necessarily can only be seen as conceptual, 'objectively' knowable.

On the other hand, if a structural view of the social is retained, as in Dilthey's 'objectifications of life', without, however, according this social field any specific modality that would differentiate it from conceptual thought, once more the social can only be seen as ultimately objectively knowable, refuting thus any nominal hermeneutic claim. In a structural approach, it is only if a degree of non-correspondence and a differential modality between the interpreted element and its interpretation are assumed, with the corresponding necessary relativity and historicity, that a 'real'

53. N. Mouzelis, *Back to Sociological Theory*, London, 1991, p. 83.

hermeneutic approach can be claimed.

In fact, Dilthey, Husserl and Mead are all suggestive of a theorization of a level of the social as a structured field of meaning, not coextensive with conceptual thought, though partially accessible to it. Such a theorization would introduce the necessary difference of modalities that could in turn necessitate a 'really' interpretive procedure. However, these remain tentative suggestions rather than a developed scheme.[54]

54. Recognizing the impasse in traditional hermeneutics, the greatest modern representative of the hermeneutic tradition, H.G. Gadamer, affirms the impossibility of any final objective knowledge of the social and the necessarily historically dependent nature of such knowledge. He bases his claim on the inherent openness of language as the necessary medium of understanding ('all human speaking is finite in such a way that there is within it an infinity of meaning to be elaborated and interpreted', Gadamer, *Truth and Method*, p. 416). It is not evident, however, why language, the medium of conceptual thought *par excellence* and hence operating on the same level as such thought could be considered as introducing such an 'openness'. Moreover, the reference to language does not cover at all social phenomena which are not primarily to do with the word – such as those pertaining to social practice – and which a hermeneutics of the social aspires to include (see also note 6, chapter 12, p. 206).

–3–

Objectivism and Rationalism

While initial approaches to the study of the social within the idealist tradition have originally seen society as the subject of history in an evolutionary perspective, subsequent theorists were less inclined to do so. What these theorists retained and which connected them with the idealist tradition, was the acceptance of certain constant and transhistorical categories which supposedly always order the social. Although these categories were not always introduced in an axiomatic way and they were instead presented as empirical generalizations, they were in fact always *a priori*. We can consider Weber, the late Parsons, and Lévi-Strauss as exemplifying this first case. However, even the assumption of the existence of these categories was abandoned in certain cases, retaining only an assertion of the possibility of an objective and complete knowledge of the social based on an ultimate susceptibility of the social to reason. We can consider the early Parsons and Althusser as representing this second approach.

Weber and Parsons

Weber's theoretical account of the social is intriguing. He starts from individual action and an interpretative viewpoint of understanding (*Verstehen*) this action. Yet, in fact, his theorization is neither individualistic nor hermeneutic. Weber constructs a typology of social actions, two forms of rational action (*zweckrational*: instrumentally rational; and *wertrational*: value rational) and two other forms (affective/traditional action).[1] In his view the first two types can form the basis of an understanding of the social through the construction of a 'purely rational course of action' – an 'ideal type'. He introduces rational action, therefore, simply as a methodological device offering the only possibility of understanding social action in general. The social as a whole is not primarily rational but is amenable to an

1. M. Weber, *Economy and Society*, Berkeley, 1978, p. 24.

analysis as if it were. Thus, in a neo-Kantian fashion, distance is introduced between what the social is and its yielding to an analysis according to the laws of the intellect.

However, the possibility of understanding the social through 'ideal types' would require either that rational action covers the majority of social action or that other types of action are also amenable to a rational analysis. Since Weber explicitly recognizes that the 'ideal type' can only be a marginal case, it is not the widespread nature of rational action that supports his assertion. Rather, it is the possibility of analysing non-rational action as if it were rational. For Weber other types of action are to be treated as 'factors of deviation from a conceptually pure type of rational action'. But if so, rational action and the ideal type cease to be simple methodological devices; they become the basis upon which the whole of the social action can be constructed, that is, as deviations from it. For Weber's notion of ideal types to be operative, the social has to be seen not only as amenable to rational analysis, but as primarily rational.

Thus tensions exist within Weber's theoretical scheme. He claims that understanding (*Verstehen*) provides the basis of the knowledge of the social. And yet, it is in fact the assumption of a primarily rational character of the social that serves this function. He explicitly recognizes the existence and even the importance of affective and traditional action, i.e. of non-rational forms of action (his theorization of charisma being an example). And yet, he introduces the notion of ideal type, reducing all types of action to deviations from the rational type.

Moreover, to pass from individual (social) action to an account of the social as such, Weber introduces broad social categories which are presented as produced by the aggregation of individual actions. For example, the economy is defined through 'economically oriented' action which, 'according to its subjective meaning is concerned with the satisfaction of a desire for "utilities"'.[2] But utilities are the 'specific and concrete, real or imagined advantages of opportunities for present or future use as they are estimated and made an object of specific provision by one or more economically acting individuals'.[3] The definition of utilities, then, presupposes 'economically acting individuals', and hence the economy. Weber cannot escape from the fact that the existence of an economy is presupposed by the type of action for which it seems to provide a foundation. A similar argument can be made for the other categories, of authority, religion and law.

2. Ibid., p. 63.
3. Ibid., p. 68.

These categories are not produced by any aggregation of individual social action, the attributes of which can be captured through 'ideal types'. Rather, they are introduced *ad hoc*, as the axes along which historical data can be ordered, axes transhistorically constant and immutable. Thus, despite supposedly starting from individual action as he claims, Weber uses, in fact, a structural approach.

The categories could of course be presented independent of a theorization of individual action, as empirical generalizations. However, the problem is that they are not in any way 'empirically' deducible from a mass of empirical material. In fact these categories are constructed through an extrapolation to the past of features of modern society, and in particular of the seemingly autonomous systemic function of the economy and the polity. Consequently, since the past is seen through the categories of the present, the present appears as the culmination of the past. When Weber refers to modern bureaucratic authority and to capitalist economy as the most rational forms of these categories, this is a necessary result of the way authority and economy are in fact defined.[4] Thus a notion of the social as primarily rational, implicit in Weber's 'ideal type', is reinforced by the introduction of transhistorical categories that can be neither deduced from individual social action, nor derived from empirical generalizations.

Therefore, despite his many contradictions and the alternative directions in which he simultaneously points, if we are to grant a cohesiveness in Weber's theorization of the social, we can only consider it as rationalist. Hence Weber shares a fundamental similarity with Marx. While for Marx there is a single dominant human element, that of production, an element that is the guiding line in the development of history and the analysis of the social, for Weber there are several such lines: the economy, authority, legitimation, among others. Marx's argument is generalized, its more extreme evolutionism is abandoned, but its nature remains unchanged: the social is ultimately founded on constant – rational – attributes of man manifested and realized in history. Because, if categories are to exist transhistorically, they can only refer to some transhistorically constant elements of human nature or intellect, certain constant needs that have to be

---

4. This is not to imply that Weber unequivocally and unambivalently considers 'modernization' to be positive. His notion of disenchantment of the world and his account of the limits of formal rationality – loss of freedom and meaning – indicate his reservations for the 'modern'. However, within Weber's theoretical scheme it is difficult – if not impossible – to see the present in any other way than as a culmination of the past.

satisfied, some facets, in general, of a human essence. It is these elements that pre-ordain history and society.

Parsons follows a path under the influence of Weber, while at the same time trying to generalize Weber's argument and to provide a more cohesive theory.[5] His starting point is the 'unit act', involving an agent (actor), an end, condition and means, and a normative orientation that allows choice between means. This classic means-end scheme is developed into what Parsons calls the 'voluntarist theory of action' by making all parameters dependent upon a system of norms. Not only the choice of means is a function of social values or norms as in the traditional model, but also the 'end' and the situation itself. In this way Parsons avoids the problems which the individualist theories that employed the model had faced, in particular the problem of societal 'order' if individuals are seen as independent entities posing disparate 'ends'. Moreover, while Parsons's scheme takes also into account the actor's rational knowledge, the social is for him primarily represented by the system of norms. Thus he is able to derive the level of society from individual action in general, avoiding the difficulties Weber faces being based exclusively on rational action.

Parsons defines norms as 'verbal descriptions of the concrete course of action regarded as desirable, combined with an injunction to make certain future actions conform to this course'.[6] This 'concrete course of action' is clearly distinguished from 'non-subjective elements of action', such as heredity and environment, which are located on the level of biology and physical nature respectively. For Parsons there is no separation of the 'desirability and injunction' of the course of action from the 'verbal description' of it. Nor is there separation of the latter from its 'symbolic expressions'.[7] Thus the 'norm' can be objectively − scientifically − known. The level of action, as norm oriented, is directly expressible by symbolic and scientific language. There is no 'interpretation' to take place; rather an unproblematic access − from the part of the observer − to the norms guiding action is assumed. Since the level of norms defines also the result of social action − the level of 'society' − Parsons's formulation ceases to pose society as primarily rational as does Weber, but rather as fully describable through a system of normative elements, coextensive with the ideal concepts referring to them. There is no proper distinction, therefore, between the social and the ideal (although there is one

5. Parsons's first major work, *The Structure of Social Action*, can be seen as roughly corresponding to chapter 1 of Weber's *Economy and Society*.
6. T. Parsons, *The Structure of Social Action* (1937), New York, 1968, p. 75.
7. Ibid., p. 78.

between the social and cultural 'systems'). Society can be fully and comprehensively analysed through the systems of norms that guide the action of its composite members.[8]

Parsons in his *The Structure of Social Action* does not present a theory of the actor. Actors appear as simply using systems of norms in a conscious, cognitive way. However, the cohesiveness of Parson's theory does not require positing the actor as merely a cognitive being, so far as the objectivism of the scientific observer is not questioned. Given this, and the difficulties inherent in assuming individuals formed outside society (especially in the light of psychoanalytic theories), Parsons in later work gradually presents a theory of the individual and in particular of the shaping of the motivational sphere by society. The initial undifferentiated system of needs is transformed into 'need–dispositions' by the social environment: 'The child's development of a "personality" (or an "ego structure") is to be viewed as the establishment of a relatively specific, definite and consistent system of need–dispositions operating as selective reactions to the alternatives which are presented to him by his object situation.'[9] These need–dispositions are subsequently, in the process of socialization, organized around role–expectations which the alter confronts the developing ego with.[10] The role–expectations are relative 'to a particular interaction context, that is integrated with a particular set of value standards which govern interaction with one or more alters in the appropriate complementary roles'.[11] Constellations of 'roles' or 'role–expectations', constitute 'social systems'.

The Freudian theory of the psyche is also acknowledged by Parsons. Initially the ego is seen as structured through a cognitive

---

8. That Parsons refuses to admit the existence of any level of the social not reducible to the systems of norms is evident also in the way he incorporates the thinking of earlier writers into his scheme. He transforms Pareto's distinction between 'derivations' (the actor's conscious beliefs) and 'residues' (the actor's sentiments guiding action and determining 'derivations') to a distinction between symbols referring to statements of sentiments (subjective) and statements of facts (objective). Thus a difference in modality between the two, as posed by Pareto, is transformed to a difference in degree. Similarly, the fact that Durkheim in his *Elementary Forms of Religious Life* tries to distinguish a social level from the ideas, values and categories it produces is disregarded and Durkheim's later work is considered only as indicating that the 'social factor becomes a normative one'. Finally, the specificity of Weber's concept of 'traditional action' referring to action that cannot be described through the means-end scheme, is also ignored by Parsons.

9. T. Parsons *et al.*, 'Some Fundamental Categories in the Theory of Action', in T. Parsons and E. Shills (eds), *Towards a General Theory of Action* (1951), New York, 1962, p. 18.

10. Ibid., p. 154.

11. T. Parsons, *The Social System*, London, 1951, p. 38.

reference system, a common set of moral standards and expressive symbolism,[12] i.e. as primarily cognitive and as separated from an id representing the biological organism. Later, though, the ego is considered, along with Freud, as the 'precipitate of abandoned object–cathexes'[13] and it is recognized that 'the categories of instinctual and learned components cut across the id, the ego and the superego'.[14] However, it remains the case that these 'instinctual and learned components' are directly and unproblematically knowable through their normative/ideal expressions. The theory of role–expectations and the theorization of the unconscious allows the incorporation of the motivational sphere within the context of the social, without implying any alteration in Parsons's fundamental thesis in *The Structure of Social Action*, namely that social systems can be conceived as coextensive with a system of concepts/ideal elements which fully describe them and which are amenable to objective knowledge.

At this stage, which can be considered as completing the first phase of his theoretical work, Parsons presents a comprehensive theorization of action that can satisfactorily take account of both the structurality and the opacity of the social. Since he does not assume any transhistorically constant elements or a human 'essence', Parsons cannot be subjected to the criticisms addressed at Marx or Weber. However, his position remains an objectivistic one. Implicit in the conception of the social as fully describable through – scientific – knowledge is the assumption of a transhistorical space: that of the rational human mind, expressions of which are both the social itself – as a system of norms – and rational knowledge. The social may not be an expression of an essence, but it springs from a transhistorically present human mind. In Parsons this rationalism is openly accepted and is not contradicting any other assumptions (which is not the case in Althusser). Yet it indicates his close links with the idealist tradition and it is open to criticism from a hermeneutic standpoint.

The more central criticisms to which Parsons is open, however, are of a different nature. First, once the motivational and cognitive levels are seen as fully determinable along role–expectations, the individual can only be considered as fully determined by the social and, moreover, as a harmonious 'construction' with no internal conflict between the different roles involved (for Parsons there are only two alternatives: the 'normal' individual and the 'deviant'). Thus any

12. T. Parsons, 'Superego and the Theory of Social Systems' (1952), in T. Parsons, *Social Structure and Personality*, London, 1964, p. 32.
13. T. Parsons, 'Social Structure and the Development of Personality' (1958), in *Social Structure and Personality*, London, 1964, p. 109.
14. Ibid., p. 110.

autonomy or independence from the part of the actor dissolve into an all determinant 'social' system. Second, once fully closed 'systems of norms' are assumed, no possibility exists to account for history – that is for change in these systems. Since the individual is also incorporated within them, no change can come from the actors. But since these systems are fully closed, no internal reason for change exists either. In *The Social System* Parsons remarks that his theorization cannot as yet account for change, but that future developments could allow it. The fact is that no theory of change is possible within the parameters of the Parsonian scheme.

Perhaps as a response to his inability to account for history, an important shift in Parsons's theoretical work occurs. Instead of simply exploring the nature of 'systems of action', in this new phase Parsons presents fixed patterns of systemic structuring and development. In his books and articles this phase runs parallel to the incorporation of the motivational sphere of the individual within the earlier scheme. It marks, however, a new phase, analytically distinct from the first. In *The Social System* these fixed patterns appear as the positing of 'foci of crystallisation for social structure' and institutions are classified into relational, regulative and cultural, depending on their respective 'function'. Later, this classification is expanded into the 'AGIL scheme' which includes four phases 'in the relationship of any system of action to its situation'.[15] The phases are *A*daptation, *G*oal attainment, *I*ntegration, *L*atent pattern maintenance. The scheme is initially derived from empirical observations in interaction contexts and Parsons considers that it reflects four fundamental functions of action systems in general. The scheme is applied to the formation of personality and its subsystems[16] and replaces the older classification of social institutions. In later papers its four functional lines are taken to define also the direction of any societal development and indeed the development of any action system.[17] Finally the AGIL scheme is seen as also describing the relation of action systems to psychochemical and biological systems.[18] Thus Parsons substitutes for his earlier theory a functional systemic one including an evolutionary claim. The scheme covers the main lines of

15. T. Parsons *et al.*, *Working Papers in the Theory of Action*, New York, 1953, p. 182.

16. T. Parsons, R. Bales *et al.*, *Family, Socialisation and Interaction Process*, London, 1956, pp. 172ff.

17. T. Parsons, 'Some Problems of General Theory in Sociology' (1970), in *Social Systems and the Evolution of Action Theory*, New York, 1977, p. 238.

18. For example in T. Parsons, 'A Paradigm of the Human Condition', in *Action Theory and the Human Condition*, New York, 1978, p. 382.

development of systems as well as the actual classification of subsystems in any given system.

Parsons tried to justify the AGIL scheme by two means: firstly by connecting it to his earlier action scheme and considering it as deducible out of a fixed number of dichotomous choices any process of action involves, either in the development of personality, or in social action. These choices were limited to five – the famous 'pattern variables'. However, despite many efforts at classification by himself and associates, Parsons has not been able to actually establish either that the pattern variables cover the entire field of orientation of human action or that the AGIL system can be indeed deduced by them.[19]

The second means by which Parsons supported the introduction of the AGIL scheme was a functional argument. The scheme was presented as covering the fundamental functions any system of action must perform in order to be self-sustainable. This assertion marks Parsons's 'structural–functional' approach. However, in order for a functional argument of this kind to hold, the borders of the 'system' in question with its environment towards which the functions of the system are addressed have to be clearly drawn. In the case of the social system, which is Parsons's central concern, neither the borders of the system nor the environment towards which its functions are performed, are ever clearly defined. What happens instead is that modern society is taken as the model of both these necessary functions and their differentiation, projecting into the past an incomplete image of the present and into the future a multiplied image of the present. The AGIL system can be supported by a structural–functional argument only by accepting that the present form of the social transhistorically defines the limits and functions of any social 'system'. A similar case can be made for Parsons's account of character formation in terms of the AGIL scheme.

The AGIL system cannot therefore be justified by either of the two arguments Parsons advances. In fact, what the scheme does, is to pose a number of categories as central and determinant in an *a priori* and axiomatic way. This kind of functionalism or systems theory[20] is only a more modern and sophisticated version of idealism's attempt to

19. For a full discussion see S. Savage, *The Theories of T. Parsons*, London, 1981, pp. 162ff.

20. Other functionalist arguments such as Merton's and other open variants of systems theory, such as Buckley's or Luhmann's, are not subject to such a criticism (R. Merton, 'Manifest and Latent Functions' (1948), in *Social Theory and Social Structure*, Glencoe, 1963; W. Buckley, *Sociology and Modern Systems Theory*, New Jersey, 1967; N. Luhmann, 'The Differentiation of Society' (1977), in *The Differentiation of Society*, New York, 1982).

ground the social (and the individual) in a hidden essence manifested and developing in history. The AGIL scheme is no less metaphysical than Weber's categories or Marx's economism (or, of course, Hegel's Universal Spirit). As for the generality Parsons attributes to the scheme in his late writings, it is indeed very reminiscent of the axiomatic generality Spencer attributed to his own scheme of evolution (and it is ironic to remember that Parsons begins his *The Structure of Social Action* with the question: 'Who reads Spencer today'?).

Thus Parsons's second phase marks a regression to an assumption of given categories determining both the structural make-up and the direction of development of the social. This phase is not incompatible with the earlier one, although it is not deducible from it. But if we consider the second phase as an attempt by Parsons to account for history, something his earlier scheme alone was incapable of, the attempt is revealing. It indicates that within a rationalistic objectivism only by the assumption of transhistorically constant categories can history be taken account of.

Lévi-Strauss and Althusser

An approach that has many common elements with Parson's first phase can be found in 1950s and 1960s French structuralism. It was the work of linguists, particularly of Saussure, that brought into attention a significantly novel notion of 'structure'. Saussure's *Course in General Linguistics*, recognized as the founding work of the movement, distinguishes language as a system (*la langue*) from the actual manifestations of language in speech or writing (*la parole*)[21] and makes the first its object: language is conceived as a structure, i.e. as 'a system of interdependent terms in which the value of each term results solely from the simultaneous presence of the other terms'.[22] Language as such a system can be objectively studied in contrast to speech, which is 'many-sided and heterogeneous' and the 'unity of which cannot be discovered'.

In parallel to a view of language as a distinct and knowable system behind the multifaced quality of speech, a notion of the social in general as similarly reducible, in principle, to such systems was developed. C. Lévi-Strauss first used this type of approach, though, as he recognizes, he takes more from Troubetzkoy than from Saussure. His aim is to establish relations between terms leading to the discovery

---

21. F. de Saussure, *Course in General Linguistics* (1916), London, 1974, p. xvii.
22. Ibid., p. 114.

of general and unconscious laws that guide social phenomena.[23]

Lévi-Strauss introduces his approach by a study of elementary structures of kinship. Kinship is seen as a definable social construction, in no way reducible to biology. The different types of kinship, however, are reducible to the combination of three 'elementary structures' which 'are always present to the human mind, at least in an unconscious form'.[24] The multiplicity of kinship structures is intelligible through the different combinations (the structuralist 'combinatory') of these constant, invariable, elementary structures. The structures arising out of these combinations are by no means a product of the individual actor who is himself 'a translation, on the plane of individual psyche, of a properly sociological structure'.[25] Moreover, these structures are, like language, 'built by the mind on the level of unconscious thought'.[26] They can, however, be objectively known since, like the laws of language, 'the observer cannot modify the phenomenon merely by becoming conscious of it',[27] due to the capacity of the subject, even when studying itself, to 'indefinitely objectify itself'.[28] Science's role is precisely to discover these 'elementary structures' as well as the 'laws of combination'.[29]

Lévi-Strauss does not provide any other analysis of a social structure similar to that of kinship. In later works he turns his attention to the modality of the 'savage mind', and to an analysis of myths, and partly regresses from the most extreme formulation of this early period (roughly up to the 1950s). Yet, these early formulations are substantial enough to delineate a specific approach that could be termed 'structuralist' in a strict sense. This approach emphasizes the structure over the individual, the unconscious over the conscious and the social over the 'natural', while retaining the assertion of a possibility of full objective knowledge of these structures, through a knowledge of their constituent, invariant 'elementary structures'.

We have here a variation of the rationalism of Marx, Weber and Parsons. We do not have a single essence (Marx), or a given set of categories (Weber), or a universal scheme (Parsons's second phase),

23. C. Lévi-Strauss, 'Structural Analysis in Linguistics and Anthropology' (1945), in *Structural Anthropology I*, London, 1968, p. 33.

24. C. Lévi-Strauss, *The Elementary Structures of Kinship* (1949), Boston, 1969, p. 464.

25. C. Lévi-Strauss, 'Introduction to the Work of M. Mauss', in M. Mauss, *Sociologie et Anthropologie*, Paris, 1950, p. xvi.

26. Lévi-Strauss, 'Structural Analysis in Linguistics and Anthropology', p. 34.

27. C. Lévi-Strauss, 'Language and the Analysis of Social Laws' (1951), in *Structural Anthropology I*, p. 57.

28. Lévi-Strauss, 'Introduction to the Work of Marcel Mauss', p. xxix.

29. Lévi-Strauss, 'Structural Analysis in Linguistics and Anthropology', p. 40.

but invariant 'elementary structures' accessible to human knowledge. As with all these approaches, the invariant elements are not and cannot be properly deduced from empirical material, despite Lévi-Strauss's assertions.[30] The 'elementary structures' can be superimposed on such material, for better or worse, but they are not empirical generalizations. They are *a priori* categories which order the material in the same way as Marx's labour, Weber's economic, political, and other categories, or Parson's AGIL scheme. Moreover, their knowledge is possible because they have the modality of human mind, that of concepts, ideas and thought.[31] The existence of a 'combinatory' is possible only through the assumption of a transcendental subject, the 'unconscious human mind' in which the different combinatories can operate and which is their linking element.[32]

The novelty of Lévi-Strauss's structuralism, within a general rationalist/objectivist framework is that it proposes a different way of conceptualizing history – different from evolutionist or teleological approaches. History appears as the play of the indefinite possibilities of combination of the invariant 'elementary structures'. Invariant elements and transhistorical categories are not seen as necessary lines of differentiation but rather as the stuff of innumerable combinations: there is no necessary teleology, no implied evolutionism in the structuralist scheme. A linear view of history is replaced by a combinatorial view of history. Lévi-Strauss's structuralism represents the other possibility to an evolutionism within an objectivist context. He himself admits it: science, he writes, 'can be either reductionist or structuralist'.[33] However, the fundamental assumption remains the same: history is determined, if only in potentiality. All the possibilities of history are already enclosed in the 'elementary structures' of the – unconscious – human mind and these elementary elements are ultimately accessible to human knowledge. We may escape from a teleological view of history but not from determinism.

---

30. See the important criticism of E. Leach in chapter six of *Lévi-Strauss*, London, 1970.

31. Lévi-Strauss recognizes that 'the term social structure has nothing to do with empirical reality, but with models which are built up after it' ('Social Structure' (1952), in *Structural Anthropology I*, p. 279), but he does not consider that there is any residue between these 'models' and the modality of the (social) empirical reality that would deny any absolute identity.

32. Ricœur has characterized the Lévi-Straussian project as 'Kantianism without the transcendental subject' (P. Ricœur, 'Structure and Hermeneutics', [1963] in *The Conflict of Interpretations*, Evanston, 1974). Yet this subject does exist, only it is no longer individual, but social (the 'human group').

33. C. Lévi-Strauss, *Myth and Meaning*, London, 1978, p. 9.

The initial definition of structure by Saussure, stressed its differential character, i.e. the inability to define its elements outside itself. Lévi-Strauss's notion of 'elementary structures' clearly violated this principle by introducing transhistorical constants that could be defined outside and independently of any particular structure. To reject any such transhistoricity was the stated purpose of L. Althusser.

Althusser rejects any 'original essence' governing the unity and development of (social) structures. The negation of any such essence is also the negation of a homogeneous and contemporaneous historical time, time as the continuum in which 'the dialectical continuity of the process of the development of the Idea is manifest [. . .] a homogeneity Lévi-Strauss's use of synchrony and diachrony in fact replicates'.[34] Instead of this unitary time, Althusser claims, we observe in history a variety of times (as F. Braudel indicated). And this variety of times refers to a variety of structures, structures not definable in general, but which would 'give its meaning to any simple category within them'. Each 'structure' is a structured unity not referring outside itself, but differentially defining all its elements and exhibiting its own internal time. It is this notion of structure that Althusser wants to establish as the basic theoretical concept for the social.

For Althusser this structured unity is the product of 'theoretical practice' (of 'true' science) and not the discovery of the 'real part of the real object'[35] or of the 'essential' as opposed to the 'inessential' that the empiricist problematic poses. A 'theoretical practice' combines 'the type of object (raw material) on which it labours, the theoretical means of production available (its theory, its method and its technique, experimental or otherwise) and the historical relations (theoretical, ideological and social) in which it produces'.[36] However, once this theoretical practice effects a break with its raw material (mainly, in the case of social knowledge, ideology) and a rigorous (rational) procedure, it seems that for Althusser it can adequately describe the 'real'. Thus he embraces an objectivism incarnated in 'true' science versus the fallacies of 'ideological constructions'.

Althusser presents all the above as an interpretation of Marx. For him it is Marx who proposes, *avant la lettre*, the differential notion of structure: Marx does not simply invert the Hegelian dialectic while retaining its principle, 'deriving successive moments not from the

34. L. Althusser, 'The Object of Capital' (1968), in L. Althusser and E. Balibar, *Reading Capital*, London, 1970, pp. 94, 96.

35. L. Althusser, 'From Capital to Marx's Philosophy', in Althusser and Balibar, *Reading Capital*, p. 38.

36. Ibid., p. 41.

Idea, but from the Economy',[37] but departs radically from this dialectic. Althusser distinguishes between the young and the mature Marx, considering that in his later phase Marx dissociates himself from Hegel. In his 'mature' works, and especially in *Capital*, Marx implicitly employs precisely the kind of structure Althusser explicitly develops. The 'capitalist and every mode of production' can be seen as such a structure, incorporating production and the economy as well as the superstructure.[38] Althusser wants to retain, simultaneously with his definition of structure and his radical anti-historicism, the determinant role Marx assigns to the economy and particularly to production, as well as the transhistorical constancy of this determinacy. However, this task proves an impossible one.

To support the argument that the economy remains determinant in historically distinct structural wholes – modes of production – which are differentially defined, Althusser considers the concept of the economic not to have the 'qualities of a given' but 'as having to be constructed for each mode of production'.[39] Moreover, the economy can be determinant only 'in that it determines which of the instances of the social structure occupies the determinant place'.[40] But how can a 'category' or 'instance' be considered to be always determinant if it has to be constructed anew for every structural whole? The very assertion of transhistorical determinacy requires certain constant and invariable elements that would support this always existing determinacy (for example a necessary function, an assumption of man as *Homo laborans*, certain categories, and so on). If the category of the economic has indeed to be constructed for every structural whole, then no *a priori* determinacy can be assumed. No transhistorically constant categories can be assumed simultaneously with a rejection of any transhistorically homogeneous essence or time. Once Lévi-Strauss's combinatory and any Hegelian type of essence are rejected, a transhistorical determinacy of the economy cannot be sustained. Althusser's formulations are simply an attempt at a verbal reconciliation of these contradictory elements, a reconciliation that does not stand close scrutiny. Correspondingly, no general theory of production (of modes of production in the limited sense) can exist

37. L. Althusser, 'Contradiction and Overdetermination' (1962), in *For Marx*, Harmondsworth, 1969, p. 108.38. This is the broad sense of the term 'mode of production' used by Althusser in *Reading Capital*. Balibar and Althusser in other writings use instead the term 'social formation' retaining the term 'mode' for production itself.

39. Althusser and Balibar, *Reading Capital*, p. 183.

40. E. Balibar, 'The Basic Concepts of Historical Materialism', in Althusser and Balibar, *Reading Capital*, p. 224.

without a prior assumption of certain transhistorically invariable elements. Balibar's attempt to do so (in *Reading Capital*) leads him back
to a version of the structuralist combinatory of constant elements.[41]

The same cul-de-sac is reached regarding a possible determinant
instance within a given structured whole (i.e. the determinacy of
production and the economy within a mode of production in the broad
sense). In order to retain such a determinacy, Althusser introduces a
number of terms: structure in dominance, principal contradiction, and
overdetermination. The 'principal contradiction' (that 'of the forces
of production and the relations of production, essentially embodied
in the contradiction between two antagonistic classes') is, within a
concrete structured whole (a 'mode of production'), 'overdetermined
in its principle by the various other levels and instances of the social
formation it animates',[42] thus producing a structure in dominance. The
economy is determinant 'only in the last instance' while the
'superstructure and other circumstances retain a specific effectivity'.[43]
Althusser here wants again to reconcile two irreconcilable assertions:
that of the 'specific effectivity' of the superstructure with that of the
determinacy of the economy. It is once more obvious, however, that
either the economy defines a whole that includes the 'superstructure',
in which case the 'relative autonomy' is simply a qualification, or the
two are distinct structures, relatively autonomous with respect to each
other. To assume that both a determinacy and an 'autonomy', however
relative, simultaneously exist, is logically unacceptable.[44]

Althusser's reading of Marx's *Capital* is also problematic. The
'determination of either an element or a structure by a structure',[45]
which is encountered in *Capital* in the form of the determinant role
of 'surplus value', is seen as reflecting not an essentialism but a
'structural causality' in which the structure determines its elements
because 'its whole existence consists of its effects'.[46] While classical
economics is based on 'a homogeneous space of given phenomena and
an ideological anthropology which bases the economic character of
the phenomena and its space on man as the subject of needs – the

41. In a less strict reading, these elements can be taken to be determined each
time by their specific relation and hence as not invariable. But if so, Balibar can
provide no theory at all since no specific meaning can be assigned to these elements
outside the capitalist mode of production (see A. Glucksmann, 'A Ventriloquist
Structuralism' (1967), *New Left Review*, no. 72, 1972).

42. Althusser, 'Contradiction and Overdetermination', p. 101.

43. Ibid., p. 113.

44. See E. Laclau and C. Mouffe, 'Post Marxism without Apologies', *New Left
Review*, no. 166, 1987, p. 93.

45. Althusser and Balibar, *Reading Capital*, p. 188.

46. Ibid., p. 189.

giveness of homo oeconomicus',[47] Marx rejects both the homogeneous space and the philosophical anthropology supporting it. This rejection can be reconciled with the essence-like notion of 'surplus value' which cannot be measured or 'seen', because 'surplus value [. . .] is not a thing, but the concept of a relationship, the concept of an existing social structure of production, of an existence visible and measurable only in its effects'.[48] However, the fact remains that surplus value, as argued in chapter 1, can only be defined if there exists 'homogeneous, simple, abstract labour' which in turn is possible only in simple commodity production with no technological change, and if there is a given 'necessary labour' on which the workers are to survive. These conditions cannot be satisfied within Marx's own description of the capitalist mode of production and can only be sustained if human labour is assumed to be a transhistorical human essence – reintroducing thus the 'homogeneous space' of classical economists. To consider that surplus value corresponds to 'structural causality' cannot make this underlying essentialism disappear.

Within a strict structural scheme in which structures are differentially defined and not reducible to a homogeneous 'outside', none of the notions Althusser proposes in his reading of Marx's work – overdetermination, determination in the last instance, structural causality – are necessary. Their need arises only if the structural scheme is to be made compatible with a theorization that contradicts it, as Marx's notion of determinacy of production and economy does. Even so, these notions cannot really reconcile the two theorizations. Althusser's attempt to retain the determinacy of the economy both within a social whole including other elements and as transhistorically existing, in other words his appropriation of Marx, can be seen as a failure in terms of his own declared objectives.

However, Althusser's own project, that of distinct 'structures', differentially defined, not subject to an overall homogeneity and directly accessible to knowledge, remains a possible, alternative approach, which retains some elements in common with Marx's work. Critics of Althusser have indicated this possibility. Hindess and Hirst, in particular, reject any general theory of modes of production which 'can be realized only by reproducing the essential structures of the idealist philosophies of history'.[49] They proceed further to consider 'social formations' as differentially definable structures, not as 'totalities governed by an organising principle' but as a 'definite set

47. Ibid., p. 162.
48. Ibid., p. 180.
49. B. Hindess and P. Hirst, *Pre-Capitalist Modes of Production*, London, 1975, p. 7.

of relations of production together with the economic, political and cultural forms in which their condition of existence are secured'.[50] This position has been in turn criticized for still retaining the 'relations of production' along with the other 'forms' as identifiable in general, irrespective of their specific structural whole.[51] However, even a general definition of 'forms' can also be discarded and the theorization presented as referring to differentially defined structures which have each time to be reconstructed. If so, Althusser's intention of a structural theorization of the social, explicitly rejecting transhistorical invariables such as a human essence or a homogeneous historical time, can be seen as realized. Such a possibility is not entirely without precedent: it bears a certain resemblance to Parsons's first phase. By employing, however, (Saussure's) differential notion of structure, it marks a specific advance over Parsons. Instead of systems of norms, roles, and role–expectations, elements that could exist independently of the system, the elements of a 'structure' do not have any meaning outside the specific differential relation within the structure. An antihistoricism, which is possible in Parsons's scheme, becomes now necessary.

However, even this modified Althusserian scheme faces important problems. The first is the contradiction that emerges if we retain the assertion of the possibility of an ultimate full and objective 'knowledge' of the social alongside the rejection of any transhistorical constant. As in the case of Parsons, the only way such an objectivism can be grounded is by assuming a transhistorical constant: a rational kernel in human mind is implied, always present, but obscured by 'ideological' constructions. This rational kernel is accessible to scientific 'theoretical practice' but not to ideology. Human rationality manifested in 'objective social structures' and accessible as such through 'science' remains as a transhistorical invariant.

Althusser in his late work[52] denounces the science–ideology distinction as 'theoreticism' and considers his project as still 'objectively true' but as representing the – historically specific – position of the proletariat. In doing so, however, he faces a dilemma: either to see this position (and hence the corresponding theory) as historically privileged and, consequently, the theory as 'true', or to

50. A. Cutler, B. Hindess, P. Hirst and A. Hussain, *Marx's Capital and Capitalism Today*, 2 vols, London, 1977, vol. 1, p. 222.
51. E. Laclau and C. Mouffe, *Hegemony and Socialist Strategy*, London, 1985, pp. 101–4.
52. Cf. L. Althusser, 'Lenin and Philosophy' (1968), 'Lenin before Hegel' (1969), in *Lenin and Philosophy*, London, 1977; and, idem, 'Eléments d'autocritique' (1974), in *Essays in Self-Criticism*, London, 1976.

see it as one possible position of a specific class in a specific social conjuncture. If the former is posited, then an evolutionary scheme of history into which such a privileged position can be grounded has to be again accepted. If the latter, a radical relativity denying any ultimate objectivity is introduced, thus subverting any 'objectivism'. Althusser's objectivism therefore necessarily negates his anti-historicism: either indirectly, by necessarily assuming a transhistorical terrain, a terrain on which 'structures' are deployed and of which 'science' is also a manifestation; or directly, by returning to an evolutionary view of history.

In addition to this contradiction, and perhaps more importantly, Althusser faces the two problems encountered also in Parson's first scheme: the impossibility of conceptualizing historical change and active agency. Once a multiplicity of self-enclosed 'structures' is assumed, no principle or indeed possibility of change can be seen to exist. Since any homogeneity of historical time is denied along with any transhistorical 'essence' and the subject – the individual – is also seen as the 'product' of the structure, there is no 'outside' which could force a change. At the same time, the Saussurian notion of structure as a differential entity is by definition static, synchronic (to which diachrony is opposed). But since no outside 'space' for the effects of diachrony exists any more, the structure can only be seen as necessarily being in equilibrium, reproducing itself and its elements. The alternative would have been for change to be already implicit in the structure, not as actual but as potential – for instance, in the existence of internal contradictions. If so, however, a transhistorical constant would have to be assumed, in the form of a kernel of initial potentialities already there at the very beginning of history (as in Lévi-Strauss's 'elementary structures').

The dilemma – the assumption of an invariable 'outside' and the possibility of a theory of history, of change, of transition from one structure to another, versus the rejection of any such 'outside' – is inescapable. Althusser recognizes the problem but wishes it away,[53] while Balibar invokes necessary 'transition periods' and 'modes of transition', without however being able to justify their necessity and their coming about with respect to the 'mode' itself. In fact, in a strict differential definition of structures, it is impossible to account for history at all. The similar problem Parsons faced in his first phase perhaps prompted him to invoke the generality of the AGIL system. With Althusser the problem is the opposite. Having rejected the Marxian model of the '1859 Preface' he is left with no theoretical

---

53. Althusser and Balibar, *Reading Capital*, pp. 196–8.

means to account for transitional periods or change.

The second problem concerns the autonomy of social actors. Unlike Marx or Lévi-Strauss, Althusser recognizes a field specific to the 'construction' of individuals: it is that of ideology which effects an imaginary 'interpellation' of the subject. In this one area – a theory of ideology – Althusser sees himself as not merely interpreting Marx but advancing beyond him. Ideology is seen as necessary, because it is the 'lived relation between man and their world', a relation that does not operate on the field of consciousness but it is 'imaginary', appearing 'as conscious on the condition that it is unconscious'.[54] The function of ideology is to constitute, to 'interpellate', 'concrete individuals as subjects'.[55] Moreover, ideology exists 'materially', i.e. embedded in apparatuses and practices, not as abstract ideas cognized by the subject and it necessarily involves a misrecognition (*méconnaissance*) 'in the very form of recognition it produces'.[56] Thus for Althusser the construction of the subject is not a mechanical procedure. It involves a specific field – that of ideology, embedded in material practices – with a specific modality – that of the imaginary – and a specific function – recognition/misrecognition.

However, despite the specificity that Althusser attributes to the 'imaginary' field of ideology, he ultimately reduces it to the underlying structure: ideology remains the main mechanism for the reproduction of the structure (the 'mode of production') and thus its specificity is determined by this structure. Consequently, the 'subject' remains passive, denied any autonomy *vis-à-vis* the 'structure'. Indeed the definition of the structure as a fully closed and determined entity does not even allow the possibility of theorizing a determination of the subject by different structures, independent of one another. If social structures are seen as fully closed entities then they can coexist only if they are compatible with and reinforce each other within a totality. Thus the subject has also to be seen as unitary and as having been subjected at least to a series of determinations compatible with and reinforcing each other, if not to one determinant structural whole. The theorization of the subject as fully determined, presented as it is within a theory claiming to be leading to political action (Marxism) is definitely problematic and fiercely attacked.[57] Asserting

54. Althusser, *For Marx*, p. 233.
55. L. Althusser, 'Ideology and Ideological State Apparatuses' (1970), in *Lenin and Philosophy*, p. 160.
56. Ibid., p. 170.
57. See, for example, L. Goldmann, 'Structuralisme, marxisme, existentialisme', *Praxis*, no. 8, 1966, or E.P. Thompson, 'The Poverty of Theory', in *The Poverty of Theory and Other Essays*, London, 1978. However, these criticisms simply indicate the problem, they do not offer a viable alternative.

simultaneously a (full) structural determination of the subject and the possibility of political action is obviously impossible.

It is, therefore, not only the question of historical change but also the question of the possibility of active agency that is closely linked with the modality attributed to social structures, as fully determinable and closed entities. Thus attempts to provide a theory of historical change through 'class struggle' while the modality of social structures is still considered the same[58] are contradictory. If classes are fully determined the outcome of class struggle is also determined. On the other hand, for classes not to be fully determined and hence for class struggle to be significant, a different conception of 'structure' is required.[59]

58. For example E. Balibar, 'Sur la dialectique historique', in *Cinq études du matérialisme historique*, Paris, 1974, p. 245. Also Hindess and Hirst, 'Pre-Capitalist Modes of Production', p. 278.

59. Foucault's work, in so far as any general theorization can be inferred from it, indicates similar assumptions and faces similar problems as the objectivist approach exemplified by the modified Althusserian scheme. Foucault's 'discursive formations' correspond to fully definable and relatively closed structural entities, being 'principles of dispersion and redistribution of elements called statements' whose the modality of existence is 'proper to a group of signs' (M. Foucault, *The Archaeology of Knowledge* 1969, London, 1972, p. 107). It comes as no surprise, then, that no theorization of history can be advanced in either the 'archaeological' method – discovering past 'formations' – or the 'genealogical' one – tracing the origins of present 'formations'. In both cases the causes of emergence or alteration of these formations remain beyond the scope of enquiry, but also, one could argue, beyond the capacities of the approach as well. As for the question of agency, Foucault refuses to theorize the subject other than as the locus of subject positions inherent in discursive formations which construct certain forms of individuality. Yet the analysis of such formations is always made in a critical vein, as if, through the analysis, the subject can discover its own history, the origin of its own construction as a subject and can thus intervene to effect a limited but nevertheless important change. Foucault stresses the critical importance of his analyses (for example in 'What Is Enlightenment', in P. Rabinow (ed.), *The Foucault Reader*, Harmondsworth, 1986) consistently refusing, at the same time, to provide a theorization that would allow the reconciliation of such an active subjectivity with the constructed nature he attributes to the subject. This remains the case in his later work where, in a change of emphasis, the possibility of such an autonomy on the part of the subject in certain limited areas is highlighted, again without being theorized. One wonders whether such a theorization would have been possible given the definition of structural formations. Foucault's relatively rigid structural framework, therefore, inevitably leads to the same type of impasse as does that of Parsons's or Althusser's. However, since Foucault does not aim to provide a fully elaborated theoretical framework and always insists on the topical and limited nature of his studies, it would be perhaps unfair to criticize him for failing to provide a theorization he never intends to. For this reason he is not discussed in the present study as Parsons or Althusser are. Needless to say, despite the shortcomings of his overall (implied) theoretical scheme, Foucault's work remains a source of inspiration and has been used in parts of the present study.

Defining a Field of Enquiry

The different attempts to provide answers to the questions that the modern notion of the social has opened up have been diverse in direction and rich in insight. However, none of them offers a fully satisfactory account of the social, either from an epistemological or ontological point of view. Individualism, in both its positivistic and hermeneutic forms, fails to deliver what it seeks: a theoretical account of how the social can be seen as 'produced' out of the action or interaction of self enclosed, autonomous individuals definable prior to and outside this 'social'.

Holistic approaches, asserting the specificity and *sui generis* nature of the social on methodological/epistemological grounds, fare no better. The social field does not appear as amenable to any 'laws' or even 'regularities' in the manner of the natural sciences to support a holistic positivism. On the other hand, structural hermeneutics, in so far as it remained structural and did not fall back to an individualism, tended to slide towards an – ultimate – objectivism, negating its own assumptions. Both approaches indicate, by default, that an epistemological claim about the nature of social knowledge cannot be convincingly asserted without a parallel supporting theorization of the specificity and of the mode of being of the social, without, in other words, an 'ontology' of the social. Pareto and Durkheim do make an attempt for such an 'ontology', specifically addressed against any reduction of the whole of the social to the realm of 'ideas'. In a surprisingly similar way, Dilthey, Husserl and Mead all indicate the necessity of accepting the existence of a level of the social that is meaningful – and thus interpretable – and yet irreducible to formal/ conceptual thought. However, in both cases the theorization remains undeveloped and not satisfactorily connected to the respective epistemological claims.

The ground was left open, thus, for an advanced and sophisticated version of objectivism/rationalism, offering a detailed theorization of the social closely articulated to an epistemological thesis. Earlier rationalist/idealist approaches were either conceiving society as the subject of history in a path of progress and evolution or claiming transhistorical validity for one or more categories organizing the social field. However, both positions failed to ground their – metaphysical – assumptions or to successfully accommodate the accumulated historico-empirical material. In their place emerged a structural objectivism – identifiable in the early work of Parsons and, in a more developed way, in a modified Althusserian scheme, asserting the possibility of a theorization of the social through its reduction to closed and fully determinable structural entities, each with its own dynamic and history, irreducible to one another and to any transhistorical constants.[60]

However, even this approach faces serious problems. To start with, there is an inherent contradiction between the asserted anti-essentialism and the simultaneous acceptance of the ultimate objectivity of social knowledge. This is because the latter necessarily introduces a transhistorical constant, that of the rational human mind, both producing and capable of 'knowing' the social. Apart from this contradiction, and more importantly, the approach faces two other problems: the inability to conceptualize change and the inability to take into account some form of active agency from the part of the social agent or agents,[61] both closely connected with the way social structure is conceptualized.

A regression to an individualistic position to take account of agency is not an answer since it faces insurmountable obstacles. Similarly, the readoption of transhistorical constants, in the manner of Parsons's later work or of Lévi-Strauss, while providing a provisional answer to the question of history, creates more problems than it solves. The way forward, then, can only be the rejection of the central assumption behind structural/objectivist approaches, namely that the social is reducible to fully determinable and closed structural entities and hence ultimately rational. In this direction alternative theoretical frameworks for the mode of being of the social have to be explored, which, while remaining structural in a general sense (since individualism is a dead end) would allow the theorization of active agency and historical

60. 'Realism' has been relatively recently proposed as an epistemological position providing an alternative to both positivism and hermeneutics (see R. Bhaskar, *The Possibility of Naturalism*, London, 1989). Realism rejects the possibility of establishing any rules or regularities in the social field due to its open nature but retains the assertion of the possibility of an objective knowledge/explanation of the social. In this sense it shares the central epistemological premiss of the objectivist theories discussed here. Its proponents, however, do not provide any theorization of the social that would back their epistemological claims (apart from a general reference to the structural nature of the social and to a 'transformational model of society/person connection', in which the individual retains a level of autonomy). Thus an evaluation of these claims cannot really be made. The modified Althusserian scheme remains the more fully elaborated example of an approach advocating a final objectivity of social knowledge – and of the problems such an approach faces.

61. The problem of agency has been in fact implicit in all structural holistic approaches, though it was not explicitly addressed by either positivist or hermeneutic ones. Indeed, the question about the limits of autonomous action, the question of morality and of politics in the broadest sense, long predates the modern notion of the social. It goes back at least as far as the problem of the limits of 'free will' from the Stoics to Christianity as well as – in a more socially oriented context – to the theorization of politics the Enlightenment produced.

change and provide the basis for an acceptable epistemological position.

In the second part of the book two such alternative lines of theorization – 'structuration' and 'post-structuralist' theories – will be evaluated, while in the third part an attempt to synthesize them, inspired by C. Castoriadis's work and drawing heavily on psychoanalytic theory, will be presented.[62] However, a fruitful line of thought has already been outlined. Marx's notion of a social 'material' level, Durkheim's late work, Pareto's 'residues', Dilthey's, Husserl's and Mead's treatment of meaning and Althusser's 'imaginary' all indicate, alongside or even in contradiction to these authors' dominant themes, the possibility of conceptualizing a level of the social as embodying meaning and yet as distinct from ideas, categories or norms – and from nature too. A different way of theorizing the mode of being part of the social is thus hinted at, a theorization that could, possibly and if sufficiently developed, provide the alternative theoretical framework sought. Indeed, the synthetic attempt presented in the third part of the book will re-examine, amplify and confirm this possibility.

62. One important figure in modern social theory is not explicitly discussed: J. Habermas, whose work, of amazing breadth, is of an undeniable importance to social theory. However, within the context of the analysis that follows, the discussion of Habermas's work is not, strictly speaking, necessary because: first, as far as Habermas's actual social theory is concerned – as expanded in *The Theory of Communicative Action* – it does not offer anything new. On the contrary, it very precariously tries to balance an action theory with a systems theory without addressing the problems each approach faces. Second, Habermas's main interest and focus is not so much in this theory of the social (which also appears relatively late in his work) as on a theory of rationality and modernity. Without a detailed reference to both these subjects, any discussion of Habermas is bound to be deficient. However, neither the question of rationality nor that of modernity is directly addressed in the present study. Our concern is more with an underlying theorization of the social that does have a connection to these questions but a connection that can not be made explicit without further amplification. Thus Habermas's theory is outside the scope of the present work.

Part II

Structuration and Indeterminacy

–4–

Giddens's Theory of Structuration

The turn from the 'structure' to the 'rules' governing its emergence and reproduction – in other words the transition from a theorization of the structure to a theory of 'structuration' – was initially introduced in linguistic theory, just as it was from linguistics that the notion of 'structure' was borrowed in a structuralist context. N. Chomsky's work is exemplary in this respect:

> The real richness of phonological systems lies not in the structural patterns of phonemes but rather in the intricate system of rules by which these patterns are formed, modified and elaborated. The structural patterns that arise at various stages of derivation are a kind of epiphenomenon [. . .] It is the properties of the systems of rules, it seems to me, that really shed light on the specific nature of the organization of language.[1]

Chomsky provided such sets of rules in his 'transformational' grammar, rules that he considered innate. The question of the transition from structure to the modalities of its existence and reproduction, however, was to be posed in the more general context of social theory. Already in 1967 Ricœur remarked:

> The philosophical interest of this new phase of linguistic theory is evident: a new relation, of a nonantinomic character, is in process of being instituted between structure and event, between rule and invention, between constraint and choice, thanks to dynamic concepts of the type structuring operation and no longer structured inventory. I hope that anthropology and the other human sciences will know how to draw the consequences of this, as they are doing now with the original structuralism at the moment when its decline is beginning in linguistics.[2]

The very manner in which the question was posed indicated an allegiance to structural as opposed to individualist accounts and yet an attempt to provide a bridge between the 'structure' and the

1. N. Chomsky, *Language and Mind*, New York, 1972, p. 75.
2. P. Ricœur, 'Structure, Word, Event' (1967), in *The Conflict of Interpretations*, Evanston, 1974, p. 91.

'individual'. It was indeed in this direction 'structuration' theories actually developed, as indicated by the work of A. Giddens and P. Bourdieu.

A. Giddens is the first to introduce the term 'structuration', to designate his theorization of the mechanisms of production and reproduction of social structures within the individual.[3] His aim is to overcome the deficiency of structural approaches such as Parsons's and Althusser's to present the subject 'as a reasoning, acting being'.[4] At the same time he wants to avoid a lapse to subjectivism: 'A theory of the subject which avoids objectivism should not slide into subjectivism'.[5] To this end Giddens proposes a series of definitions for the structural side of the social, as well as a theory of the individual. He considers that his formulations introduce a 'duality of structure', referring to structure as 'both the medium and the outcome of the conduct it recursively organizes: the structural properties of social systems do not exist outside action but are chronically implicated in its production and reproduction'[6] and transcending 'the dualism of individual and society or subject and object'.[7]

Giddens defines social structure as 'rules and resources, recursively implicated in the reproduction of social systems. Structure exists only as memory traces, the organic basis of human knowledgeability, and as instantiated in action.'[8] Giddens employs also the notion of (social) system defined as 'the patterning of social relations across time–space, understood as reproduced practices. Social systems should be regarded as widely variable in terms of the degree of "systemness" they display.'[9] At an intermediate level, between 'structure' and 'system', 'structures' in the plural indicate the more enduring sets of structures as 'rule–resource sets, implicated in the institutional articulation of

3. Giddens's 'theory of structuration' appears in 1976 in his *New Rules of Sociological Method*; it was further developed in *Central Problems in Social Theory* in 1979 and finally in *The Constitution of Society* in 1984. More recent books (*The Consequences of Modernity* [1990], *Modernity and Self-Identity* [1991], *The Transformations of Intimacy* [1992]) built upon this theory to provide a theorization of modernity. In our analysis we will focus mainly on the *Central Problems in Social Theory* and on *The Constitution of Society*. It must be noted that the theory of structuration represents only part of an extensive œuvre, from theoretical critiques to substantive studies of capitalism and the nation–state.
4. A. Giddens, *Profiles and Critiques in Social Theory*, London, 1982, p. 8.
5. Ibid.
6. A. Giddens, *The Constitution of Society*, Cambridge, 1984, p. 374.
7. Giddens, *Central Problems in Social Theory*, London, 1979, p. 5.
8. Giddens, *The Constitution of Society*, p. 377.
9. Ibid.

social systems'.[10] Correlatively, institutions are subdivisions of social systems created by structural sets.

While in the definition of structure the notion of 'rules' is accompanied by that of 'resources', it is the former that primarily describes structure for Giddens. The concept of resources is introduced to emphasize the enabling aspects of structure. Resources, however, only operate within systems of rules and not independently of them. Giddens stresses this point: 'Resources might seem to exist in a temporal–spatial sense in a way in which rules do not. But I want to say that the material existents involved in resources (a) are the content, or the "vehicles" of resources in a parallel manner to the "substance" of codes and norms and (b) as instantiated in power relations in social systems, only operate in conjunction with codes and norms.'[11] Consequently, we can refer to rules as the defining element of the concept of structure.

Rules are defined as 'techniques or generalizable procedures applied in the enactment/reproduction of social practices'.[12] They do not have to be formulated: 'Formulated rules, those that are given verbal expression as canons of law, bureaucratic rules, rules of games and so on, are codified interpretations of rules rather than rules as such.'[13] Giddens considers that the most germane of all examples of rules is that of a mathematical formula, such as $a_n = n^2 + (n-1)$. This is so not because of its mathematical character, but because 'to understand the formula is not to utter it. For someone could utter it and not understand the series; alternatively, it is possible to understand the series without being able to give verbal expression to the formula.'[14] The formula, therefore, is an example of a 'generalizable procedure' and Giddens considers linguistic rules to be similar in character. The example reveals a central assumption underlying Giddens's definition of rules: while a rule can be understood without being formulated, it remains, in principle, perfectly definable and determinable independently of the particular context within which it is used. The fact that the actor can perhaps 'use' the series 1, 5, 11, 19, 29,. . .without knowing the expression that produces them does not change the fact that such an expression does exist and can be clearly formulated. The precise and objective knowledge of 'rules', therefore, and thus of 'structures', is always possible. Giddens's definition of structure remains close in this respect to that of structural/

10. Ibid.
11. Ibid., p. 104.
12. Ibid., p. 21.
13. Ibid.
14. Ibid., p. 20.

objectivist theories discussed above.

Giddens's notion of 'structure' is complemented by his theory of the actor. Three levels are distinguished within the individual in a 'stratification' model: discursive consciousness, practical consciousness and the 'basic security system' (unconscious motivation). The triad is intended to replace the psychoanalytic model of ego, super-ego and id.

The 'basic security system' developed early in life, includes the 'basic existential parameters of the self and social identity', while it develops as 'basic anxiety controlling mechanisms hierarchically ordered as components of personality'.[15] It is unconscious and, unlike practical consciousness, separated by bars and repressions from the conscious level that discursive consciousness represents. The moving force within this 'system' is the establishment and preservation of 'ontological security'[16] corresponding to 'confidence and trust that the natural and social worlds are as they appear to be'. The quest for ontological security provides the general motivation for the monitoring of action performed by practical and discursive consciousness.

Giddens does not deny that the 'ontological security' refers to a 'social' setting, i.e. that the constitution of the subject is effected within society: 'The generation of feelings of trust in others as the deepest lying element of the basic security system, depends substantially upon predictable and caring routines established by parental figures.'[17] He argues, however, that the establishment of the 'basic security system' corresponds mainly to biological, and hence transsocial 'capacities of tension management in relation to organic wants'.[18] Thus the 'basic security system' corresponds to a biological mechanism of homoeostatic adjustment, indicating a central core of subjectivity independent of any 'social' influence. Giddens's appropriation of psychoanalysis is telling in this respect. It is to justify the view of a socially independent and 'given' level of subjectivity that he uses ego-psychology, Freud and psychoanalysis in general. For example, Giddens accepts Lacan's 'mirror stage', which provides a biologically determined model of primary subjectivity, while discarding the other elements of Lacan's theory: 'I want to claim only that in respect of *interpreting the emergence of subjectivity*,

---

15. Ibid., p. 50.
16. Ibid., p. 375. Giddens borrows the term from R.D. Laing.
17. Ibid., p. 50.
18. Giddens, *Central Problems in Social Theory*, p. 122.

Lacan's Freud can be drawn upon with profit.'[19]

If the 'basic security system' corresponds to motivation and is primarily non-social, the levels of discursive and practical consciousness correspond to the 'cognitive' side of the individual and to the internalization of the 'social' by the individual. Discursive consciousness is defined as an 'awareness which has a discursive form',[20] while practical consciousness consists of 'all the things actors know tacitly how to go on in the contexts of social life without being able to give them discursive expression'.[21] No bar or repression protects practical consciousness, unlike the unconscious 'basic security system'.[22] The common origin of the two levels of consciousness is 'memory': 'Discursive and practical consciousness refer to psychological mechanisms of recall, as utilised in contexts of action. Discursive consciousness connotes those forms of recall which the actor is able to express verbally. Practical consciousness involves recall to which the agent has access in the durée of action without being able to express what he or she thereby knows.'[23] What is recalled are 'memory traces' formed by perceptual residues, perception being understood as 'a set of temporal ordering devices'.

With respect to the social what is recalled is the structural 'rules'. How are the rules perceived in the first place? We saw that, despite the definition of rules as 'techniques and procedures', it is a formal and abstract model that Giddens has in mind for the social 'rules'. Correspondingly, 'rules' can only be perceived as formal and abstract entities of an ideal nature which, subsequently, become memory traces. Giddens makes no distinction between perception corresponding to practical consciousness and perception corresponding to discursive consciousness. It is only the mechanisms of recall that differentiate the two levels. Consequently, a change of mode of recall, i.e. a transition from practical to discursive consciousness does not imply any change in the context (the 'rules') recalled. Between the practical and the discursive level exists only a threshold of (higher) awareness. By becoming 'discursive' the rules do not 'change'. Hence, practical consciousness is only a less complete, an impoverished variant of the discursive consciousness.

19. Ibid., p. 121 emphasis added. M. Gane's remark seems justified: 'Giddens is attracted to elements of the analysis of Freud and Lacan only in so far as something can be taken in order to justify the primacy of the subject and the primacy for the subject of his 'ontological security' (M. Gane, 'Giddens and the Crisis of Social Theory', *Economy and Society*, vol. 12, no. 3, 1983, p. 379).

20. Giddens, *The Constitution of Society*, p. 374.

21. Ibid., p. xxiii.

22. Ibid., p. 5.

23. Ibid., p. 49.

For the notion of practical consciousness to introduce a new level of theorization of the actor, there would have to be presented a new modality of operation of this 'consciousness', distinct from the one discursive consciousness refers to. In other words, a level of 'practical' knowledge of rules would be significant only if to know 'practically' meant something different than to know 'discursively'. This in turn would require a different modality of the 'rules' which are practically and not discursively used and reproduced. The 'rules' of practical consciousness would have to exist in consciousness differently from the 'rules' of discursive consciousness. The transition between the two would then involve a 'translation' or an 'interpretation'. Giddens recognizes this when he writes: 'The discursive formulation of a rule is already an interpretation of it.'[24] Yet his actual definitions of the two levels of consciousness do not allow any disjuncture between them that would justify such an 'interpretation'.

Giddens's theorization of the actor introduces, therefore, two, rather than three, significant levels: a biologically determined 'basic security system', in the mechanisms of which the social has no influence or relevance, and, second, a level of primarily cognitive 'memory traces' expressible either in practical or discursive consciousness. The difference between the two modes of consciousness is one of degree rather than one of modality. The structural 'rules' are inscribed as memory traces and can be expressed in either mode of consciousness.

At this point the question of the relationship between the actor and the structure can be posed: do social rules form part of the make-up of the actor, an inseparable element of the 'self'? Or, are they external to the individual, being manipulated at will by a subject definable independently of them?

Since the rules exist as 'memory traces', they are in a sense internal to the actor. However, the central core of subjectivity lies beyond these rules, in the 'basic security system', which as we saw develops independently of the social. The 'deep' unconscious, as well as all motivation processes, lie within this basic security system. Thus Giddens retains, in a modified form, one of the basic postulates of traditional individualism: a unitary, primary subject irreducible to any 'social' determinations. However, given that the structural 'rules' also exist also within the individual, the possibility remains that s/he can be relatively less autonomous with respect to the structure than individualist theories assert.

Giddens's theorization of the actor does not allow us to judge the

24. Ibid., p. 23.

extent of this autonomy. He himself, however, provides a direct and unambiguous answer on this matter. The actors are both 'knowledgeable' about these rules and 'capable' of using them in an active way. 'Knowledgeability' is defined as 'everything the actors know (believe) about the circumstances of their action and that of others [. . .] including tacit as well as discursively available knowledge'.[25] How extensive is this 'knowledgeability'? Giddens admits that 'social actors can be wrong some of the time about what these rules and tactics might be', but he stresses that, 'if there is any continuity to social life at all, most actors must be right most of the time'.[26] Moreover, this 'knowledgeability' is supported by the 'capability' of actors 'of doing otherwise, generally exercised as a routine, tacit feature of everyday behaviour'.[27] It is this 'capability' that 'marks the conceptual boundary of action'.[28] Giddens insists that the possibility that the actor 'might act otherwise' exists even when 'constraints so narrow the range of (feasible) alternatives that only one option or type of option is open to the actor'.[29] Therefore actors not only 'know' the rules, they are capable of either following them or ignoring them at will, of using them in a non restrained, active way.[30]

Thus Giddens, in his desire to stress the autonomy and activeness of the individual, reproduces in fact almost intact the traditional individualistic account of the actor. He superimposes on a theory of social structure as 'rules' a theory of the actor in which, for all important purposes, the individual is independent of the social and can use these rules at will. He can, in this way, claim with justification that he provides a theorization of the subject as a 'reasoning, acting being'. He does so, however, by abandoning basic premisses of structural approaches and by borrowing too liberally the assumptions of individualistic ones.

Giddens is open, therefore, to the same criticisms that individualistic theories are subject to: first, can we indeed sustain that

25. Ibid., p. 90.
26. Ibid.
27. Giddens, *Profiles and Critiques in Social Theory*, p. 9.
28. Giddens, *The Constitution of Society*, p. 69.
29. Ibid., p. 309.
30. This has been remarked on by many commentators of Giddens. For example, J. Thompson notes that 'Giddens manages to preserve the complementarity between structure and agency only by defining agency in such a way that any individual in any situation could not not be an agent' (J. Thompson, *Studies in the Theory of Ideology*, Cambridge, 1984, p. 169). M. Archer remarks that 'the systematic underplaying of constraints artificially inflates the degrees of freedom for action' (M. Archer, 'Morphogenesis vs. Structuration', *British Journal of Sociology*, vol. 33, no. 4, 1982, p. 464).

the social does not enter into the very constitution of the individual psyche in both a cognitive and a motivational way? Can we consider that individuals are not influenced in a profound and permanent way by their social surroundings? Second and more important, given that individuals may always 'have acted otherwise', how can we account for the structurality and the relative permanence of the social? The question, the traditional 'problem of order' is one that Giddens cannot avoid.

Of course Giddens is too much of a sociologist to fully accept the implications of his theorization of the actor. When he refers to society he presents certain 'axes of structuration' through which he can produce constant categories of social structures and institutions (in a manner reminiscent of Weber). These 'axes of structuration' are considered to be signification, domination and legitimation. Through 'modalities' of structuration upon which actors draw in the reproduction of systems of interaction, these basic structures appear on the level of interaction as communication, power and sanction as in the following figure:[31]

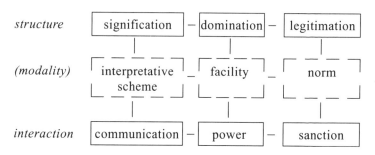

Figure 2

These three axes can also be combined in different ways to produce the actual institutions of a society (symbolic orders, political, economic and legal institutions).[32] Thus a theory of constant types of structures and institutions at a social level becomes possible. This theorization, however, is not connected to Giddens's theory of the actor. It is introduced to provide some 'structural' account of the social within an otherwise individualistic theorization. Not surprisingly, in his more concrete studies – such as his study of the nation–state[33] –

31. Giddens, *The Constitution of Society*, p. 29.
32. Ibid., p. 33.
33. A. Giddens, *The Nation–state and Violence*, Cambridge, 1985.

Giddens uses neither these 'axes of structuration' nor his theory of the actor. Structural wholes (the nation–state, capitalism, and so on) are treated in a conventional way, as *sui generis* entities not necessarily traceable to actors. Indeed Giddens asserts the possibility of an 'institutional analysis', placing 'in suspension the skills and awareness of actors, treating institutions as chronically reproduced rules and resources'.[34] Of course the lack of connection between the two levels of analysis cannot simply be wished away through a play of words. Giddens's uneasiness on the matter, however, is indicative of the impossibility of deriving a plausible theorization of the social from an account of the actor such as his.

We can justifiably assert, therefore, that, the kind of 'theory of structuration' Giddens provides, despite his claims, does not represent an advance over structural theories nor does it provide a bridge between 'action' and 'structure' or 'subject' and the 'social'. It can take account of the subject as 'reasoning and active' only by neglecting any deep, enduring determination on the part of the 'structure'. The structure's reproduction rests entirely on the whim of the individual actor, an actor presented as independent of this structure. Far from introducing any 'duality', Giddens's theory reproduces the traditional dualism of subject and structure.[35]

Giddens's epistemological position is also worth discussing. He considers that the mode of knowledge proper to the social sciences is that of 'double hermeneutics'. While hermeneutics has tended to equate positivism with natural sciences, newer developments in the philosophy of science 'have made it plain that (natural) science is as much about "interpreting" the world as about "explaining" it'.[36] Therefore hermeneutics as such should not be limited to the social sciences. To indicate the specific nature of the hermeneutics of these sciences Giddens uses the concept of 'double hermeneutic'. Unlike the hermeneutics of natural science which 'has to do only with the theories and discourse of scientists analysing an object which does not answer back',[37] 'double hermeneutic' refers to 'the intersection of two frames of meaning as a logically necessary part of social science, the

---

34. Giddens, *The Constitution of Society*, p. 375.

35. Giddens could have followed the other path open to him and asserted that the internalized rules do limit the actor's autonomy and that, in most cases, the actor could not have acted otherwise. He could have thus retained a real structural determination of the actor and avoided the problem of order. In that case his position would have been similar to Parsons's in *The Structure of Social Action* and would have faced the problems Parsons encounters in theorizing historical change and active agency.

36. Giddens, *Profiles and Critiques in Social Theory*, p. 12.

37. Ibid.

meaningful social world as constituted by lay actors and the metalanguages invented by social scientists'.[38] There is a constant 'slippage from one frame of meaning to another involved in the practice of the social sciences'.[39] The logical tie between first and second order concepts 'depends upon the social scientific observer accurately understanding the concepts whereby the actors' conduct is oriented'.[40] 'Second-order' concepts 'can become "first-order" by being appropriated within social life itself'.[41]

However, the relation of 'first' to 'second order' concepts is similar to that proposed by Schutz and others as (simple) 'hermeneutics'. The specificity of Giddens's 'double hermeneutics' lies not in the epistemological position he advocates for the social sciences but in the rejection of the equation of natural sciences with positivism. The concept of 'double hermeneutic' does not introduce anything new regarding the epistemological claims of the hermeneutic tradition. Concerning these claims, it was argued in the first part of the book that there is no real discontinuity between 'first order' concepts and 'second order' concepts, i.e. 'scientific' knowledge. First order concepts have the same modality as the concepts science uses and there is, in principle, no obstacle to the ultimate full and 'objective' knowledge of them. This type of hermeneutics, therefore, cannot avoid falling into an ultimate objectivism. Giddens's 'double hermeneutics' is liable to the same criticism. Indeed, Giddens's definition of 'rules' implies that they are always amenable to a 'formal' and 'discursive' formulation. In fact Giddens explicitly recognizes the possibility of an ultimately objective knowledge of the social: 'The sociologist has a field of study phenomena which are already constituted as meaningful,'[42] but this does not inhibit him from 'accurately understanding the concepts whereby the actors' conduct is oriented'.[43] An 'accurate' understanding is both possible and desirable.[44]

However, Giddens's notion of 'practical consciousness' does introduce the possibility of an alternative theorization of social

---

38. Giddens, *The Constitution of Society*, p. 374.
39. Ibid.
40. Giddens, *Profiles and Critiques in Social Theory*, p. 13.
41. Giddens, *The Constitution of Society*, p. 284.
42. Ibid., p. 284.
43. Giddens, *Profiles and Critiques in Social Theory*, p. 13.
44. Giddens's ultimate alliance to an objectivism is also demonstrated in his discussion of structuralism and functionalism (for example in *Profiles and Critiques in Social Theory*, pp. 9–49, and in *Studies in Social and Political Theory*, London, 1979, pp. 96–129). Giddens's criticism focusses almost exclusively on the neglect of the active role of the subject by these approaches while he does not indicate that he considers their epistemological position as problematic.

knowledge. If the level of 'practical consciousness' had a modality different from that of discursive consciousness and of science, a hermeneutic procedure in the proper sense would have been required to have access to this level and the discursive formulation of a rule would indeed be an interpretation of it. Yet, the actual theorization of practical consciousness Giddens advances introduces no real discontinuity between the two levels of consciousness. 'Practical', 'discursive' and 'social scientific' modes of knowledge are presented simply as divisions along a continuum, at one end of which is the concept of rules and at the other an 'accurate' knowledge of them. It remains possible, though, that an alternative theorization of a level similar to Giddens's 'practical consciousness' could support a truly 'hermeneutic' mode of knowledge of social phenomena.

To conclude: Giddens's intentions and criticisms of structural/ objectivist and subjectivist theories indicate a possible path that would allow an escape from the obstacles they face and would, specifically, allow a satisfactory answer to the question of agency. However, in his willingness to provide an account of the active role the individual actor plays, Giddens simply regresses to a thinly veiled individualistic theory. The actor is presented both as definable outside any structural/ social influences and as capable of 'always acting otherwise' than his structural position would require. Thus the real question is avoided, namely locating the level of the actor's 'activeness' while accepting that s/he remains to a great extent socially constructed and constrained. Moreover, despite his claims to making a 'double hermeneutic' approach, Giddens's conception of the social remains objectivist, close to the objectivist approaches he criticizes.

However, the clarity with which Giddens poses the aims a theory of structuration should have is exemplary. Moreover, the intention behind the introduction of concepts such as 'duality of structure' or 'practical consciousness' – though not their actual use – points the way towards a direction of theoretical development that could be fruitfully pursued if any return to individualism is to be firmly rejected.

–5–

Bourdieu's Theory of Practice

Bourdieu has a similar starting point to Giddens's. He wants to go beyond the reification and objectification of the social that structural approaches usually imply, for all that without accepting subjectivist assumptions.[1]

Bourdieu regards objectivistic approaches as equating the model an observer constructs to theoretically represent the social with the social itself. They transpose, in other words, 'the reality of the model for the model of the reality'. The result is the reification of the social, a reification which treats 'objects constructed by science, whether "culture", "structures" or "modes of production" as realities endowed with a social efficacy'.[2] On the other hand, Bourdieu is equally opposed to subjectivism, for a similar reason: '"Second order" concepts or "accounts of accounts" already transpose a mode of being of scientific accounts, of social science, to the "first order" concepts of the actors. It replaces a causal link between hypostasized entities and practice, as in objectivism, by the supposition that these entities exist already within practice.'[3]

To go beyond the 'objective limits of objectivism' while avoiding the 'imaginary anthropology of subjectivism', a specific theory of practice is required: 'We shall escape, from the ritual either/or choice between objectivism and subjectivism [. . .] only if we are prepared to inquire into the mode of production and functioning of the practical mastery which makes possible both an objectively intelligible practice and also an objectively enchanted experience of that practice.'[4] Bourdieu constructs such a theory around two central concepts, that

---

1. Bourdieu's first statement of a 'theory of practice' appears in 1972 in *Esquisse d'une theorie de pratique* and further expanded in the 1977 English edition (*Outline of a Theory of Practice*). The final development appears in 1980 in *Le sens pratique*, translated in English under the title *The Logic of Practice*. Bourdieu covers an extensive field of studies, from analyses of education to the state, art and culture. It is for his more substantive studies that Bourdieu is best known.
2. P. Bourdieu, *Outline of a Theory of Practice*, Cambridge, 1977, p. 27.
3. Ibid., p. 21.
4. Ibid., pp. 3–4.

of 'habitus' and that of the 'logic of practice' (*sens pratique*).

'Habitus' describes, for Bourdieu, the way social agents are constructed by the social:

> The structures constitutive of a particular type of environment (e.g. the material conditions of existence characteristic of a class condition) produce habitus, systems of durable, transposable dispositions, structured structures predisposed to function as structuring structures, that is, as principles of the generation and structuring of practices and representations which can be objectively 'regulated' and 'regular' without in any way being the product of obedience to rules, objectively adapted to their goals without presupposing a conscious aiming at ends or an express mastery of the operations necessary to attain them.[5] [. . .] The habitus could be considered as a subjective but not individual system of internalized structures, schemes of perception, conception, and action common to all members of the same group or class and constituting the precondition for all objectification and apperception.[6]

The 'durable dispositions' of the habitus allow agents to 'inhabit institutions, appropriate them practically, and so keep them in activity, continuously pulling them from the state of dead letters'.[7] The habitus, as internalized dispositions and as a set of principles of structuration, is a central determinant in the context of practice: 'It produces practices which tend to reproduce the regularities immanent in the objective conditions of the production of their generative principle.'[8] The homogeneity of a group, a class, a 'society', is precisely the result of the structured character of these dispositions: 'The objective homogenizing of group or class habitus, which results from the homogeneity of the conditions of existence, is what enables practices to be objectively harmonised without any intentional calculation or conscious reference to a norm and mutually adjusted in the absence of any direct interaction or, *a fortiori*, explicit co-ordination.'[9]

The habitus does not consist of a system of ideas that a person 'internalizes', but rather of a series of identities the person acquires and 'embodies'. It exists primarily in an embodied form, as 'a bodily hexis':

> Bodily hexis is political mythology realised, em-bodied, turned into a permanent disposition, a durable way of standing, speaking, walking, and,

---

5. Ibid., p. 72.
6. Ibid., p. 86.
7. P. Bourdieu, *The Logic of Practice* (1980), Cambridge, 1990, p. 57.
8. Bourdieu, *Outline of a Theory of Practice*, p. 89.
9. Ibid., p. 80.

thereby of feeling and thinking[10] [. . .] Every successfully socialised agent thus possesses, in their incorporated state, the instruments of an ordering of the world, a system of classifying schemes which organizes all practices, and of which the linguistic schemes (to which the neo-Kantian tradition – and the ethnomethodological school nowadays – attribute unjustified autonomy and importance) are only one aspect.[11]

It is this 'em-bodied' modality of habitus that accounts for its durability: 'The principles em-bodied in this way are placed beyond the grasp of consciousness, and hence cannot be touched by voluntary, deliberate transformation, cannot even be made explicit; nothing seems more ineffable, more incommunicable, more inimitable, and, therefore, more precious, than the values given body. . .'[12] Thus the habitus is 'not something that one has, as a knowledge that one can keep in front of him, but something that one is'.[13]

The 'durable dispositions' that constitute a habitus are gradually acquired as the child grows up within a particular environment, with earlier experiences structuring to an extent the acquisition of later ones: 'The habitus acquired in the family underlies the structuring of school experiences (in particular the reception and assimilation of the specifically pedagogic message) and the habitus transformed by schooling, itself diversified, in turn underlies the structuring of all subsequent experiences [. . .] and so on, from restructuring to restructuring.'[14] A habitus is thus the product of the simultaneous effect of many 'structures'. Indeed it constitutes the 'space' within which different structures coexist and articulate with each other: 'The unifying principle of practices in different domains which objectivist analysis would assign to separate "subsystems" such as matrimonial strategies, fertility strategies, is nothing other than the habitus, the locus of practical realization of the "articulation" of fields which objectivism lays out side by side.'[15]

10. Ibid.
11. Ibid., p. 123.
12. Ibid., p. 94.
13. Bourdieu, *The Logic of Practice*, p. 73. Providing an example of the deep level on which the habitus operates, Bourdieu analyses class differences in 'taste' as precisely an indication of the deep individual differences differential (class) positions entail. Individuals belonging to the different classes are not simply endowed with different quantities of capital or power; they are different in their most 'personal', 'intimate' characteristics: their tastes, their likes and dislikes, conceptions and beliefs (P. Bourdieu, *Distinction: A Social Critique of the Judgement of Taste* [1979], London, 1984).
14. Bourdieu, *Outline of a Theory of Practice*, p. 87.
15. Ibid., p. 83.

The crucial difference between Bourdieu and Giddens, together with the whole of the individualist tradition, is now obvious: Bourdieu really accepts the constructed nature of the 'person', the 'subject', the 'agent' and his/her determination by the structure, stressing the durable, unconscious and embodied character of this construction as opposed to 'ideas' or 'rules' the person internalizes.

The question arises whether the notion of habitus negates any activeness and autonomy from the part of the actor. Bourdieu's answer is in the negative. He claims that the social actor in the context of practice always invents directions of action which are in no way reducible to given 'rules': 'It is necessary, to abandon all theories which explicitly or implicitly treat practice as a mechanical reaction, directly determined by the antecedent conditions and entirely reducible to the mechanical functioning of pre-established assemblies, "models" or "roles" which we would, moreover, have to postulate in infinite number.'[16] Instead, Bourdieu proposes, we have 'to substitute strategy for the rule (and thus) to reintroduce time, with its rhythm, its orientation, its irreversibility'.[17] Practice always has a temporal dimension within which the activeness of the actors is manifested and which cannot be captured in the 'spatial' representations of objectivist approaches.

As an example, Bourdieu cites Mauss's theory of the gift as exchange, a theory taken up by Lévi-Strauss. He observes that if the relations of exchange are simply mapped in a spatial sense, as in Lévi-Strauss, the importance of the timing of the counter gift, which is as important as its content, is not taken into account. The gift exchange cannot be simply represented as a mathematical structure of exchange. What has to be incorporated in it is the notion of time and its possible variations which are never reducible to a formal model. But the timing rests entirely with the actor. The choice of the time of the counter gift is part of the overall strategy that any gift exchange entails. The temporal dimension, therefore, a dimension not taken into account by formal structural models, is an indication of the active role the subject has to play for any 'rules' to operate in practice.

Bourdieu provides another example in his analysis of the way kinship rules are used by the Kabyles in Algeria. The genealogical rules (of parallel cousin marriage) operate neither as judicial rules nor as norms. They are simply elements within a complex strategy the actors deploy, for example to enhance their position within the group. In fact these rules cannot be approached in any 'objective' way.

16. Ibid., p. 73.
17. Ibid., p. 9.

Different individuals present them in different ways, all equally legitimate: 'Informants constantly remind us by their very incoherences and contradictions that marriage can never be fully defined in genealogical terms, and that it may take on different, even opposite meanings and functions, according to its determining conditions.'[18]

However, the autonomy the social actor has in deploying 'strategies' instead of following fixed structural rules is limited. Bourdieu rejects approaches such as Sartre's that 'make each action a sort of unprecedented confrontation between the subject and the world'. The habitus forms, in a way, the boundaries within which the social actor can deploy strategies and pursue 'aims', the limits of any autonomy:

> Because the habitus is an endless capacity to engender products – thoughts, perceptions, expressions, actions – whose limits are set by the historically and socially situated conditions of its production, the conditioned and conditional freedom it secures is as remote from a creation of unpredictable novelty as it is from a simple mechanical reproduction of the initial conditionings.[19]

Though Bourdieu does not use the term, his notion of habitus fulfils the basic requirements of a theory of structuration. It allows the theorization of structural elements internalized in the individual – and 'constructing' him – in a durable way. These 'structured dispositions' ensure the reproduction of social structures through the action of the individuals they determine. Moreover, for Bourdieu, the existence of these structured dispositions does not imply that the individual is passive. On the contrary, social actors have to be seen as exhibiting a degree of autonomy: they do not follow rules, they deploy strategies. For Bourdieu the assertion that the actor is constructed within a set of structures is separate from the assertion that – therefore – his/her actions can be derived in a mechanistic way from these structures.

However, the notion of habitus remains a generic one. It indicates the requirements of a theorization of the structural construction of the individual – permanence, unconscious and non-ideal level of operation, relevance to the motivational sphere, and production through participation in a series of environments. But it does not provide a proper and extensive theory of the way in which these structural dispositions are constructed. The attributes of the habitus are simply evoked, in an additive way, without for that being properly

18. Ibid., p. 49.
19. Ibid., p. 73.

related to one another, without their level of operation within the individual being clarified and without the mechanism of their production being sufficiently theorized.[20] Bourdieu's empirical illustrations of the relevance of the notion of habitus, although extremely useful in order to establish the need of such a concept, confuse rather than facilitate a proper theorization. The notion is used to cover both fundamentally defining characteristics and dispositions (as, for example, in the analysis of taste in *Distinction*) and more superficial and 'external' to the individual elements (as when Bourdieu refers to an 'academic habitus')[21]. Moreover, the question of whether theoretical knowledge can provide a satisfactory account of the non-ideal but 'embodied' principles that constitute a habitus is not addressed at all.

The insufficiency of the theorization of habitus becomes pronounced when Bourdieu simultaneously asserts the possibility of active agency. The empirical illustrations of Bourdieu's concept of 'strategy' as a way to assert the – limited – autonomy of the individual cannot, by themselves, do more than indicate that indeed a certain autonomy exists. A theory of the existence of this autonomy, however, is not presented. Thus a number of questions remain open: how is it possible to have within the subject and side by side both the structured dispositions of the habitus and the locus of an active agency? Do these two requirements refer to the same level within the individual or to different ones? How can the limits of active agency *vis-à-vis* the habitus be drawn? In what sense are the structured dispositions more 'permanent' than the 'reasoning' subject?

The habitus refers to the socially constructed individual. To assert a certain autonomy, as Bourdieu does, however bounded, a socially irreducible part of the person has to be assumed. For the 'structured dispositions' to produce 'strategies', they have to be supported by a certain individuality outside of and not reducible to the habitus. Bourdieu's theorization of the habitus does not allow us to locate this 'irreducible' individuality, its level, or its limits. A more precise and detailed theorization of the individual is necessary, therefore, if the aims Bourdieu proposes for the notion of habitus are to be fulfilled.

---

20. As DiMaggio remarks, 'We are told that the initial habitus (inculcated primarily by early childhood experience) is durable, but, since it is also transformable, we are never sure just what difference this durability makes, or under what circumstances it makes a difference for what phenomena. This question, that of the stability and plasticity of personality, is one about which Bourdieu has little concrete to say' (P. DiMaggio, 'Review Essay on P. Bourdieu', *American Journal of Sociology*, vol. 84, no. 6, 1979, p. 1468).

21. P. Bourdieu, *Homo Academicus* (1984), Cambridge, 1988, p. 143.

The notion of habitus is pivotal also in constructing a 'theory of practice'. The habitus, as internalized dispositions and a set of principles of structuration, is a central determinant in the context of practice. The structured dispositions, as 'schemes of perception, appreciation and action, which are acquired through practice and applied in their practical state without acceding to explicit representation, function as practical operators'.[22] Thus the habitus 'produces practices which tend to reproduce the regularities immanent in the objective conditions of the production of their generative principle'.[23] Because the 'practical operators' of the habitus are activated within the specific context of practice, no preconceived ideational schemes are necessarily implied:

> An agent who possesses a practical mastery, an art, whatever it may be, is capable of applying in his action the disposition that appears to him only in action, in the relationship with a situation [. . .] Agents can adequately master the *mondus operandi* that enables them to generate correctly formed ritual practices, only by making it work practically, in a real situation, in relation to practical functions.[24]

A 'practical mastery' is always different from theoretical accounts of practice, irrespective of whether it is the agent himself who gives this account or an external observer:

> As soon as he reflects on his practice, adopting a quasi theoretical posture, the agent loses any chance of expressing the truth of his practice, and especially the truth of the practical relation to practice [. . .] he cannot communicate the essential point which is that the very nature of practice is that it excludes this question (of its theoretical elaboration).[25]

Practice, therefore, has a specific modality that cannot be theoretically represented and understood without a transformation, an interpretation that transforms it to a discourse. Bourdieu introduces thus a break with the whole rationalistic tradition for which social practice is the product of ideal entities – norms, rules, or individual meanings – and hence is directly amenable to a theoretical knowledge. This specific modality of practice Bourdieu indicates as 'logic of practice', as '*sens pratique*', remarking at the same time that 'the idea of practical logic, a logic in itself, without conscious reflection or logical control, is a contradiction in terms, which defies logical logic.

22. Bourdieu, *Outline of a Theory of Practice*, p. 97.
23. Ibid., p. 78.
24. Bourdieu, *The Logic of Practice*, p. 90.
25. Ibid., p. 91.

This paradoxical logic is that of all practice, or, better, of all *sens pratique*.'[26]

Bourdieu proceeds to further analyse this '*sens pratique*': 'Practical logic is able to organize the totality of an agent's thoughts, perceptions, and actions by means of a few generative principles, themselves reducible in the last analysis to a fundamental dichotomy.'[27] This organization, which implies a loss of rigour for the sake of greater simplicity and generality, is the mode of operation of practical condition in general. Practical logic functions 'as an analogical sense, a sort of "sense of the contrary" which gives rise to the countless applications of the few basic contrasts capable of providing a minimum of determination (a man is not a woman – a toad is not a frog) and cannot give any information about the relations it relates, because it is precisely their indeterminacy and fuzziness that permit it to operate'.[28] This 'indeterminacy or fuzziness' can, among other things, account for 'the application to the same objects or practices of different schemes (such as opening/closing, going in/coming out, going up/going down, etc.) which, at the degree of precision (i.e. of imprecision) with which they are defined, are all *practically* equivalent, is the source of the polysemy characterising the fundamental relationships in the symbolic system'.[29]

Similarly, because practical logic functions through a simple generative scheme of oppositions, it is the specific universe of practice as relevant in each case that determines the meaning of a term: 'the house' in the Kabyles, for example, 'is globally defined as female, damp, etc., when conceived from the outside, from the male point of view, i.e. in opposition to the external world, but it can be divided into a male–female part and a female–female part when is treated instead as a universe – of practice and discourse – on its own right'.[30] A preeminent example of practical logic is provided by rites which are often

> simply a practical mimesis of the natural process that is to be facilitated. As opposed to explicit metaphor and analogy, mimetic representation links phenomena as different as the swelling of grain in the cooking pot, the swelling of a pregnant woman's belly and the sprouting of wheat in the ground, in a relationship that implies no spelling-out of the properties of the terms thus related or the principles applied in relating them.[31]

26. Ibid., p. 92.
27. Bourdieu, *Outline of a Theory of Practice*, p. 110.
28. Ibid., p. 113.
29. Ibid., p. 111.
30. Ibid., p. 110.
31. Bourdieu, *The Logic of Practice*, p. 92.

Bourdieu observes that Lévi-Strauss and others, who noted this reliance on simple pairs of opposites functioning analogically, failed to note that it does not correspond so much to a different 'mode' of thought as to the modality of practical logic, immanent in practice. They have passed 'in silence the transformation leading from operations mastered in their practical state to the formal operations isomorphic to them, failing by the same token to inquire into the social conditions of production of their transformation'.[32]

However, Bourdieu's analysis of practical logic in terms of opposing concepts remains very much under the spell of Lévi-Strauss. The actual theorization of this logic assumes what Bourdieu claims must be avoided: it reduces practice to concepts, its only difference from theoretical/formal logic being the use of the same oppositions in a variety of circumstances and a less developed form. The female/damp, male/female notions in the above example are presented as concepts only operating, in the case of practice, in a less explicit and less developed mode. Still, they remain 'objectively' knowable.

Moreover, Bourdieu in his more empirical analyses often presents schemata for the social in a purely objectivist way, completely disregarding the level of practice and its specificity. In these studies social actors are presented as endowed with different quantities and types of capital (economic, cultural, social, symbolic), which constitute a 'social field' as a 'multidimensional space' and can even be graphically represented:

> The social field can be described as a multidimensional space of positions such that every actual position can be defined in terms of a multidimensional system of co-ordinates. Thus agents are distributed within it, in the first dimension, according to the overall volume of the capital they possess and, in the second dimension, according to the composition of their capital i.e. according to the relative weight of the different kinds of assets within their total assets.[33]

The different kinds of habitus that characterize classes are thus attributable, in the last instance, to the different quantities and compositions of capital, i.e. to the different positions within this objective space the actors occupy. Within such a given 'field' the agents are seen as trying to maximize their total capital or specific forms of it in constant power struggles (this principle is used by

32. Bourdieu, *Outline of a Theory of Practice*, p. 117.
33. P. Bourdieu, 'The Social Space and the Genesis of Groups', *Theory and Society*, vol. 14, no. 6, 1985, p. 724. See also the tables in *Distinction*, pp. 262, 266, 340 and 452.

Bourdieu whenever he attempts a 'dynamic' analysis, as, for example, in his discussion of education[34] and of the May 1968 events)[35]. Here is a type of analysis that combines a structuralist conception of the structure as an objective entity (the social space appears as immediately and unproblematically accessible to scientific knowledge, measurable and even graphically representable) and a utilitarian principle of motivation of agents, a motivation considered to be of the same kind in a number of different fields. On these grounds it is possible to comment both that 'the utilitarian concept of social action is at the basis of Bourdieu's social theory and analysis of culture'[36] and that 'the relationship Bourdieu eventually poses between "objective structures", the habitus and social practice becomes one of determination. The analytical emphasis falls upon causes rather than reasons. Structures produce the habitus, which generates practice, which reproduces the structures, and so on.'[37]

Thus not only does Bourdieu not provide a satisfactory theorization of the 'logic of practice' he introduces, but he completely disregards any relevance such a 'logic' may have for his empirical studies. In particular, it seems difficult for him to escape from some version of objectivism, despite his willingness to do so. Moreover, Bourdieu does not sufficiently clarify the relation between 'practice', 'habitus' and 'strategies'. If the specific modality of practice to which he refers is the result of the manifestation of the 'practical operators' of habitus, then what is the connection of practice with the 'strategies' agents employ? Do we have to distinguish two kinds of practice – active and passive – to take account of the two levels? A theorization of practice that would support the differential modality Bourdieu attributes to it, therefore, and that would clarify its relationship with the agent, still remains to be elaborated. Only through such a theorization the specificity of the level of practice and its irreducibility either to ideal entities or to fully determined individuals can be fully supported.

Bourdieu shares with Giddens the aim of transcending 'subjectivism' and 'objectivism' by offering a theorization of processes of reproduction of the social through the individual. He, too, insists on

34. P. Bourdieu and J.C. Passeron, *Reproduction in Education, Society and Culture* (1970), London, 1977.

35. Bourdieu, *Homo Academicus*.

36. A. Honneth, 'The Fragmented World of Symbolic Forms: Reflections on P. Bourdieu's Sociology of Culture', *Theory, Culture and Society*, vol. 3, no. 3, 1986, p. 58.

37. R. Jenkins, 'Pierre Bourdieu and the Reproduction of Determinism', *Sociology*, vol. 31, 1982, p. 273.

a certain autonomy with respect to the individual, but, unlike Giddens, he stresses the deeply social nature that the 'structured dispositions' of the habitus imply. Thus a return to individualism is firmly ruled out. Bourdieu also stresses the need to theorize social practice as a field with a specific modality, irreducible to objectivist conceptual schemes. He moves away, therefore, from the objectivism Giddens still adheres to, introducing the possibility of a modality of the social different from what structural/objectivist approaches advocate and raises the question of practice as the locus of such a modality. Finally, Bourdieu indicates the connection between the modality of practice and the specific characteristics of the habitus which reproduce it.

However, Bourdieu has not elaborated the concepts to their fullest extent. The notion of habitus, although suggestive, remains generic and cannot support his assertion about individual autonomy beyond structural determinations. It cannot as such provide a satisfactory theorization of the question of agency and thus an alternative to the obstacles that structural/objectivist approaches face. Similarly, when Bourdieu provides a more detailed account of his 'theory of practice', he must revert to an objectivist Lévi-Straussian scheme, while in his more empirical studies he often uses the very objectivist theorization he denounces. Thus, although he introduces an alternative theorization of the modality of the social in the case of practice, and connects this modality with the reproduction of the social through the individual, Bourdieu's theory does not constitute a fully elaborated alternative.

The move from 'structure' to 'structuration', therefore, even in its more developed form proposed by Bourdieu, does not, by itself, provide an alternative to structural/objectivist approaches either in theorizing the social in a different way or in addressing the questions of agency and history more satisfactorily. Bourdieu's contribution is significant and points out a promising direction but requires further elaboration if it is to achieve its aims.

–6–

Derrida and 'Différance'

While Bourdieu introduces the possibility of theorizing an alternative mode of being of the social only in relation to practice, there is an identifiable current of thought that seeks to present a similar theorization for the social as a whole. This current starts as a challenge to structuralism and its assumptions of full determination and closure. J. Derrida exemplifies the approach in its general form, and theories that specifically address the modality of the social include the work of E. Laclau and C. Mouffe and, more significantly, C. Castoriadis, who aim to theorize an alternative, 'open' modality of the social.

Derrida presents his critical account of philosophy as a critique of the 'metaphysics of presence' that have dominated Western thought.[1] The metaphysics of presence represents

> the historical determination of the meaning of being in general as *presence*, with all the subdeterminations which depend on this generic form and which organize within it their system and their historical sequence (presence of the thing to the sight as *eidos*, presence as substance/ essence/ existence [*ousia*], temporal presence as point [*stigmè*] of the now or of the moment [*nun*], the self-presence of the cogito, consciousness, subjectivity, the co-presence of the other and of the self, intersubjectivity as the intentional phenomenon of the ego, and so forth).[2]

It is this whole tradition that Derrida characterizes as 'logocentrism' or 'phonocentrism' (the latter because phonetic writing considers words themselves to be endowed with a meaning, referring to a signified outside any context, in contrast to written modes, such as ideograms or hieroglyphics, which acquire a specific meaning only within each context). In the history of this 'logocentrism', 'the most

---

1. We focus here on Derrida's earlier and more groundbreaking work – up to the early 1970s – which introduces his central concepts – principally, *Of Grammatology*, the collections of articles in *Writing and Difference* and *Margins of Philosophy*, and his interviews in *Positions*. His later work does not introduce any differentiation of these concepts.

2. J. Derrida, *Of Grammatology* (1967), Baltimore, 1976, p. 12.

decisive separation appears at the moment when, at the same time as the science of nature, the determination of the absolute presence is constituted as self-presence, as subjectivity.'[3] This is so even when naïve anthropologism is criticized, as in Hegel, Husserl or Heidegger. In Hegel and Husserl, 'the critique of empirical anthropologism is only the affirmation of a transcendental humanism' with a transcendental *telos*: 'The end of man (as a factual anthropological limit) is announced to thought from the vantage of the end of man (as a determined opening or the infinity of a *telos*).'[4] In Heidegger, 'Dasein, though *not* man, is nevertheless *nothing* other than man. It is a repetition of the essence of man permitting a return to what is before the metaphysical concepts of *humanitas*.'[5]

Structuralism affords, for Derrida, a first step towards a way out of this 'logocentrism'. He defines as 'structuralist' 'a method for which everything within the structural totality is interdependent and circular'. What constitutes the decisive rupture is exactly this interdependence, i.e. the relational character of the structure. Before structuralism, although 'structure – or rather the structurality of structure – has always been at work, it has always been neutralized or reduced, and this by a process of giving it a centre or by referring it to a point of presence, a fixed origin'.[6] This centre – an *arche* or a *telos* – has been the expression of the metaphysics of presence within structural thought. It was through this 'centre', at once inside and outside the structure, that the structure was ordered by '*telos*, *aletheia* or *ousia*', or that a meaning was attributed to it.

In contrast, the relational definition of the structure allows the 'determination of the possibility of meaning on the basis of a "formal" organization which in itself has no meaning, which does not mean that it is either the non-sense or the anguishing absurdity which haunt metaphysical humanism'.[7] The definition of structure as relational, however, is not sufficient because, as Derrida remarks apropos of Lévi-Strauss, it is accompanied by a denial of time and history: '[T]he respect for structurality, for the internal originality of the structure, compels a neutralisation of time and history.'[8] The appearance of a new structure can be described only 'by omitting to posit the problem

3. Ibid., p. 16.
4. J. Derrida, 'The Ends of Man' (1968), in *Margins of Philosophy*, Brighton, 1982, p. 123.
5. Ibid., p. 127.
6. J. Derrida, 'Structure, Sign and Play in the Discourse of the Human Sciences' (1966), in *Writing and Difference*, London, 1978, p. 278.
7. Derrida, 'The Ends of Man', p. 134.
8. Derrida, 'Structure, Sign and Play', p. 291.

of the transition from one structure to another, by putting history between brackets'.[9] Therefore a step beyond the relational definition of structure is necessary.

Derrida's critique of metaphysics has many points of contact with a critique internal to social thought. Indeed social theories can be seen as a specific instance of the 'metaphysics of presence' to which Derrida refers: the traditional individualistic paradigms are a direct continuation of the 'great rationalisms of the seventeenth century' in which 'the determination of absolute presence is constituted as self-presence, as subjectivity'. Their opposing structural approaches in the idealist/rationalist tradition substitute for the self-presence of subjectivity society as the subject of history, a history determined and determinable, with a beginning and/or an end. Later, transhistorical categories always ordering society and history are assumed. In both cases an 'outside', itself transhistorical and directly accessible to reason, determines the successive structural totalities of the social and neutralizes the 'structurality of structure' as Derrida notes. With structuralism and its presentation of a social structure as a system of differences which does not refer to an outside 'centre', a beginning of a break with such transhistorical constants is made. A 'beginning', because a 'centre' and an 'outside' is reestablished not only in the case of Lévi-Strauss as Derrida notes, but also in the case of Althusser. Overcoming the problems structuralism faces, which seems to be a starting point for Derrida, is also the starting point of the present study. Derrida's alternative to structuralism, therefore, may be of interest also within a theorization of the social.

Derrida introduces the notion of *différance*, a neologism in French aiming at indicating in one term the double meaning of 'differing' and 'deferring'. To the differential definition of structure – structure as a system of differences – a temporal difference is added. Structure is seen as deferring itself, opening itself in time: '*Différance* will be the playing moment that "produces" – by means of something that is not simply an activity – these differences, these effects of difference.'[10] The notion of *différance* introduces a *necessary* openness which can

---

9. Ibid. Moreover, Lévi-Strauss still aspires, for Derrida, in a romantic way, like Rousseau to a possible totalization to an absolute discourse, to a primal innocence, to 'a sort of ethic of presence, an ethic of nostalgia for origins, an ethic of archaic and natural innocence, of a purity of presence and self-presence in speech' (ibid., p. 292; also see *Of Grammatology*, pp. 97ff).

10. J. Derrida, 'Différance' (1968), in *Margins of Philosophy*, p. 11.

provide an alternative to the metaphysics of presence.[11] However, the notion is not to be seen as a new expression of an essence: 'The *différance* that produces differences is not somehow before them, in a simple and unmodified – in-different – present. *Différance* is the non-full, non-simple, structured and differentiating origin of differences. Thus the name "origin" no longer suits it.'[12] It has rather to be seen as a movement: 'We will designate by *différance* the movement according to which language, or any code, any system of referral in general, is constituted "historically" as a weave of differences.'[13] *Différance* is 'neither a word nor a concept', it does not have the modality of 'being', it is rather the 'pre-opening of the ontico-ontological difference'.[14] Derrida also uses the terms 'trace' or 'archi-trace' to indicate the modality *différance* refers to. This 'trace' is one that does not lead anywhere, it is an 'archi-trace' without any presence in its end.[15] Trace, *différance* have

> to be thought before the opposition between nature and culture, animality and humanity, inside and outside: The outside, 'spatial' and 'objective' exteriority which we believe we know as the most familiar thing in the world, as familiarity itself, would not appear without the *grammè*, without *différance* as temporalization, without the nonpresence of the other inscribed within the sense of the present, without the relationship with death as the concrete structure of the living present.[16]

The opening *différance* designates cannot be seen as the result of a 'need' or a 'desire' within a consciousness because 'the speaking or signifying subject could not be present to itself, as speaking, or signifying without the play of linguistic or semiological *différance* [. . .] The subject as consciousness has never manifested itself except as self-presence.' This self-presence itself presupposes *différance*: 'Thus one comes to posit presence – and specifically consciousness,

---

11. Derrida notes that the possibility of openness exists, for example, in Husserl, as *genesis*. But this genesis is '*logos* produced in history which it differs from itself in order to re-appropriate itself', it is the 'infinite opening of what is experienced, which is designated at several moments of Husserlian analysis by reference to an Idea in the Kantian sense, that is, the irruption of the infinite into consciousness' (J. Derrida, '"Genesis and Structure" and Phenomenology' (1959), in *Writing and Difference*, pp. 162, 166). Derrida's aim is to retain this infinite opening without, however, accepting a metaphysics of an atemporal and transcendental reason.

12. Derrida, 'Différance', p. 11.

13. Ibid., p. 12.

14. J. Derrida, 'Freud and the Scene of Writing' (1966), in *Writing and Difference*, p. 198.

15. Derrida, *Of Grammatology*, p. 62.

16. Ibid., p. 71.

the being beside itself of consciousness – no longer as the absolutely central form of Being but as a "determination" and as an "effect".'[17] In fact, without *différance* 'there would be neither "subject", nor "history", nor the "symbolic"'.[18]

Différance is manifested best in 'writing', if writing is 'no longer understood in the narrow sense of linear and phonetic notation' but rather as introducing the very possibility of signification, 'of bringing classificatory difference into play'[19] and thus as behind the existence of language as such. However, writing in the usual sense, that of the text, is also the preeminent field of *différance*: the text is never closed, it always defers itself, it incorporates its 'outside' as the limits of its 'inside'. The principle of *différance* consequently can also be used as a tool of textual analysis: this is what Derrida has called the deconstructive method.

Finally, the modality Freud attributes to the unconscious is an example of the 'existence' and function of *différance*:

> A certain alterity – to which Freud gives the metaphysical name of the unconscious – is definitely exempt from every process of presentation by means of which we would call upon it to show itself in person. In this context, and beneath this guise, the unconscious is not, as we know, a hidden, virtual, or potential self-presence. It differs from, and defers, itself; which doubtless means that it is woven of differences, and also that it sends out delegates, representatives, proxies; but without that the giver of proxies might 'exist', might be present, be 'itself' somewhere, and with even less chance that it might become conscious.[20]

Does the concept of *différance* have something to offer to a theory of the social? Derrida considers that the notion provides an alternative to the 'metaphysics of presence' and any essentialism. However, *différance*, being 'the pre-opening of the ontico-ontological difference', the 'primordial non self-presence', it seems to operate on the same level, and in the same manner, as Heidegger's *Dasein*[21] (*différance* does not, however, refer to the subject in any way.) *Différance* is not an 'essence' since it precisely denies any essentialism and yet – to play with Derrida's own words – is nothing more than a (negative) essence. *Différance* is supposed to negate essentialism and yet simultaneously to organize the whole question of being through

17. Derrida, 'Différance', p. 16.
18. J. Derrida, *Positions* (1972), London, 1987, p. 88.
19. Derrida, *Of Grammatology*, p. 109.
20. Derrida, 'Différance', p. 21.
21. As J. Habermas also argues in *The Philosophical Discourse of Modernity* (1985), Cambridge, 1990, pp. 161ff.

its (non)self-presence. We have, therefore, a negation of traditional metaphysics while retaining a discourse and concepts that continue to function on the same level and with the same ambitions. In fact, the notion of *différance* (and all the other notions that Derrida introduces to indicate the same) neutralizes the radicalism Derrida's own critique of traditional metaphysics had entailed by reestablishing, albeit in an oblique way, just such a metaphysics. Derrida does retain, after all, a nostalgia for an all encompassing philosophical discourse, whose criticism was his starting point.

The notion of *différance* operates at a level beyond and behind that of actual social phenomena and refers exclusively to thought. The 'pre-opening of the ontico-ontological difference' pre-exists and defines the level of any 'positive' science of the social. Indeed, Derrida's theory implies the irrelevance of history and society for the actual movement of thought. As Habermas remarks: '[Derrida], too [like Heidegger], degrades politics and contemporary history to the status of the ontic and the foreground, so as to romp all the more freely, and with a greater wealth of associations, in the sphere of the ontological and the archewriting.'[22] Therefore, the notion of *différance* as such cannot be used within a theorization of the social.

Could, however, the notion be relevant to a theory of the social in a less direct way? A certain reading of Derrida's work has focussed on the epistemological implications of *différance*. Derrida is seen as advocating a necessary and unavoidable relativity of knowledge and truth, introducing a general theory of knowledge.[23] If so, social theory could be also inscribed within this theory of knowledge which has some parallels with the hermeneutic tradition. However, to indicate the openness or the lack of any final closure of scientific thought does not imply anything about the *content* of this thought and the assumptions it makes about its object – in our case, the 'social'. Moreover, as argued in the first part of the book, to support an epistemological position on social knowledge, an ontological account

---

22. Ibid., p. 181.
23. Such an interpretation is offered, for example, by R. Gashe. He sees Derrida as addressing the ultimate foundations of reflection and reflexivity, 'engaged in the construction of the "quasi-synthetic concepts" which account for the economy of the conditions of possibility and impossibility of the basic philosophemes' (R. Gashe, *The Tain of the Mirror*, Cambridge, 1986, p. 7). However, it has been argued that Derrida's account, taken at its word, does not imply a relativization of meaning, but its destruction: 'Just as the regress of reflection renders the phenomenon of consciousness inexplicable, so – on Derrida's account – there would never be an emergence of meaning: there would be nothing but an unstoppable mediation of signs by other signs [. . .] not the volatization of meaning, but its destruction' (P. Dews, *Logics of Disintegration*, London, 1987, p. 30).

of the social has to be provided as well, which is not the case with Derrida. Thus Derrida's importance for an epistemology of the social sciences is very small.

A more restricted interpretation of the relevance Derrida's work has for a theory of the social focusses on the 'deconstructive' method as a tool in the analysis of different ideologies.[24] Although Derrida does indicate how through a reading of a text the intrusion by the 'outside' (what is not said or written) into the inside (what is said or written) can be discerned,[25] such a method does not offer much more than traditional critical analyses of such 'ideologies'. Moreover, though it can indicate implicit assumptions, it cannot specify the source and origin of these assumptions within the wider social context.

Despite the common ground that Derrida's critique of metaphysics shares with an antiessentialist critique of social theory, therefore, his work seems to have no direct relevance to a theory of the social. Yet, Derrida's intention of affirming a necessary and inescapable openness as an alternative to structuralism – a temporal deferring alongside a differential definition of structures – is too important to be lost in either an obscure metaphysics or in sterile relativism. Derrida himself considered structuralism as a starting point. But structuralism, in either its linguistic or social theoretic versions, was referring to positive (though not positivistic) sciences and to a theorization of their objects (language or the social). Moreover, Derrida establishes a connection between *différance* and the level of the unconscious, a positive level of operation of the psyche. All the above point towards a possible theorization of the openness *différance* refers to otherwise than as a negative essence. Indeed, the possibility of locating such an openness *within* a level of the social, introducing 'alterity' to otherwise immobile 'structures' and offering thus an alternative to structural/objectivist theories, presents itself. And it is such a possibility we shall investigate in the work of Laclau and Mouffe and of Castoriadis.

24. For example M. Ryan, *Marxism and Deconstruction*, Baltimore, 1982.
25. Derrida himself orients his work towards such a critical reading of major figures – mainly philosophical but also literary – both in the context of a critique of 'metaphysics of presence' and also in order to establish the concept of *différance*. Textual analysis – as 'deconstruction' – occupies a central role in his work, because it is through a reading of texts that he proceeds and because 'the text' is for him the outstanding example of the play of *différance*.

Laclau and Mouffe's 'Discursive Articulations'

Laclau and Mouffe's theoretical project has ultimately a political aim: the affirmation of the possibility of radical democracy. To ground this possibility, however, they also provide a general theorization of the social as open and contingent.[1]

Structuralist Marxism constitutes a starting point for Laclau and Mouffe, Marxism being '*one* of the traditions through which it becomes possible to formulate a new conception of politics'.[2] They remark that it is not enough to reject the determinant role of the economy or of any 'objective interests' and 'objective destiny' of the working class – an objectivity that can be supported only within a teleological conception of history. A simple 'logical deconstruction of the Althusserian totality' (like Hindess and Hirst's critique of Althusser) still assumes that 'the disconnected "elements" have a full and unequivocal identity attributed to them'. To be radical the critique has to be directed against 'every type of fixity, through an affirmation of the incomplete, open and politically negotiable character of every identity'.[3]

Consequently, Laclau and Mouffe propose that a structural totality should be seen as 'an ensemble of differential positions [which] [. . .] is not the expression of any underlying principle external to itself'.[4] Such structural totalities, termed 'discourses', have the modality Foucault attributes to his 'discursive formations' – namely, 'regularity in dispersion'. They are the result of an 'articulatory practice', being 'any practice establishing a relation among elements such that their identity is modified as a result of the articulatory practice [. . .] The

1. See, principally, E. Laclau and C. Mouffe, *Hegemony and Socialist Strategy*, London, 1985, and, idem, 'Post Marxism without Apologies', *New Left Review*, no. 166, 1987; E. Laclau, 'New Reflections on the Revolution of Our Time' (1990), in idem, *New Reflections on the Revolution of Our Time*, London, 1990. (The NLR article is found in the same volume, but reference here is to the first publication of the article.)
2. Laclau and Mouffe, *Hegemony and Socialist Strategy*, p. 3, emphasis in the original.
3. Ibid., p. 104.
4. Ibid., p. 106.

differential positions, insofar as they appear articulated within a discourse, we will call moments. By contrast, we will call element any difference that is not discursively articulated.'[5] In a 'discursive articulation, as a systematic structural ensemble, the relations are unable to absorb the identities; but as the identities are purely relational, this is but another way of saying that there is no identity which can be fully constituted'. Every ensemble of differential entities is constantly subverted by the 'surplus of meaning' which is 'the necessary terrain for the constitution of every social practice' and is called 'the field of discursivity.'[6] The distinction between 'elements' and 'moments' corresponds to the distinction between the 'field of discursivity' and its partial closures that are the discursive articulations. Within this field, and prior to their articulation within a discourse, 'the status of elements is that of floating signifiers, incapable of being wholly articulated to a discursive chain'.[7] As floating signifiers the elements have no real identity. Any identity, always partial, is constructed when they become moments, i.e. when they form part 'of a totality resulting from an articulatory practice'.

Despite the terminology, Laclau and Mouffe do not see their theorization as referring to 'discourse' in the limited sense, i.e. to ideas or ideologies. They explicitly reject 'the distinction between discursive and non-discursive practices' emphasizing that 'every social configuration is meaningful'[8] and affirming:

(a) that every object is constituted as an object of discourse, insofar as no object is given outside every discursive condition of emergence; and (b) that any distinction between what are usually called the linguistic and behavioural aspects of a social practice, is either an incorrect distinction or ought to find its place as a differentiation within the social production of meaning, which is structured under the form of discursive totalities.[9]

Laclau and Mouffe also advance a theorization of the subject: 'Subjects cannot be the origin of social relations',[10] but are the locus of 'subject positions' defined within 'discursive structures'. However, precisely because a 'discourse' is always open and never fully constituted, the subject is also never fully determined: '[E]very subject position, as a discursive position, [. . .] partakes of the open character

5. Ibid., p. 105.
6. Ibid., p. 111.
7. Ibid.
8. Laclau and Mouffe, 'Post Marxism without Apologies', p. 82.
9. Laclau and Mouffe, *Hegemony and Socialist Strategy*, p. 107.
10. Ibid., p. 115.

of every discourse.'[11] Laclau is to further amplify: 'The field of social identities is not one of full identities, but of their ultimate failure to be constituted[12] [. . .] the location of the subject is that of dislocation. Far from being a moment of the structure, the subject is the result of the impossibility of constituting the structure as such – that is as a self-sufficient object.'[13]

Because of the open character of every subject position, the determination of the subject by many structures, of a fusion between them becomes possible.[14] The subject has, in addition, a specificity beyond what a multiple determination would allow and hence an autonomy in the strict sense, although it remains bounded: '[T]he degree of autonomy may vary, but the concept of total autonomy is devoid of all meaning.'[15]

It is the existence of this autonomy that allows the emergence of a 'hegemonic subject' and of a 'hegemonic project'. 'Hegemony' is an articulatory practice in which subjects use 'elements' not yet crystallized into 'moments' to form a new 'discursive articulation'. The hegemonic subject is partly exterior to the 'elements' articulated but this exteriority does not imply any privileged level of the social (as the level of production remains in the traditional definition of hegemony)[16]. For the possibility of a hegemonic project to exist, however, the existence of 'antagonisms' is necessary (the term 'antagonism' retains, for Laclau and Mouffe, the usual connotations of two antagonistic sides – classes or persons). Though this does not predetermine the form of a hegemonic project – as it can be articulated

11. Ibid.
12. Laclau, 'New Reflections on the Revolution of Our Time', p. 38.
13. Ibid., p. 41.
14. Laclau and Mouffe remark that Freud introduced the term 'overdetermination' in order to describe this 'very precise type of fusion entailing a symbolic dimension and a plurality of meanings' (*Hegemony and Socialist Strategy*, p. 97).
15. Laclau, 'New Reflections on the Revolution of Our Time', p. 38.
16. Laclau had proposed a theory of hegemony – mainly following Gramsci – in his previous work (E. Laclau, *Politics and Ideology in Marxist Theory*, London, 1977). In that work hegemony is the result of a dominant class – defined as such on the level of production – manipulating and organizing different ideological elements to form a unity that would ensure a hegemonic position in the political/ideological field as well. Through a hegemonic articulation, demands from other classes can be channelled in ways compatible with the interests of the hegemonic class. Thus a distinction is made between relations of production, which determine class relations, and the ideological and political levels which are not reducible to class relations. In *Hegemony and Socialist Strategy* the process of creation of a hegemonic articulation remains the same. The privileged role of production is, however, abandoned: 'Both the hegemonic force and the ensemble of hegemonised elements would constitute themselves on the same plane – the general field of discursivity' (Laclau and Mouffe, *Hegemony and Socialist Strategy*, p. 135).

to different projects and to different discourses. The possibility of 'hegemonic projects' allows, in turn, the possibility of a 'radical democratic hegemonic project' through an articulation of 'new social movements' within an overall strategy.

Laclau and Mouffe's theorization provides an example of how the direction of thought indicated by Derrida can be used within a theory of the social. The central assumption of rationalist/objectivist structural approaches, that of closed and fully determinable social structural entities is explicitly challenged and an alternative provided.[17] What is claimed is a necessary openness and contingency of the social field as a whole, rather than of a part or level of it, as in Bourdieu's theory of practice. As a result, the 'subject' can be seen as structurally determined, but never fully, exhibiting a degree of autonomy beyond the effect of multiple determinations by different structures. This autonomy, though not unlimited, is sufficient to allow the emergence of hegemonic projects and thus of 'politics' in the broad sense. The question of agency, therefore, seems to be satisfactorily addressed. Moreover, though Laclau and Mouffe do not explicitly discuss it, since a non-fully-constituted, open structure, can always alter itself, 'becoming' can be introduced and the question of alterity and change can be also addressed. Thus the general direction of Laclau and Mouffe's argument indicates a new path. However, specific aspects of the argument are not fully elaborated.

Laclau and Mouffe base their assertion that the social is never fully constituted and thus 'open', on the assumption that the social is always 'meaningful'. Drawing particularly on Wittgenstein, they consider that the totality of social phenomena includes both linguistic and non-linguistic elements ('the distinction between linguistic and non-linguistic elements does not overlap with the distinction between "meaningful" and "not meaningful"')[18] and that 'it has become increasingly accepted that the meaning of a word is entirely context-dependent.'[19] Given the 'meaningfulness' of the whole of the social and given that 'a number of contemporary currents of thought – from Heidegger to Wittgenstein – have insisted on the impossibility of

17. The theorization of 'openness' refers simply to its possibility. It does not necessarily imply that 'everything is an undifferentiated flux' (A. Hunter, 'Post-Marxism and the New Social Movements', *Theory and Society*, no. 17, 1988, p. 894), and does not make impossible, in principle, to conceptualize durable institutions (as N. Mouzelis argues in 'Marxism or Post-Marxism?', *New Left Review*, no. 167, 1988, pp. 113–14) though of course it does not facilitate such a conceptualization.
18. Laclau and Mouffe, 'Post Marxism without Apologies', p. 83.
19. Ibid.

fixing ultimate meanings,'[20] the social is also necessarily open. The argument seems clear and persuasive.

However, in which sense the social can be seen as 'meaningful', except through a reference to thought and language, is not sufficiently clarified. That the meaning of a 'word' or a 'rule' is context-dependent does not alter the fact that it is the word or the rule that carries the meaning and not the 'context'. Laclau and Mouffe assert, of course, that the 'material character' of discourse and 'the material character of ideologies, inasmuch as these are not simple systems of ideas but are embodied in institutions, rituals and so forth'.[21] However, the 'embodiment' of these systems of ideas to institutions or rituals does not change the fact that they are primarily 'ideas' and it is as such that we should approach them. Similarly, while it is affirmed that there are differentiations 'within the social production of meaning', such as that between the 'so-called non-discursive complexes (institutions, techniques, productive organization, and so on)'[22] and 'discursive' complexes in the narrow sense, this differentiation is presented as one of degree and not kind. The 'so-called non-discursive complexes' cannot, therefore, be analysed otherwise than as if they were fully discursive ones.

Moreover, since Laclau and Mouffe do not offer any account of the meeting of the 'subject' and the 'structure' – any theory, that is, of subjectivity proper – they cannot locate, within the individual, a level of 'meaning' different from thought. As it is, their theorization seems perfectly compatible with a scheme of action guided by (ideal) norms such as Parsons's in his early work. Finally, the political project of hegemony, referring, as it does, to (political) discourse in the narrow sense, is not helpful in locating any alternative level of meaning. Unless, however, a level distinct from ideas and yet meaningful is conceptualized, any affirmation of meaning beyond ideas or ideologies cannot but ultimately refer back to these ideas. This is exactly what happens with Laclau and Mouffe's theory. Therefore, they can be justifiably accused of idealism,[23] despite their intentions. The fact that the non-reductionism of the social to the ideal is affirmed, is not enough to provide an alternative theorization for the way the social is 'meaningful'.

20. Laclau and Mouffe, *Hegemony and Socialist Strategy*, p. 111. In these currents Laclau and Mouffe include Derrida who 'generalises the concept of discourse in a sense coincidental with that of our text'.

21. Ibid., p. 109.

22. Ibid., p. 107.

23. As, for example, by N. Geras in 'Post Marxism?', *New Left Review*, no. 163, 1987, or by E.M. Wood in *The Retreat from Class*, London, 1986.

If the 'meaningfulness' of the social is not sufficiently clarified, the actual way the social can be seen as non-closed, as open and indeterminate, necessarily remains even more so. The authors Laclau and Mouffe cite all specifically refer to the lack of ultimate fixity in the meaning of thought or language. Moreover, this openness is always asserted through a reference to 'something' beyond thought: to the motivations lying behind a perlocutionary act (Austin), to the practice of application of the rule (Wittgenstein), or even to a pre-ontico/ontological level as that on which Heidegger's *Dasein* or Derrida's *différance* are seen as operating. This 'something' relates thus either to a social or psychological datum or to the postulation of an arch-level beyond the positivity of 'ontic' – as opposed to ontologic – being. Laclau and Mouffe transpose the 'openness' assigned by these authors to thought or language to the social at large. But if so, no empirical/concrete 'outside' (of the type Austin or Wittgenstein refer to) supporting this openness can be claimed. Nor do Laclau and Mouffe indicate that they accept Heidegger's or Derrida's transcendental argument. Thus the validity of a transposition of the contingency and openness claimed for thought or language to the social in general is questionable.

In his later 'New Reflections on the Revolution of Our Time', Laclau modifies the argument somewhat. It is 'antagonism' that becomes the principal determinant of the 'openness' of the social: 'antagonism is the *limit of all objectivity* [. . .] It is an "outside" which blocks the identity of the "inside" (and is, nonetheless, the prerequisite for its constitution at the same time) [. . .] it is pure facticity which cannot be referred back to any underlying rationality.'[24] But what constitutes the 'pure facticity' of antagonism? Discussing Marx, Laclau locates 'antagonism' in class struggle ('class struggle is an antagonism without contradiction')[25], being the 'constitutive outside' which 'cannot be reintegrated into the forces and relations of production schema'.[26] Thus it is social actors – in this case classes – that are at the origin of antagonisms. What is implied here is a certain indeterminacy in the actors relative to the structure. It is on the subject as an 'outside' and on the autonomy of this subject that antagonism, and hence the openness of the structural totalities, are based. However, within Laclau and Mouffe's theoretical framework, if the subject is 'something more' than its structural determinations, if it has a specificity and autonomy, it is *because* of the openness of the structure.

24. Laclau, 'New Reflections on the Revolution of Our Time', p. 17.
25. Ibid., p. 7.
26. Ibid., p. 11.

Therefore the subject's autonomy cannot be the cause of the structure's openness. The argument would be valid only within some version of individualism in which the subject is seen as external to the structure and possessing an unlimited autonomy. Thus Laclau's reference to 'antagonism' does not provide a better grounding for the affirmation of a necessary openness of the social.[27]

There are problems also in Laclau and Mouffe's theorization of the subject. It is not clear what exactly the autonomy attributed to the subject implies and what are its limits. At times Laclau and Mouffe refer simply to the contradiction generated by a simultaneous determination by more than one structure: 'A fall in a worker's wage, for example, denies his identity as a consumer. There is therefore a "social objectivity" – the logic of profit – which denies another objectivity – the consumer's identity. But the denial of an identity means preventing its constitution as an objectivity.'[28] The lack of a 'full' identity in this case – and any subsequent 'autonomy' – is simply due to the simultaneous determinations to which the worker is subject. In other instances Laclau and Mouffe tend to imply an absolute rather than a relative autonomy, as in their discussion of hegemony. The structural limitations and constraints of a 'hegemonic subject' are nowhere discussed. Moreover, 'who' could be a hegemonic subject, under what conditions such a subject could emerge (apart from the necessity of 'antagonism') and 'why' it would pursue such a project are never clarified.

In fact Laclau and Mouffe's account of the subject, though suggestive, is very limited. They do not provide any theorization proper of subjectivity, of the way the structure operates within the individual, or of social action. This, coupled with the insufficiencies of their theorization of the 'openness' of the social, makes their claims for the possibility of autonomy and indeed of 'hegemonic projects' lack any firm grounding. Thus, in the case of their project of 'radical democracy', the social agent that could and would be the initiator of such a project is never identified, nor are the 'objective' structural limitations such an agent may be subject to.

---

27. S. Zizek tried to relate Laclau and Mouffe's notion of 'antagonism' to the notion of the 'real' in Lacan's late work, the 'real' being a 'certain fissure which cannot be symbolised' (S. Zizek, 'Beyond Discourse Analysis', in Laclau, *New Reflections on the Revolution of Our Time*, p. 249). Zizek does not clarify the way in which 'antagonism' can be seen as homologous to the Lacanian 'real', and therefore he does not offer an alternative to Laclau's argument. However, the establishment of a relationship between the (open) modality of the social and the unconscious is significant and will be elaborated in the third part of the book (see, in particular, note 85, chapter 10, p. 164 and note 2, chapter 12, p. 190).

28. Laclau, 'New Reflections on the Revolution of Our Time', p. 16.

Thus Laclau and Mouffe's theorization remains incomplete, though it marks a definite step in the development beyond Derrida by introducing an openness and indeterminacy as necessarily implied in any definition of social structure. The 'meaningfulness' of the social in general is not satisfactorily argued, nor is the 'openness' of the social grounded on it. As for the autonomy of the subject claimed, it is not backed by a theory of subjectivity proper. Laclau and Mouffe's work, though evocative, indicates a direction to be followed rather than mapping this development itself.

—8—

Castoriadis and the 'Social Imaginary Significations'

C. Castoriadis[1] wants to break with any determinism in thinking 'the being proper to the social-historical'. Traditional theories have

> always split [the social–historical] into a society, related to something other than itself and, generally, to a norm, end or *telos* grounded in something else, and a history, considered as something that happens to this society, as a disturbance in relation to a given norm or as an organic or dialectical development towards this norm, end or *telos*. In this way, the object in question, the being proper to the social-historical, is constantly shifted towards something other than itself and absorbed in it.[2]

Underlying these theories is the 'inherited logic–ontology' within which the traditional conceptualization of the social has been elaborated: 'For the past 25 centuries Greco-Western thinking has constituted, developed, amplified and refined itself on the basis of the thesis: being is being something determined (*einai ti*), speaking is saying something determined (*ti legein*).'[3] For Castoriadis this thesis corresponds to what he terms 'ensemblist-identitary logic' (*logique ensembliste-identitaire*)[4]. The logic is 'identitary' because it posits each thing 'as distinct and definite [which] implies, at the very least,

---

1. Discussion here is mainly about the later phase of Castoriadis's work, roughly from 1965 onwards, which culminates in the *Imaginary Institution of Society* (1975) ('Marxism and Revolutionary Theory', part 1, written in 1965) and includes three collections of articles under the rubric 'Crossroads in the Labyrinth' (*Crossroads in the Labyrinth* [1978], *Domaines de l'homme* [1986], *Le monde morcelé* [1990]). Castoriadis's earlier work, of a more Marxist and more grounded nature, is by no means incompatible with this later phase, and Castoriadis himself repeatedly traces the continuities through references to his earlier work.

2. C. Castoriadis, *The Imaginary Institution of Society* (1975), Cambridge, 1987, p. 167.

3. Ibid., p. 221.

4. The term has been translated also as 'set-theoretical/identitary logic' (*Crossroads in the Labyrinth*, Brighton, 1984, p. vii).

that it is posited in its pure self-identity and in its pure difference with respect to everything that is not itself'.[5] And it is 'ensemblist' because it is perfectly expressed in the classic definition of a set (*ensemble*) by Cantor, as 'a collection into a whole of definite and distinct objects of our intuition or of our thought'.[6] This logic is adequate in theorizing a level of existence of the social, because

> If society is to exist, if a language is to be established and if it is to function, if a thoughtful practice is to develop, if people are to be able to relate to one another other than through fantasies, then, in one way or another, on a certain level, on a certain layer or stratum of social doing and representing, everything must be made consequent with what Cantor's definition implies.[7]

There is, therefore, an identitary dimension of the social that can be fully determined and which is manifested both in social representing (*legein*) and in social doing (*teukhein*): *legein* is 'distinguishing – choosing – positing – assembling – counting – speaking'.[8] Its principal manifestation is through the identitary/ ensemblist aspect of language, i.e. of language as a formal system, 'to the extent that language [. . .] is a system of ensembles (or of ensemblizable relations)'.[9] *Teukhein* is 'assembling – adjusting – fabricating – constructing. It separates "elements", fixes them as such, orders them, combines them, unites them into totalities and organised hierarchies of totalities within the field of doing'.[10] The two are closely interrelated: '*Legein* is not *legein* if it is not an organised totality of efficacious operations with a "material" basis. *Teukhein* is not *teukhein* if it is not the positing of distinct and definite elements involved in functional relations.'[11]

However, *legein* and *teukhein*, as complementary activities within the social field which can be analysed as fully determinable sets, do not 'exhaust' the social. The ensemblist/identitary level of social representing/doing they refer to is only *one* layer of the social. This layer is 'surrounded' by, based on, transcended by, limited by, another 'layer', one that cannot be fully subsumed under identitary logic, which cannot even be fully grasped since understanding operates

5. Castoriadis, *The Imaginary Institution of Society*, p. 224.
6. Ibid., p. 223.
7. Ibid.
8. Ibid.
9. Ibid., p. 238. It is this aspect of language that is analysed by structural linguistics.
10. Ibid., p. 260.
11. Ibid., p. 261.

through identitary logic. This other layer Castoriadis calls the *magma of social imaginary significations*. It operates in the *imaginary* dimension, is presupposed by *legein* and *teukhein* and institutes the social.

The notion of 'magma' introduces a mode of being that breaks with ensemblist/identitary logic: 'A magma is that from which one can extract (or in which one can construct) an infinite number of ensemblist organizations but which can never be reconstituted (ideally) by a (finite or infinite) ensemblist composition of these organizations.'[12] The mode of being of significations in general can serve as an example. A signification is 'infinitely determinable without thereby being determined'.[13] What escapes determination is the flow of meaning that surrounds it and always allows a different determination to be added without, for that, ever exhausting its 'meaning'. Thus an intuitive support for the notion of magma can be 'all the significations of the English language or all the representations of one's life'.[14]

The social/historical is also, primarily, a magma, that of 'social imaginary significations': 'The institution of society is the institution of a magma of social imaginary significations.'[15] 'Society is not a set, neither a structure nor a hierarchy of sets or structures: it is a magma and a magma of magmas.'[16] Social imaginary significations are manifested through *legein* and *teukhein*, they form the 'background' out of which *legein* and *teukhein* may emerge. *Legein* in language – i.e. language as a code – is based on language as 'langue, to the extent that it refers to a magma of significations'.[17] As for *teukhein*, 'ends and significations are posited together in and through technique and *teukhein* [. . .] In a sense, the tools and instruments of a society are significations; they are the "materialization" of the imaginary significations of that society in the identitary and functional dimension. An assembly line is (and can only exist as) the "materialization" of a host of imaginary significations central to capitalism.'[18]

12. Ibid., p. 343. Castoriadis has also proposed a formal definition of 'magma' in a logico/mathematical way in 'La logique des magmas et la question de l'autonomie' (1981), in *Domaines de l'homme*, Paris, 1986, pp. 394–5.
13. Castoriadis, *The Imaginary Institution of Society*, p. 346.
14. Ibid., p. 344.
15. Ibid., p. 359.
16. Ibid., p. 228.
17. Ibid., p. 238.
18. Ibid., p. 361.

The social imaginary significations do not 'exist' only through their materialization in *legein* and *teukhein*. They also, and more importantly, 'exist' within the individuals, as a constituent part of the psyche and especially of the (individual) unconscious. The unconscious itself, as 'an indissociably representative/affective/intentional flux'[19] has, for Castoriadis, the modality of magma: 'The a-logic of the unconscious is something quite different from the juxtaposition of several different exemplars of the same logic. The unconscious does not belong to the domain of identitary logic and determination. A product and continuing manifestation of the radical imagination, its mode of being is that of magma.'[20]

Castoriadis presents a modified psychoanalytic theorization of the development of the psyche in the early years of life, a theorization that indicates the way in which social imaginary significations are internalized within the psyche. The psyche is characterized from the very beginning, by an inherent, and irreducible, ability to create representations: 'One must admit that originary phantasmatization, which I term the radical imagination, pre-exists and presides over every organization of drives, even the most primitive one, that it is the condition for the drive to attain psychical existence.'[21] In its initial, monadic state, this originary phantasmatization is all that operates within a psyche totally enclosed to itself: 'Unconscious desire is fulfilled ipso facto as soon as it arises, fulfilled on the only level that matters, that of the unconscious representation.'[22] However, this monadic state is soon breached. The breakup leans on somatic needs, mainly hunger: 'An "outside" is created so that the psyche can cast off into it whatever it does not want, whatever there is no room for in the psyche, non-sense or negative meaning, the breast as absent, the bad breast[23] [. . .] At the same time, the other side of the breast, the present or gratifying breast, continues to submit to the schema of inclusion.'[24] These two sides are gradually 'connected to a third entity which is the ground of both of them without being identical with either of them'.[25] This third entity is the other person, usually the mother.

Through the 'other', the whole world of social significations is

19. Ibid., p. 274.
20. Ibid., p. 281. Indeed it could be said that it is the unconscious that primarily serves Castoriadis as a model for the notion of 'magma'.
21. Ibid., p. 287.
22. Ibid., p. 298.
23. Ibid., p. 303.
24. Ibid., p. 304. Castoriadis accepts here Klein's distinction of good and bad objects and the mechanisms of introjection and projection.
25. Ibid.

transmitted to the child. The other 'speaks to the child and speaks of himself both in his words and his behaviour, his corporeal manner of being and of doing, of touching, of taking and handling the child, he embodies, presentifies, figures the world instituted by society and refers to this world in an indefinite diversity of ways'.[26] At this stage the 'private objects' of cathexis of the psyche are replaced by socially instituted ones.[27] However, the 'other' is still seen by the infant as a projection of the infant's own imaginary scheme of omnipotence. It is only when the other ceases to be the 'origin and master of signification' and it is realized that no specific person can be such a master that the social reality as such is established. This second breakup corresponds to the Oedipal phase in its most general sense, i.e. not only in the form it appears in Western family institutions: '[T]he encounter with the Oedipal situation sets before the child the unavoidable fact of the institution as the ground of signification and vice versa, and forces him to recognize the other and human others as subjects of autonomous desires, which can interrelate with one another independently of him to the point of excluding him from this circuit.'[28] The Oedipal phase corresponds to the establishment of the social origin of meaning and marks the beginning of the process of creation of a fully social individual.

Castoriadis stresses that although social imaginary significations are internalized within the psyche, there is no one-to-one correspondence between them and individual psychical representations. This is because only *some* of the social imaginary significations become internalized within each individual: 'Sublimation is in each case specific [. . .] the institution of society renders obligatory for the innumerable individuals of society particular objects of sublimation to the exclusion of others.'[29] But it is also, and more importantly, because there is a *qualitative* difference between social imaginary significations and individual psychical representations:

> The world of instituted significations cannot be reduced to actual individual representations or to their 'common', 'average' or 'typical part'. Significations are obviously not what individuals represent to themselves, consciously or unconsciously, or what they think. They are that by means of which and on the basis of which individuals are formed

26. Ibid., p. 306.
27. Ibid., p. 312.
28. Ibid., p. 310. A similarity with Lacan's theorization of the Oedipal phase is evident.
29. Ibid., p. 318.

as social individuals [. . .] This entails – and, to be sure, even requires – that part of the social imaginary significations has an actual 'equivalent' in the individuals (in their conscious or unconscious representation, their behaviour, etc.) and that the other can be 'translated' into them, either directly or indirectly. But this is something quite different from their 'actual presence' or their existing 'in person' in the representation of individuals.[30]

Moreover, 'the constitution of the social individual does not and cannot abolish the psyche's creativity, its perpetual alteration, the representative flux as the continuous emergence of other represent-ations.'[31] Thus, while the social imaginary significations – and the social in general – are irreducible to their effects on the individual, the individual psyche is also irreducible to its social determinations: '[S]ociety and psyche are inseparable and irreducible one to the other.'[32] For Castoriadis the relationship between the social and the individual is a complex one, 'which cannot be thought under the categ-ories of the whole and the part, the set and its elements, the universal and the particular, etc. [. . .] it has no analogy elsewhere, has to be reflected upon for itself, starting from itself and as a model of itself'.[33]

Castoriadis stresses the consequences that his theorization of the social and of the individual has for the emergence of the new in history and for the theorization of the autonomy of the individual, i.e. for the questions of history and agency.

Because the social is primarily a 'magma of social imaginary significations', it retains a degree of indeterminacy both in relation to nature and in the context of history. For Castoriadis, society 'leans' on nature but is not determined by it in any way. In nature society finds only 'a series of conditions, supports and stimuli, stops and obstacles'.[34] For example, 'the *natural* fact of being-male and being-female [is transformed] into an *imaginary social signification* of being-man and being-woman which refers to the magma of all the imaginary significations of the society considered. Neither this transformation itself nor the specific tenor of the signification in question can be deduced, produced or derived on the basis of the natural fact, which is always and everywhere the same.'[35]

30. Ibid., p. 366.
31. Ibid., p. 321.
32. Ibid., p. 320.
33. C. Castoriadis, 'Power, Politics, Autonomy' (1988), in *Philosophy, Politics, Autonomy*, Oxford, 1990, p. 145.
34. Castoriadis, *The Imaginary Institution of Society*, p. 234.
35. Ibid., p. 229.

In a similar way, history is never predetermined. 'What is given in and through history is not the determined sequence of the determined but the emergence of radical otherness, immanent creation, non-trivial novelty[36] [. . .] what emerges [has to be seen as] not in what exists, not even "logically" or as an already constituted "potentiality" nor as the actualization of pre-determined possibilities[37] [. . .] history is the emergence of the radical otherness or of the absolutely new.'[38] Historical time has to be thought as 'not simply and not only indetermination but [as] the springing forth of determinations, or, better yet, of other eide – images-figures-forms'.[39] Thus, while 'there can be and, in fact, there always is a persistence or a subsistence of certain determinations', there never exists, in history, a full, principal, or essential determinacy. Historical change is characterized – for Castoriadis – by an essential indetermination.[40] The 'immanent creation and radical otherness' is, by definition, a central element of the mode of being of magma. Therefore it is *because* the social is seen as fundamentally a 'magma' that the 'absolutely new' can emerge in history.

The modality of magma is pivotal also for the affirmation of the possibility of autonomy, an affirmation that constitutes a central tenet of Castoriadis's work. Castoriadis defines autonomy on the level of the individual as 'the possibility that the activity proper to the "subject" becomes an "object", the possibility of putting oneself into question.'[41] The autonomy of the individual 'consists in the instauration of an other relationship between the present and the history which made the individual such as it is. This relationship makes it possible for the individual to [. . .] look back upon himself, to reflect on the reason for his thoughts and the motives of his acts guided by the elucidation of his desire and aiming at truth.'[42]

'Self objectification' can be also translated into action and

36. Ibid., p. 184.
37. Ibid., p. 190.
38. Ibid., p. 172.
39. Castoriadis, *The Imaginary Institution of Society*, p. 190. Thus historical time regains its specificity and its 'spatialization' , its reduction to extension – which happens if time is seen as a scheme of succession between already given entities – is avoided (ibid., p. 188).
40. Ibid., p. 199. The manner in which this indetermination appears in history is the 'creative capacity of the anonymous collectivity, as it is manifested clearly, for example, in and through the creation of language, of family forms, of morality, of ideas, etc.' (idem, 'Psychanalyse et politique' (1987), in *Le monde morcelé*, Paris, 1990, p. 148).
41. C. Castoriadis, 'The State of the Subject Today' (1986), translation in *Thesis Eleven*, no. 24, 1989, p. 26.
42. Castoriadis, 'Power, Politics, Autonomy', p. 165.

represents the specificity of human subjectivity which is distinct from simple consciousness or self-referentiality: 'One can perfectly well conceive of a consciousness that remains a simple spectator, recording the processes that unfold in individual life.'[43] The possibility of autonomy can be asserted, despite the fundamentally social nature of the human individual, because both the social (as social imaginary significations) and the individual unconscious have the modality of 'magma':

> If ensemblist-identitary logic totally exhausted what exists, there could never be any question of rupture of any kind, and even more of autonomy. Everything would be deducible/producible from the 'already given' [. . .] A subject existing totally within a ensemblist-identitary universe, not only it could not change anything, it could not even know that it exists with such a universe[44] [. . .] It is because the human being is imagination (non-functional imagination) that it can posit as an 'entity' something that is not so: its own process of thought.[45]

However, only the *possibility* of autonomy can be generally asserted. The actualization of this possibility is historically specific: 'Individuals aiming at autonomy cannot appear unless the social-historical field has already altered itself in such a way that it opens a space of interrogation without bounds (without an instituted or revealed truth, for example).'[46] It is only with societies that 'put into question their proper institutions and significations',[47] (i.e. autonomous societies) that autonomous individuals can emerge. Such societies, for Castoriadis, have appeared only twice in history: 'in Greece from the eight century B.C. onward and in Western Europe from the twelfth to thirteen centuries onward'.[48]

Even if actualized, autonomy can never lead either on an individual or a social level to full transparency. Castoriadis, introducing a theorization of autonomy alongside a structural theorization of the

43. Castoriadis, 'The State of the Subject Today', p. 37.
44. Castoriadis, 'La logique des magmas et la question de l'autonomie', p. 412.
45. Castoriadis, 'The State of the Subject Today', p. 27.
46. Castoriadis, 'Power, Politics, Autonomy', p. 166.
47. Castoriadis, 'La logique des magmas et la question de l'autonomie', p. 411.
48. Castoriadis, 'Power, Politics, Autonomy', p. 167. Correlatively, the political project of autonomy is defined by Castoriadis as the 'creation of the institutions which, by being internalized by individuals, facilitate most their accession to their individual autonomy and their effective participation in all forms of explicit power existing in society' (ibid., p. 173).

social and an affirmation of the deeply social nature of the individual, indicates also the bounded nature of this autonomy:[49]

> No society will ever be totally transparent, first because the individuals that make it will never be transparent to themselves, since there can be no question of eliminating the unconscious. Then, because the social element implies not only individual unconscious, nor even simply mutual intersubjective inherencies, [but also] the relationships between persons, both conscious and unconscious, which could never be given in its entirety as a content to all [. . .] the social implies something that can never be given as such.[50]

Through his notion of 'magma of social imaginary significations', Castoriadis offers a way to conceptualize the kind of modality that a radical openness/indeterminacy of the social would necessitate. Moreover, he provides an extensive theorization of the different levels of the social and of the meeting between the social and the individual, building on the psychoanalytic theory of the psyche. Finally, he traces in detail the consequences his theorization has for the questions of agency and history, presenting a detailed theorization of autonomy and indicating beyond any doubt the need to theorize the social as open and indeterminate if a satisfactory answer to these questions is to be provided. Castoriadis's work constitutes a significant step further in the direction Laclau and Mouffe also indicate.[51] It establishes a theory of the mode of being of the social as structural and yet as different from that of fully determined and closed structural entities, providing an alternative to structural/objectivist theories and avoiding the problems such approaches face. However, once the general lines of Castoriadis's theoretical framework have been accepted, certain questions remain.

The question of totality: Castoriadis often refers to *a* society, considering the magma of imaginary significations as determining one totality, that of society. Although he does not dwell on this point particularly, he does nowhere recognize a possible existence of

49. The very emergence of the social individual depends on the satisfactory internalization of social imaginary significations. Attempts, therefore, to consider Castoriadis's emphasis on the possibility of autonomy as reintroducing a sovereign subject (as, for example, A. Elliott in *Social Theory and Psychoanalysis in Transition*, London, 1992, who appropriates Castoriadis within a theoretical scheme reminiscent of Giddens) are definitely misplaced.
50. Castoriadis, *The Imaginary Institution of Society*, p. 111.
51. Castoriadis's theorization is more comprehensive and fully argued than Laclau and Mouffe's and avoids the reduction of the social to the level of ideas that their work seems to imply.

different magmas of signification within particular spatio-temporal co-ordinates, or, to put it differently, he does not consider 'partial' structures of a 'society' to correspond to distinct 'magmas'. For example, the economy in capitalism is seen as 'representing the economic signification which in certain *societies* had emerged first as important and then as central and decisive'.[52] Capitalism, then, is not a magma of significations in its own right, is not a relatively autonomous totality but represents the economic signification of a greater totality, of a society.

However, a 'society' can be defined as such only in the presence of a degree of closure *vis-à-vis* 'other' societies, a closure that cannot be assumed but has to be demonstrated. A 'society' can be defined generally, i.e. transhistorically, only in the context of transhistorical constancy of certain elements (as, for example, are the 'functions' in functionalist approaches); and Castoriadis explicitly denies the presence of any such elements. Moreover, a reference to society as a general totality implies a pre-established harmony among its different parts, which makes difficult the conceptualization of contradictions and conflict (as also the possibility of certain structural wholes being more dominant than others) and Castoriadis would be the last to deny their existence.

One of the important contributions of structuralism was the emphasis it placed on the possibility of analysing the social through a reference to many structures, irreducible to one another and not necessarily belonging to a greater totality. Since Castoriadis theorizes the social as open, he does not have to depart from this position but simply to improve it. It may be that particular 'segments' of a world of significations represent relatively autonomous and self-sustainable magmas of significations, not necessarily belonging to a greater totality. Indeed, the modality of magmas implies that any cohesiveness and closure has to be established in every particular case. Moreover, the recognition that the unconscious has the modality of magma allows precisely the possibility of a simultaneous determination of the subject by a plurality of 'magmas of social imaginary significations', not necessarily in harmony with each other, which can be seen to operate on the individual psyche and to fuse with one another on the level of the unconscious. The magmas of social imaginary significations can be regarded as corresponding to partial social structures rather than to an overall 'society' without this changing anything for the notion of a magma of significations or the implications drawn from it.

---

52. Castoriadis, *The Imaginary Institution of Society*, p. 362, emphasis added.

The level of existence of social imaginary significations: If Castoriadis's reference to a totality can be seen as a simple lack of precision, the case of the level on which the magma of social imaginary significations might be considered as operating is not so straightforward. Social imaginary significations are presented as operating behind and beyond the identitary aspects of social doing/ representing (*legein* and *teukhein*), behind and beyond individuals and things, assuring the always indeterminate and open nature of this doing and representing. Castoriadis is not very forthcoming, however, about the level of operation (of 'existence') of these significations as such.[53] The reference to the institution of society, to the instituting instance, could be taken to introduce something like Derrida's *différance* (or Heidegger's *Dasein*), subverting any closure but as such not existing, a kind of negative essence. If so, we are faced with the application of a transcendental ontology of the Derridian/Heideggerian type within the field of the social.

It is doubtful, however, whether Castoriadis would endorse an explicitly Derridian stand. Moreover, he does indicate at least one level at which the social imaginary significations exist, to a certain extent, as such, i.e. as a magma: it is the level of the (individual) unconscious which also has the modality of magma (insisting, at the same time that 'the world of instituted significations cannot be reduced to actual individual representations'). Could it be, then, that it is *because* the social imaginary significations exist – in some way – within the unconscious and *because* the unconscious has the modality of magma that significations and the social in general also has this modality? Could it be, in other words, that the openness the modality of the magma introduces within the social, passes through the mode of existence of the social within the individual and specifically within the level of the unconscious? If so, any reference to a transcendental level as the foundation of the 'openness' of the social would be unnecessary. Castoriadis does indicate the possibility of such an interpretation. He does not, however, commit himself to it.

---

53. For example, Castoriadis writes in *The Imaginary Institution of Society* (p. 368): 'The world of social significations is to be thought of not as an irreal copy of a real world; nor as formed by that which is 'expressible' in individual representations [. . .] not, finally, as a system of relations which would be added onto subjects and objects which themselves are given fully and which would modify, in this or that historical context, their properties, effects or behaviour. We are to think of the world of social significations as the primary, inaugural, irreducible positing of the social-historical and of the social imaginary as it manifests itself in each case in a given society.'

Is the social primarily significations?: Castoriadis's theorization of social openness is based on the modality social imaginary significations have, that of 'magma'. Can we confine, however, the indeterminacy and openness the mode of being of magma introduces only to 'significations'? Is the social 'open' only because social imaginary significations have the modality of magma?

Referring to the psyche, Castoriadis recognizes that the unconscious is an 'indissociably representative/ affective/ intentional flux' and accepts that 'I have spoken mainly the language of representation because [. . .] it is the aspect about which we can more easily and directly speak.'[54] Yet he does reduce the social determination of the unconscious to the internalization of social imaginary significations. Also, Castoriadis often gives the impression that for him the social in general is simply the actualization of some 'central imaginary significations', which, however 'imaginary' and 'materialized' in practice they may be, they remain a kind of idea, a *Weltanschaung*.[55] Moreover, if we want to theorize social practice and social action and its specificity – a specificity that Bourdieu forcefully indicates – within Castoriadis's scheme we can not. The only way to theorize practice is as the actualization of (pre-existing) social imaginary significations.

There is a possibility, though, that the social may operate on the structuring of the psyche in general and on the unconscious in particular in some other way besides the internalization of social imaginary significations. Social determinations may exist which, though expressible through representations on the level of the individual psyche, in their 'social' form do not originate from and are not transmitted as representations. A more detailed theorization of the ways in which the social determines the individual – apart from the internalization of social imaginary significations – and a corresponding theorization of social practice and social action could extend Castoriadis's reference on significations and provide the basis for a more comprehensive theorization of 'openness'.

54. C. Castoriadis, 'Fait et à faire' in G. Busino *et al*, *Autonomie et autotransformation de la société: La philosophie militante de C. Castoriadis*, Genève, 1989, p. 476.

55. This is the case in Castoriadis's reference to significations 'giving a meaning' to the social world and being thus the 'religious core' of the institution of society ('Institution de la société et religion' (1982), in *Domaines de l'homme*, p. 369) or his reference to capitalism as corresponding to a central core of significations indicating 'the unlimited expansion of the 'rational' matrix' ('Le régime social de la Russie' (1978), op. cit., p. 197).

The existence of different levels of autonomy: Castoriadis focusses on the level of autonomy defined by the possibility of 'putting oneself into question', a possibility linked to society itself being able to question its 'institution'. This is the highest possible degree of self-reflectiveness and self-objectification in the sense that it addresses the greatest possible number of determinations both at an individual and at a social level. There is also, however, a lower level of autonomy, referring to a self-reflexivity of a more instrumental type, one that does not imply any 'putting into question' but rather the successful use of existing norms or rules. It is this 'activeness' of the social actor that hermeneutically oriented micro-sociology highlights and that Giddens and Bourdieu have primarily attempted to theorize. Castoriadis's own earlier work, repeatedly focusses on such a creativity at a 'micro' level, as for example in the case of the workers in a factory creating new forms of organization or resistance. This 'creation', though it presupposes some degree of 'putting into question', it does not refer to a questioning of the totality of instituted society. Thus, besides autonomy in the strict sense Castoriadis theorizes, we would have to distinguish 'degrees' or 'levels' of autonomy, and to articulate these levels with one another. This is not Castoriadis's primary aim, but it is necessary if a comprehensive theory of the levels of autonomy is to be presented.

Castoriadis's work can be considered as a landmark in the direction we identified Derrida as introducing and Laclau and Mouffe as further developing. He completes the move from a general theorization of 'openness' and indeterminacy to the affirmation that such an 'openness' refers to the social itself and provides an elaborate theorization of the social and the individual grounding this claim. Moreover, the necessity of theorizing the social as open in order to fruitfully address the questions of agency and history is conclusively argued for. A novel and in many aspects very promising way of theorizing the social at a general and abstract level is thus established, providing an alternative to structural/objectivist approaches.

However, the 'level of existence' of the 'magmas of social imaginary significations' and the limitation of the social to these significations remain problematic. How do social imaginary significations exist if not as a kind of negative essence behind and beyond the positivity of the social, somehow introducing an 'openness' and a 'radical indeterminacy'? The danger of assuming a level beyond that of the social, a kind of transcendental level, to ground such an indeterminacy is present. Moreover, the question emerges whether the theorization of indeterminacy can be limited to the mode of being of significations alone. Does not the realm of social practice have a specific relevance and modality, of the kind Bourdieu claims? Further theoretical elaboration and clarification towards the direction Castoriadis's work establishes seems to be necessary.

At this point the possibility of a synthesis between the theorization of the social as 'open' and the direction in which theories of structuration have moved presents itself. A theorization of a certain 'openness' and indeterminacy of the social could be located *within* the processes of production and reproduction of the social through the individual, within, in other words, a theory of 'structuration'. Such a move could avoid the shortcomings of either approach while retaining their insights.

In fact, Castoriadis, by stressing the specific mode of being of the individual unconscious as also its social nature, indicates the way such a synthesis can go. Instead of simply asserting a similarity in modality between the 'magma of social imaginary significations' and the individual unconscious, a causal chain could be introduced. It could be claimed that the social is 'open' and indeterminate – i.e. it has the modality of magma – because it is reproduced through the level of the (individual) unconscious (or, in a generalized version, through the psyche). Castoriadis never commits himself to such a thesis, but it seems promising enough. It could even allow a broader theorization of the 'openness' of the social so that it is not limited to the mode of being of 'significations'. If so, it would be possible to integrate a theory of practice – on the lines of Bourdieu's suggestions – within the same theoretical framework.

In order to evaluate this possibility, a more detailed account of the ways and the levels of interaction between the social and the individual psyche is needed. To provide such an account, we turn to the psychoanalytic theorization of the psyche in general and of the unconscious in particular, from Freud's original formulations to later developments.

Part III

Psyche and Society

–9–

The Specificity of the Unconscious

Psychoanalysis has repeatedly proclaimed its uniqueness, its irreducibility to a sociology and its indissociable link with analytic practice. However, if the psychoanalytic approach can offer a theorization of the psyche in general, as it claims, it cannot avoid facing, sooner or later, the question of the social (no doubt within analytic practice as well). We shall concentrate, therefore, precisely on these elements of psychoanalytic theory that are of interest in the context of the interface of the individual psyche and the social, before proceeding to theorize the interface itself. The account of psychoanalysis presented is, consequently, limited and partial. Freud's own writings will be used as the base reference throughout not only because of his being the founder of psychoanalytic discourse but also because his work remains the most comprehensive and profound account of psychoanalytic theory and its implications. While others have made important contributions in particular areas (and we will refer to such contributions that are of interest to the present analysis) none has matched Freud's amazing breadth, insight and profundity.

If we were to indicate in one word Freud's most important contribution, it would undoubtedly be the 'unconscious'.[1] The notion of 'something' beyond consciousness, of an un-conscious, is not alien to the history of Western thought. Specifically in the modern period, from the eighteenth century onwards, many such references can be found.[2] Indeed, the modern notion of the social necessarily introduces a level of phenomena that, though produced by individuals, are nonetheless to a certain extent opaque to them. The modern notion of the social necessitates, therefore, a certain notion of the unconscious.[3] However, it was Freud who elaborated the distinction between

1. See also J. Laplanche and J.B. Pontalis, *The Language of Psychoanalysis* (1967), London, 1988, p. 474.
2. A detailed account is presented in L. Whyte, *The Unconscious before Freud*, London, 1962.
3. Foucault has remarked that 'the unconscious and the human sciences are, at an archaeological level, contemporaries' (M. Foucault, *The Order of Things* (1966), London, 1974, p. 326).

consciousness and the unconscious and provided a theorization of the specificity and irreducibility of the unconscious as a level of human psychical functioning.

For Freud the 'Unconscious' represents one of three levels of psychical functioning, the other two being the 'Preconscious' and 'Consciousness' (*Ucs.*, *Pcs.*, *Cs.*, respectively). This distinction came to be known as the first Freudian topography of the psyche. However, since the preconscious 'shares the characteristics of the system *Cs.*'[4] the central distinction is that between the 'unconscious' and 'consciousness'.

Consciousness is necessarily linked with perception, either external or internal and with the residues of perception: 'The process of something becoming conscious is above all linked with the perceptions which our sense-organs receive from the external world.'[5] But 'in men internal processes in the ego also acquire the quality of consciousness. This is the work of the function of speech, which brings material in the ego into a firm connection with mnemic residues of visual, but more particularly of auditory perceptions.'[6] Consciousness is thus always connected to a certain kind of 'representatives'.

In contrast to consciousness, the unconscious is a field of energy in continuous movement, a field of force. It is the field of the energy of the instincts, of the drives (*Triebe*): 'The chief characteristic of these processes [of the primary process in the dreamwork] is that the whole stress is laid upon making the cathecting energy mobile and capable of discharge; the content and the proper meaning of psychical elements, to which the cathexes are attached are treated as of little consequence.'[7] Yet even this field should always be seen as connected with 'representations':

> An instinct can never become the object of consciousness – only the idea that represents the instinct can. Even in the unconscious, an instinct cannot be represented otherwise than by an idea. If the instinct did not attach itself to an idea or manifest itself as an affective state, we could know nothing about it. When we nevertheless speak of a repressed instinctual impulse, the looseness of the phraseology is a harmless one. We can only mean an

4. S. Freud, 'The Unconscious' (1915), Penguin/Pelican Freud Library (P.F.L.) 11, Harmondsworth, 1984, p. 175. The edition used here is the Penguin/Pelican Freud Library (P.F.L.) in fifteen volumes which is a reprint of the *Standard Edition* in paperback form.
5. S. Freud, 'An Outline of Psychoanalysis' (1938), P.F.L. 15, Harmondsworth, 1986, p. 395.
6. Ibid.
7. S. Freud, *The Interpretation of Dreams* (1900), P.F.L. 4, Harmondsworth, 1976, p. 765.

instinctual impulse the ideational representative of which [*den Trieb repräsentierende Vorstellung*] is unconscious, for nothing else comes into consideration.[8]

'Affects', 'emotions' and 'feelings' are also connected to representatives in both consciousness and the unconscious, though in a different way from ideas being directly cathected. A difference between conscious and unconscious affects is the repression of the 'proper representative' of an affect and the connection of the affect to another 'idea' in order to become conscious.

Thus, despite the fact that the unconscious is energy, it operates always through a connection with 'representatives'. Freud uses the term *Repräsentanz* – which has been translated as 'representative' or 'presentation'– and the term besetzen (to cathect; literally to occupy, with a connotation of force, as in military occupation). He reserves the term *Vorstellung* – a term with a philosophical past, for example in Kant or Schopenhauer, usually rendered as 'ideational' or 'idea' – for elements derived from memory traces, i.e. ultimately from perception, elements which can also form the representatives of the instincts. However, an instinct (drive), even in the absence of such a *Vorstellung*, is never present as such. It is always connected to a *Repräsentanz*. The psyche on the level of the unconscious – as on the level of consciousness – is always and necessarily 'represented':

> At a certain point the question of force and the question of meaning coincide; that point is where instincts are indicated, are made manifest, are given in a psychical representative, i.e. in something psychical that 'stands for' them; all the derivatives in consciousness are merely transformations of this psychical representative, of this primal 'standing for' [. . .] But we must not speak of representation in the sense of *Vorstellung*, i.e. an 'idea' of something, for an idea is itself derived from this 'representative' which, before representing things – the world, one's own body, the unreal – stands for instincts as such, presents them purely and simply.[9]

If the psyche has to be seen as always employing 'representatives' the question of their origin emerges, especially regarding unconscious representations. An obvious source is perception, providing memory traces (*Erinnerungsspuren*), a cathexis of which provides, in turn,

8. Freud, 'The Unconscious', p. 179.
9. P. Ricœur, *Freud and Philosophy*, New Haven, 1970, p. 135.

Vorstellungen.[10] However, at the beginning, *before* any *Vorstellungen* can be supplied by memory, does the unconscious and the psyche in general exist in a state of pure energy, as a 'pure' field of energy?

Freud addresses obliquely the question about the original state of the unconscious in his theory of 'primal repression'. For repression to operate, 'something' to attract the contents of consciousness which are to be repressed is needed. In order to make subsequent repressions possible, 'a primal repression, a first phase of repression, which consists in the psychical (ideational) representative of the instinct being denied entrance into the conscious'[11] has to be postulated. In this primal repression 'we are dealing with an unconscious idea which has as yet received no cathexis from the *Pcs.* and therefore cannot have that cathexis withdrawn from it'. It is 'an anticathexis by means of which the system *Pcs.* protects itself from the pressure upon it of the unconscious idea'.[12] Thus the possibility of an 'unconscious idea' which does not originate in consciousness, but which is already there in the beginning is introduced. Indeed the notion of primal repression has no other function in Freudian theory than to denote precisely this fact. As Ricœur remarks: 'Primal repression means that we are always in the mediate, in the already expressed, the already said.'[13] Therefore the unconscious can be said to be 'represented' in the psyche even before memory traces are cathected to provide presentations. The same assumption is made by Freud when he refers to primal phantasies (primal scene, castration, intra-uterine existence) as phantasies operating 'regardless of the personal experience of different subjects'.

Thus we are faced with two kinds of 'representatives' in the unconscious. On the one hand the ones deriving from memory traces. On the other the 'primal' representatives, those operating in the origin, the very beginning, manifested in primal phantasies or primal repression. Yet within Freud's discussion there is nowhere established a distinction in quality between these two types of representatives. It is as if the innate 'representatives' of the psyche are of the same nature as the ones acquired through memory traces. If the two categories can be distinguished, is not because of a qualitative difference but because of a difference in origins. In fact we are nowhere faced with any primal

10. Freud is not explicit about the nature of the perceptual engraving on the surface of memory. It seems that there are grounds suggesting that he does not uphold an empiricist notion of direct, immediate and unproblematic engraving of outside 'objects' on the 'inside' of the psyche (see Laplanche and Pontalis, *The Language of Psychoanalysis*, pp. 247–8).

11. S. Freud, 'Repression' (1915), P.F.L. 11, Harmondsworth, 1984, p. 147.

12. Ibid., p. 184.

13. Ricœur, *Freud and Philosophy*, p. 141.

representatives as such. The representatives of the instincts as manifested through consciousness can almost always be seen as coming through memory traces, attributable to some past experience, however early. Even the case of primal phantasies can be seen as referring more to a specific structure organizing the contents of the unconscious, rather as having specific contents.[14]

The question of the origin of psychical representatives remained central after Freud, and many psychoanalysts have contributed to the discussion. We shall briefly refer to the contributions of Jung, Klein, Lacan and Castoriadis.

Jung accepts the existence of primal representatives and accords them a much greater role than Freud does. He introduces the notion of a 'collective unconscious' beneath the personal unconscious, in which past experiences of the human race are 'stored'. The collective unconscious is the source of the 'archetypes', 'inborn forms of intuition, of perception and apprehension, which are the necessary *a priori* determinants of all psychic processes'.[15] These archetypes are connected with the instincts, they are 'simply the forms which the instincts assume'.[16] However, despite stressing the existence of certain innate structures and symbolic predispositions of the psyche, Jung does not equate the archetypes with representations as such. The archetypes define the structure of representations rather than the representations themselves, in the same way that Freud's primal phantasies can be considered to do:

> The archetypal representations (images and ideas) mediated to us by the unconscious should not be confused with the archetype as such. They are very varied structures which all point to one essentially 'irrepresentable' basic form. The latter is characterized by certain formal elements and by certain fundamental meanings, although they can be grasped only approximately.[17]

M. Klein, investigating the first years of life, indicates that there may be 'private symbols' before the acquisition of socially derived ones. The infant is seen as having an innate capacity to produce unconscious phantasies, related both to external situations (the breast, the mother, for example) and to internal ones coming from the function

14. J. Laplanche and J.B. Pontalis, 'Fantasy and the Origins of Sexuality', *The International Journal of Psychoanalysis*, vol. 49, 1968, p. 17.

15. C.G. Jung, 'Instinct and the Unconscious' (1919), in *Collected Works*, vol. 8, London, 1960, p. 133.

16. Ibid., p. 157.

17. C.G. Jung, 'On the Nature of the Psyche' (1947), in *Collected Works*, vol. 8, London, 1960, p. 213.

of the organism. Even these earlier phantasies, though, are not entirely arbitrary from individual to individual since they relate to essentially the same type of experiences. The early phantasies form the basis on which symbol formation gradually develops as the child grows up.[18] Externally acquired symbols gradually take the place of the earlier, 'private' symbols of the phantasies. In general Klein and her followers attribute a greater importance to innate, primal capabilities of symbol/ fantasy formation than Freud does. Along with Freud, though, they see the content of these phantasies as being smoothly replaced by external acquired elements, symbols or representatives.

The distinction between the two levels of representation has been presented by J. Lacan as that between the imaginary and the symbolic. The imaginary refers to primary 'imagos' and specifically to the imago of the self which the child recognizes 'from the sixth month in its encounter with his image in the mirror'.[19] This marks the 'mirror stage' at which a pre-verbal, pre-symbolic individuality is constituted. To this primary 'I' (*Moi*) subsequently operates the 'symbolic' – the symbolic order mediated through language – through the 'discourse of the other' and creates a 'subject'. Lacan sees the imaginary order as having certain common elements with processes of identification with a *Gestalt* in animals to which ethological studies refer; yet at the same time he considers this order as having a specificity, a 'prematuration', in human beings, allowing the 'symbolic' to operate: '[T]he gap opened up by this prematuration of the imaginary and in which the effects of the mirror stage proliferate [allows] the symbiosis with the symbolic to occur.'[20]

For Lacan the symbolic order is mediated through language. Language is not seen as a code but as evoking subjects through meaning: 'The function of language is not to inform but to evoke. What I seek in speech is the response of the other. What constitutes me as subject is my question.'[21] Language totally shapes the unconscious so that the unconscious has the structure of language: '[for interpretation is based on the fact that] the unconscious is structured in the most radical way like a language, that a material operates in it according to certain laws, which are the same laws as

18. M. Klein, 'The Importance of Symbol-Formation in the Development of the Ego' (1930), in M. Klein, *Love, Guilt and Reparation: Works 1921–1945*, London, 1988, p. 220.
19. J. Lacan, 'Aggressivity in Psychoanalysis' (1948), in *Ecrits: A Selection*, London, 1977, p. 18.
20. J. Lacan, 'On a Question Preliminary to Any Possible Treatment of Psychosis' (1958), *Ecrits: A Selection*, London, 1977, p. 196.
21. J. Lacan, 'The Function and Field of Speech and Language in Psychoanalysis' (1953), *Ecrits: A Selection*, London, 1977, p. 86.

those discovered in the study of actual languages.'[22] It is the symbolic order, acquired through language, that structures the unconscious. Lacan is thus the first to draw specific attention to the social origin of the externally acquired symbols, i.e. to the fact that these symbols do not naturally exist embedded in 'things' but that they are constructed within the human community and primarily expressed through language. His attention only to language to the exclusion of other possible symbolic systems does not invalidate this fundamental insight. The imaginary origins of representations give their place to socially constructed symbolic systems. This transition is, as with the Kleinians, in principle smooth and unproblematic. Despite the difference in names, the two orders, the imaginary and the symbolic, do not represent for Lacan different modalities.

Castoriadis also insists on a primary, innate 'capacity to make representations arise', an 'originary phantasmatization [which] pre-exists and presides over every organization of drives, even the most primitive one, that it is the condition for the drive to attain psychical existence'.[23] This capacity predates therefore also the emergence of an 'I', however elementary. Thus it cannot be attributed to a 'lack' (against Lacan) or 'desire' (against Deleuze and Guattari) since any lack or desire presupposes precisely a subject. Even Freud's primal phantasies, remarks Castoriadis, cannot be really 'primary' in the sense that they already presuppose a certain organization and the distinction between 'contents', 'characters' and 'acts' to operate.[24] Gradually, however, the originary representations are replaced by the 'social imaginary significations', socially constructed and originating ones.[25]

Freud's reference to primal repression and primal phantasies, Jung's archetypes, Klein and her followers' primal phantasies, Lacan's imaginary, Castoriadis's original phantasmatization, all indicate that certain primal representatives of the instincts, lying beyond individual experience and perception do exist. They also indicate that even in the most original, primary state, the field of energy of the

22. J. Lacan, 'The Direction of Treatment and the Principles of Its Power' (1958), *Ecrits: A Selection*, London, 1977, p. 234.

23. C. Castoriadis, *The Imaginary Institution of Society*, Cambridge, 1987, p. 287.

24. Ibid., p. 286.

25. For Lacan and Castoriadis the passage from the early, innate representations to the later, socially originating ones, is associated with the Oedipus complex which acquires thus a more general meaning. Lacan, drawing upon Lévi-Strauss's 'universal law' of the prohibition of incest, sees the Oedipal crisis as lying 'at the origin of the whole process of the cultural subordination of man' (*Ecrits: A Selection*, p. 24). Similarly Castoriadis considers that 'the encounter with the Oedipal situation sets before the child the unavoidable fact of the institution as the ground of signification and vice versa' (*The Imaginary Institution of Society*, p. 310).

(unconscious) psyche is presented through representatives and never 'as such', as a state of 'pure' energy. These primal representatives though, are seen (with the exception of Jung who gives them greater weight) as readily being replaced by ones acquired through perception and the (external) environment. This is facilitated by the fact that the two levels of representatives are considered as sharing essentially the same modality. As Lacan and Castoriadis have noted, moreover, the environment at the origin of the second category of representatives is not a natural one, but a humanly constructed, social one.

The above indicate that the use of representations cannot be a criterion of distinguishing between consciousness and the unconscious. What could then such a criterion be? Three possible criteria, used by Freud in different parts of his work, are: repression, type of representatives and the mode of functioning of the unconscious. We shall discuss each in turn, trying to establish the specificity of the unconscious as a psychical level.

The unconscious is introduced by Freud as repressed, i.e. as separated from consciousness by a barrier that has to be lifted in order for the unconscious representatives to be able to become conscious. The lifting of repression is in principle possible: indeed this is the task of analysis. Repression does not indicate an impassable barrier, only one to be removed. However, the repressed is not to be equated with the unconscious in general. Initially Freud held this view, but he was gradually forced to admit that 'the unconscious has the wider compass: the repressed is part of the unconscious'.[26] Thus, while the repressed is necessarily unconscious, the unconscious as a level of the psyche is not necessarily repressed.

Freud tried also to differentiate the kind of representatives consciousness and the unconscious use. He distinguished between *Sachvorstellung* and *Wortvorstellung*, rendered as thing-presentation and word-presentation respectively. In the case of word-presentations memory traces are connected with words as well as with 'images' of objects, while thing-presentations are connected only with 'images'. Freud proposed that the distinction between the two kinds of presentations corresponds to the distinction between conscious and unconscious. For a representative to advance to consciousness, it has necessarily to be a *Wortvorstellung*, i.e. it has to be connected with words. This connection usually happens in the preconscious. On the contrary, on the level of the unconscious the instinct is represented usually by thing-presentations:

26. Freud, 'The Unconscious', p. 167.

> The conscious presentation comprises the presentation of the thing plus the presentation of the word belonging to it, while the unconscious presentation is the presentation of the thing alone. The system *Ucs.* contains the thing-cathexes of the objects, the first and true object-cathexes; the system *Pcs.* comes about by this thing-presentation being hypercathected through being linked with the word-presentations corresponding to it.[27]

However, thing presentations are not restricted to the unconscious: preconscious phantasies, preconscious 'thinking in pictures', for example, use also 'images' rather than word-presentations.[28] On the other hand, the unconscious can also use word-presentations as is the case in schizophrenics: 'In schizophrenia words are subjected to the same process as that which makes the dream-images out of latent dream-thoughts – to what we have called the primary psychical process.'[29] In dreams, also, 'we find associations based on homonyms and verbal similarities treated as equal in value to the rest'.[30] Freud insists that consciousness is necessarily linked with word-presentations and that any presentation coming from the unconscious to consciousness has, in the preconscious, to be 'brought into connection with word-presentations'.[31] Yet it seems that there is no specifically unconscious presentation. In later writings Freud admits that an idea is carried out in the unconscious 'on some material which remains unknown'.[32] Thus the distinction between thing- and word-presentation is only partially useful to differentiate between the conscious and the unconscious.

While neither repression nor the limitation to thing-presentations are sufficient criteria of differentiation of the unconscious, there is another difference between the two levels which can be considered such a criterion. As the examples of unconscious use of words indicate, even when the presentations used are of the same kind, within the unconscious they are subjected to a specific way of operating, different from conscious thought. This is confirmed by the analysis of dreams: due to the relaxation of overimposed logical functions during sleep, dreams allow the specific way of unconscious operation to appear, in the 'dream work', characterized by 'condensation, displacement, absence of contradiction'. It is worth, at this point, quoting Freud in full:

27. Ibid., p. 207.
28. S. Freud, *The Ego and the Id* (1923), P.F.L. 11, Harmondsworth, 1984, p. 359.
29. Freud, 'The Unconscious', p. 204.
30. Freud, *The Interpretation of Dreams*, p. 755.
31. Freud, *The Ego and the Id*, p. 358.
32. Ibid.

The nucleus of the *Ucs.* consists of instinctual representatives which seek to discharge their cathexis; that is to say, it consists of wishful impulses. These instinctual impulses are co-ordinate with one another, exist side by side, without being influenced by one another, and are exempt from mutual contradiction [. . .] In this system there is no negation, no doubt, no degrees of certainty [. . .] The cathectic intensities (in the *Ucs.*) are much more mobile. By the process of *displacement* one idea may surrender to another its whole quota of cathexis; by the process of *condensation* it may appropriate the whole cathexis of several other ideas. I have proposed to regard these two processes as distinguishing marks of the so-called *primary psychical process*. In the system *Pcs.* the *secondary process* is dominant [. . .] The processes of the system *Ucs.* are *timeless*; i.e. they are not ordered temporally, are not altered by the passage of time; they have no reference to time at all [. . .] The *Ucs.* processes pay just as little regard to *reality*. They are subject to the pleasure principle; their fate depends only on how strong they are and on whether they fulfil the demands of the pleasure–unpleasure regulation.[33]

The unconscious has, therefore, a number of characteristics indicating a way of psychical functioning not only different from but even opposed to that of consciousness – that of conscious thought: exception from mutual contradiction, primary process (mobility of cathexes), timelessness,[34] and replacement of external by psychical reality. Though the unconscious operates through representations just as consciousness does, the *mode* of this operation is different. We can consider this mode of operation, the manner presentations are used, as the primary distinguishing characteristic of the unconscious. Thus the specificity of the Freudian notion of the unconscious can now be established: while the system *Cs.* consists of all the characteristics that have been traditionally attributed to man (rational/logical thought, perception, and so on), the unconscious has a unique mode of functioning.[35]

33. Freud, 'The Unconscious', pp. 190–1.
34. How this 'timelessness' is to be understood? While the other characteristics of the unconscious Freud proposes are relatively clearly defined, 'timelessness' is not. Derrida proposes that 'Timelessness is no doubt determined only in opposition to a common concept of time, a traditional concept, the metaphysical concept: the time of mechanics or the time of consciousness' (J. Derrida, 'Freud and the Scene of Writing' (1966), in *Writing and Difference*, London, 1978, p. 215).
35. Lacan's argument that 'the unconscious is structured like a language' is definitely misplaced if it is taken to imply that the unconscious can be formally analysed in the way language to a certain extent can. The representatives of the unconscious as such can neither be formalized nor approached without their being 'interpreted' and transposed to consciousness. As Laplanche and Leclaire remark: 'As to the ontological status of the unconscious [. . .] need we recall that, if that system is linguistic, such a language can by no means be assimilated to our "verbal" language?' (J. Laplanche and S. Leclaire, 'The Unconscious: A Psychoanalytic Study' (1961), *Yale French Studies*, no. 48, 1972, p. 162). Similarly, Ricœur considers 'that

Having established the specificity of the unconscious as a level of psychical functioning, we may pose the question of the possibility of its knowledge. 'How are we to arrive at a knowledge of the unconscious?' Freud asks, to reply: 'It is of course only as something conscious that we know it, after it has undergone transformation or retranslation into something conscious.'[36] We can recognize the existence of the unconscious in everyday life (as in the case of 'parapraxis'), in analytic practice, or in dreams (the 'royal road to the unconscious' for Freud because it was the analysis of dreams that provided him with an indication of the unconscious' specific modality). Even dreams, however, are not directly observable. They have to be 'recalled' and 'remembered' and, moreover, 'translated' into words, that is, they have to be made conscious. Thus what Freud and psychoanalysis offer are inferences on a level of psychical functioning whose existence and operation we can recognize in its effects only, always mediated through consciousness.

The possibility of this 'transformation' or 'translation' to consciousness has been established: representatives can operate in both the unconscious and consciousness, thing-presentations can be connected with word-presentations, repression can be lifted. Indeed the whole therapeutic structure of psychoanalysis rests precisely on the existence of this possibility, to which we can attest in the analysis of dreams or analytic practice in general.

However, the passage from the unconscious to consciousness is not immediate or direct. While the common origin of presentations as memory traces and the fact that they can be used by both consciousness and the unconscious establishes a continuity, a possibility of communication between the levels of the unconscious and consciousness/preconscious, the different modality of the unconscious implies that the way these presentations exist in the two levels is radically different. A change of state, a certain 'translation' is always necessary for unconscious representatives to become conscious (in addition to overcoming the barrier of repression, when it exists). Freud stresses that even representatives that were initially connected with words, once they have been incorporated within the unconscious cannot simply be reconnected with their own word-presentations:

---

the universe of discourse appropriate to analytic experience is not that of language but that of image'. And the 'image' is 'semiotic' though not 'linguistic' (P. Ricœur, 'Image and Language in Psychoanalysis' (1976), in J. Smith (ed.), *Psychoanalysis and Language: Psychiatry and the Humanities*, vol. 3, New Haven, 1978, pp. 293, 311).

36. Freud, 'The Unconscious', p. 167.

The question might be raised why presentations of objects cannot become conscious through the medium of their own perceptual residues. Probably, however, thought proceeds in systems so far remote from the original perceptual residues that they have no longer retained anything of the qualities of these residues, and, in order to become conscious, need to be reinforced by new qualities.[37]

Despite the existence of their own, original, word-presentations, therefore, unconscious presentations cannot pass smoothly into consciousness by simply 'recalling' them. They have 'no longer retained anything of the qualities of these residues', they exist in a state where a change of 'quality' is necessary in order to become conscious again. A 'retranslation' of these presentations onto conscious material is necessary. The necessity of such a 'change of state' of representatives is valid in the case of affects as well. For affects to become conscious they have to be connected with 'new', conscious representatives. In the case of repressed affects the lifting of repression connects them with their 'proper representatives', which had been repressed.

The need for a 'translation', an 'interpretation', is more evident when an unconscious 'thought' (which, as we saw, is subjected to the specific modality of the unconscious: primary process, lack of contradiction, timelessness, and so on) is to be 'translated' into conscious/logical thought. Such is the case, for example, with the interpretation of dreams, where a conscious/rational account of the dream is sought. Freud indicates that such an interpretation can never be final or fully completed: '[I]t is in fact never possible to be sure that a dream has been completely interpreted. Even if the solution seems satisfactory and without gaps the possibility always remains that the dream may have yet another meaning.'[38] In addition, a passage of an unconscious 'thought' into consciousness does not somehow replace the original – unconscious – registration. Freud writes: 'What we have in mind here is not the forming of a second thought situated in a new place, like a transcription which continues to exist alongside the original; and the notion of forcing a way through into consciousness must be kept carefully free from any idea of a change of locality.'[39] The two systems – that of consciousness and that of the unconscious – have to be thought as standing side by side in a double inscription: 'An idea may exist simultaneously in two places in the mental apparatus and, if not inhibited by the censorship, it regularly

37. Ibid., p. 208.
38. Freud, *The Interpretation of Dreams*, p. 383.
39. Ibid., p. 770.

advances from the one position to the other, possibly without losing its first location or registration.'[40] Thus, 'what is unconscious is in relation to the manifest not as a meaning to a letter, but on the same level of reality'.[41]

The always represented character of the unconscious, therefore, though it does establish a path of communication with consciousness, it does not annul the specificity of the unconscious. The existence of unconscious representations does not imply a simple transposition of (conscious) symbolic systems within the unconscious. The transition from the unconscious to consciousness, though in principle possible, is neither direct, nor immediate. It necessarily requires a certain alteration of modality, a 'translation', a certain 'interpretation'. And this interpretation can never be full and final nor does it replace the unconscious transcription. It represents a 'hermeneutic process' in the most radical sense of the term.

Establishing the specificity of the process of communication between consciousness and the unconscious, after stressing the always represented nature of the psyche on all its levels and the specific way of functioning of the unconscious, complements the main defining lines Freud attributes to the notion of the unconscious. The theorization remains, however, a static description, presented in essentially spatial terms. Perhaps recognizing this, Freud was to gradually proceed to a theorization of the ways the field of the psychical energy is structured, a dynamic theory of the psyche, presented principally in his second psychical topography.

---

40. Freud, 'The Unconscious', p. 177.
41. Laplanche and Leclaire, 'The Unconscious', p. 126. Of course, a certain alteration of the unconscious content is possible when it becomes (also) conscious. This is, for example, one of the tasks of analysis. But this alteration is only that – an alteration – and not an effacement of the unconscious transcription.

–10–

The Structuring of the Psyche

The development of psychical structuring, of the structuring of psychical energy, was approached by Freud initially through a theory of drives (*Triebe*) and specifically of the sexual drive. Gradually, however, Freud came to theorize psychical structuring as the development of specific agencies within the psyche. The full theory of these agencies was developed in the seminal *The Ego and the Id* in which he outlined what was termed the second Freudian topography of the psyche.

A Theory of Drives

To denote the energy of the psyche Freud chooses the term *Trieb*, which can be rendered as 'drive', and not the available *Instinkt*, which he reserves for explicit references to animal instincts.[1] The choice of term implies a desire to differentiate the energy of the human psyche from that of animal instincts. Moreover, the term *Trieb* 'accentuates not so much a precise goal as a general orientation, and draws attention to the irresistible nature of the pressure rather than to the stability of its aim and object'.[2]

Drives originate within the organism: the 'source' of a drive is 'the somatic process which occurs in an organ or part of the body and whose stimulus is represented in mental life by an instinct'.[3] While,

1. For example: 'If inherited mental formations exist in the human being – something analogous to instinct [*Instinkt*] in animals – these constitute the nucleus of the *Ncs*' (Freud, 'The Unconscious', Penguin/Pelican Freud Library (P.F.L.) 11, Harmondsworth, 1984, p. 200).
2. J. Laplanche and J.B. Pontalis, *The Language of Psychoanalysis* (1967), London, 1988, p. 214. The *Standard Edition* translates *Trieb* as 'instinct', making thus Freud's distinction untranslatable. However, *Trieb* can be rendered as 'drive', retaining some of the connotations of the original term, though the long established use of 'instinct' makes it unfamiliar. We shall use 'drive' when the specificity of the term needs to be emphasized, but 'instinct' and its derivatives – e.g. instinctual – otherwise. All the extracts from Freud's works use 'instinct'.
3. S. Freud, 'Instincts and their Vicissitudes' (*Triebe und Triebschicksale* (1915), P.F.L. 11, Harmondsworth, 1984, p. 119.

however, the 'source' of the drive is biologically given, the 'object' of a drive is not: this object, 'the thing through which the instinct is able to achieve its aim (which is in every instance satisfaction) [. . .] is what is most variable about an instinct and is not originally connected with it'.[4] Thus, a level of plasticity of the drive that would be inconceivable within the traditional notion of (animal) instinct is assumed.

The plasticity of the object of the drive becomes obvious in the case of sexual drives (libido), the only kind of drives Freud explicitly theorized. Despite the impression of the given nature of sexual objects, the 'object' of the sexual drive is indeed most variable. Sexuality in the infant may 'attach itself to other somatic functions'[5] before attaching itself to the genitals (thus we can have an oral and then an anal sexual organization). In addition, it has an 'external' object-choice: '[T]he choice of an object, such as we have shown to be characteristic of the pubertal phase of development, has already frequently or habitually been effected during the years of childhood: that is to say, the whole of the sexual currents have become directed towards a single person.'[6] After the latency period, puberty brings again forcefully the need of an object-choice which this time is exclusively a person. 'The resultants of infantile object-choice are carried over [but] the object choice of the pubertal period is obliged to dispense with the objects of childhood and to start afresh [. . .] focussing all desires upon a single object.' If the 'two currents fail to converge, the result is often that one of the ideals of sexual life, the focussing of all desires upon a single object, will be unattainable'.[7]

Although the type of object-choice available to libido and the temporal sequence of these types seems to be predetermined (from the early autoerotic and somatic ones to the person–objects of infantile sexuality to the person–objects of puberty), the actual object-choice each time is not. Consequently, the actual development of the drive, the specific path it will follow, is never fully determinable. As Freud remarks, 'every step can become a point of fixation, every juncture in this involved combination can be an occasion for a dissociation of the sexual instinct.'[8] The development of the sexual drive is always 'the precarious result of a historical evolution'.[9] Freud's account of

4. Ibid.
5. S. Freud, *Three Essays on the Theory of Sexuality* (1905), P.F.L. 7, Harmondsworth, 1977, p. 102.
6. Ibid., p. 118.
7. Ibid., p. 119.
8. Ibid.
9. J. Laplanche, *Life and Death in Psychoanalysis* (1970), Baltimore, 1977, p. 15.

sexual drives, therefore, introduces a degree of indeterminacy *vis-à-vis* the biological order, though certain (biological) constants regarding the type of object-choices and the (ideal) path of development are also postulated.[10]

In attempting to present a general theory of drives as a dynamic theory of the psyche, initially Freud opposed the sexual drives – the libido – to another category of drives he termed 'ego-drives'. The postulation of the existence of this category Freud considered necessary 'from the study of transference neuroses'.[11] Yet at the same time he admitted that 'the hypothesis of separate ego-drives and sexual drives rests scarcely at all upon psychological basis, but derives its support from biology.'[12] Freud did not advance further than this preliminary argument, nor did he specify which actual functions of self-preservation he referred to, except passing references to 'hunger'. In fact, he never used the notion of ego-drives as self-preservative ones in case studies. Indeed, the analysis of transference neuroses justifies nothing more than a certain 'conflict between the claims of sexuality and that of the ego',[13] i.e. not necessarily a qualitatively different category of drives.

At a later stage Freud introduces, parallel to the postulation of (self-preservative) ego-drives, the notion of ego-libido. Ego-libido is seen as having a similar origin with libido proper – that of sexual drives – but has the ego as its locus. The ego appears as a 'reservoir of libido'[14] and can orient this libido to external objects. The object-choice and cathexis depend only on the ego and not on the – originally – libidinal nature of this energy: 'We form the idea of there being an original

10. M. Balint has argued that even early autoerotic libido choices are not (biologically) predetermined. Instead, Balint claims, these choices can be traced back to earlier, external, object-choices: 'Pregenital object-relations, the pregenital forms of love [. . .] can no longer be explained biologically [. . .] they do not succeed one another according to biological conditions, but are to be conceived as relations to actual influence of the world of objects – above all, to methods of upbringing' (M. Balint, 'Critical Notes on the Theory of Pregenital Organisations of the Libido' (1935), in *Primary Love and Psychoanalytic Technique*, London, 1952, pp. 53, 58). The only biological basis for such primary object relations, is 'the instinctual interdependence of mother and child' (idem, 'Early Developmental States of the Ego. Primary Object-love' (1937), op. cit., p. 85). If Balint's claim is accepted, the postulation of even the few biologically given constants Freud still adheres to is not necessary.

11. Freud, 'Instincts and Their Vicissitudes', p. 120.

12. S. Freud, 'On Narcissism: An Introduction' (1914), P.F.L. 11, Harmondsworth, 1984, p. 71.

13. J. Laplanche and J.B. Pontalis, *The Language of Psychoanalysis* (1967), London, 1988, p. 148.

14. S. Freud, *Beyond the Pleasure Principle* (1920), P.F.L. 11, Harmondsworth, 1984, p. 324.

libidinal cathexis of the ego, from which some is later given off to objects, but which fundamentally persists and is related to the object-cathexes much as the body of an amoeba is related to the pseudopodia which it puts out.'[15] For a time Freud continued to hold the view of the existence of ego-drives separate from ego-libido, but gradually the references to non-libidinal ego-drives cease and he admits that 'psychoanalysis has not enabled us hitherto to point out to any [ego] instincts other than the libidinal ones.'[16] Freud acknowledges that the notion of ego-libido can satisfactorily accommodate the opposition between ego and sexual drives as a cause of neuroses without postulating a qualitatively different origin of psychical energy: 'The distinction between the two kinds of instinct which was originally regarded as in some sort of way qualitative, must now be characterized differently – namely as being topographical.'[17]

Thus the second great category of drives postulated by Freud is eventually admitted to be directly linked and emanating from the agency of the ego rather than being predetermined and related to self-preservation. Indeed the notion of ego-libido heralds the introduction of the second Freudian topography of the psyche, theorizing precisely the ego as one of the agencies of the psyche (the others being the super-ego and the id). With the introduction of the second topography Freud abandons any attempt to provide a dynamic theory of the psyche through a theory of drives and puts all his efforts to the theorization of psychical agencies.

At the same time, he introduces a new instinctual dualism, that of life (Eros) and death drives. Death drives are seen as 'representing an urge inherent in organic life to restore an earlier state of things'[18] while life drives 'work against the death of the living substance and preserve life itself for a comparatively long period'.[19] The new dualism retains two essentially opposed groups of instincts, but the opposition is now between abstract principles of overall orientation and no longer between specific groups of drives as in the libido/ego-drives dualism. It is a distinction between *kinds* of psychical energy and does not have any implications for the development or structuring of this energy.

The intention behind the introduction of the new dualism is not to provide a dynamic theory of instinctual energy, but to allow a more satisfactory answer to the question of emotional ambivalence, of the transformation of love into hate and vice versa. Freud had earlier

15. Freud, 'On Narcissism', p. 68.
16. Freud, *Beyond the Pleasure Principle*, p. 326.
17. Freud, *The Ego and the Id* (1923), P.F.L. 11, Harmondsworth, 1984, p. 325.
18. Freud, *Beyond the Pleasure Principle*, p. 308.
19. Ibid., p. 313.

considered this ambivalence as a characteristic, a vicissitude of drives and had given a theorization of it based on the ego.[20] He is now in a position to offer a better answer, the fusion of the two categories of instincts: '[B]oth kinds of instinct would be active in every particle of living substance, though in unequal proportion, so that some one substance might be the principal representative of Eros.'[21] Such a fusion is possible because 'for purposes of discharge the instinct of destruction is habitually brought into the service of Eros.'[22] Ambivalence can be accounted for either as a 'defusion', or, since it is a 'fundamental phenomenon', probably as 'an instinctual fusion that has not been completed'. Thus the actual manifestation of the death drive, as a destructive and aggressive force, is always tied with the life drives. Indeed, the existence of two classes of drives is only a postulate for the purpose of theoretical analysis. The two categories of drives can be conceptualized as distinct only 'as an extreme situation of which clinical experience can furnish merely approximations'.[23]

It has been argued that, given the fused nature of drives, the death drive should be considered as 'not possessing its own energy' but as being 'the constitutive principle of libidinal circulation' in the sense that it is opposed to the 'bound and binding form' of libido which is Eros, the life instinct.[24] If so, the opposition of life and death instincts can be regarded as an opposition of bound and unbound forms of psychic energy. Life instincts are destined to create bounded forms and to this death instincts are opposed.[25] Even if the argument is rejected, however, the necessarily fused nature of the two types of drives has to be accepted and be considered as the primary justification for the introduction of the new dualism.

Thus, in so far as Freud presents a theorization of psychical energy, its development or structuring through a theory of drives, he limits himself to a theory of the sexual drives to which he adheres throughout his life (as successive editions of the *Three Essays on the Theory of Sexuality* indicate). However, in order to provide a general theory of psychical structuring and development, Freud abandons any attempt to construct a general theory of drives – his dualism of life/death drives

20. In Freud, 'Instincts and Their Vicissitudes'.
21. Freud, *Beyond the Pleasure Principle*, p. 381.
22. Ibid., p. 382.
23. Laplanche and Pontalis, *The Language of Psychoanalysis*, p. 181.
24. Laplanche, *Life and Death in Psychoanalysis*.
25. However, Laplanche remarks: 'This does not mean that we have to promote binding, or that we have to conclude that binding always works to the advantage of biological or even psychical life; extreme binding means extreme immobilization' (J. Laplanche, *New Foundations for Psychoanalysis*, Oxford, 1989, p. 148).

having other intentions – and turns instead to his second topography of the psyche.

The Second Freudian Topography

Though the roots of the second topography of the psyche go back almost to the beginning of Freud's writings, it is presented explicitly only relatively late (in 1923). It distinguishes between the 'Ego' (*Ich*), the 'Super-Ego' (*Über-Ich*), and the 'Id' (*das Es*). The id is seen as 'chaotic' instinctual energy, 'open at its end to somatic influences'.[26] In the id the 'pleasure principle [. . .] reigns unrestrictedly'.[27] In contrast, the ego is the bearer of the 'reality principle' and of rational/ conscious processes necessary for the organism. The ego operates 'by becoming aware of stimuli, by storing up experiences about them (in the memory), by avoiding excessively strong stimuli (through flight), by dealing with moderate stimuli (through adaptation) and finally by learning to bring about expedient changes in the external world to its own advantage (through activity)'.[28] Finally, in the notion of the super-ego Freud synthesizes that of ego-ideal (presented in 1914) and of an aggressive agency within the psyche, its aggression directed towards the ego.

For the ego and the super-ego Freud provides a theory of the mechanisms of their construction, their instinctual investment and their function as sources of psychical energy. The ego is 'constructed' as the 'precipitate' of abandoned object cathexes:

> When it happens that a person has to give up a sexual object, there quite often ensues an alteration of his ego which can only be described as a setting up of the object inside the ego, as it occurs in melancholia; the exact nature of this substitution is as yet unknown to us. It may be that by this introjection, which is a kind of regression to the mechanism of the oral phase, the ego makes it easier for the object to be given up or renders that process possible. It may be that this identification is the sole condition under which the id can give up its objects. At any rate the process, especially in the early phases of development, is a very frequent one, and it makes it possible to suppose that the character of the ego is a precipitate of abandoned object-cathexes and that it contains the history of those object-choices.[29]

26. S. Freud, *New Introductory Lectures on Psychoanalysis* (1933), P.F.L. 2, Harmondsworth, 1973, p. 106.
27. Freud, *The Ego and the Id*, p. 364.
28. S. Freud, 'An Outline of Psychoanalysis' (1938), P.F.L. 15, Harmondsworth, 1986, p. 377.
29. Freud, *The Ego and the Id*, p. 368.

Thus the ego constitutes a register within the psyche of its own history.[30] A similar process constructs the super-ego. It is the outcome of the Oedipus complex, in which boys identify with the father while at the same time direct a certain aggression towards him as an opponent in love for the mother, with an analogous mechanism in girls. In fact there is a double identification involved here, with both parents:

> The broad general outcome of the sexual phase dominated by the Oedipus complex may, therefore, be taken to be the forming of a precipitate in the ego, consisting of these two identifications [with the father and the mother] in some way united with each other. This modification of the ego retains its special position; it confronts the other contents of the ego as an ego ideal or super-ego.[31]

The super-ego retains 'the character of the father' and 'dominates the ego'. Both the ego and the super-ego, therefore, appear as registers of abandoned object-cathexes. What differentiates them is the type of psychical energy each agency contains and of which it becomes the source in turn.

With the introduction of the second topography of the psyche Freud further qualifies the type of energy emanating from the ego which he had earlier introduced as ego-libido. This energy is seen as 'an indifferent and displaceable' one, which can be added 'to a qualitatively differentiated erotic or destructive impulse and augment its total cathexis'.[32] Hence the ego becomes the locus of an energy that has the 'uniting and binding' characteristics of the life instincts.[33] Since the only determinant of this energy seems to be the ego itself, we can suppose that its direction, its object-choices, can only be determined by the past history of the ego, i.e. by the already internalized abandoned object-cathexes. As for the super-ego, it is the locus of aggression and guilt directed towards the ego. In extreme cases, such as melancholia, the super-ego can even become 'a pure

---

30. Freud had already made a preliminary reference to such a mechanism in a passage of the *Three Essays on the Theory of Sexuality* added in 1915: 'The sexual aim [in oral, pregenital sexual organisation] consists in the incorporation of the object – the prototype of a process which, in the form of identification, is later to play such an important psychological part' (p. 117).

31. Freud, *The Ego and the Id*, p. 373.

32. Ibid., p. 385.

33. Freud insists as late as 'An Outline of Psychoanalysis' (1938) that 'throughout the whole of life the ego remains the great reservoir from which libidinal cathexes are sent out to objects' (p. 382), an assertion he introduces in *Beyond the Pleasure Principle* (1920). Apparently this should not be seen as contradicting the fact that in *The Ego and the Id* he considers the id as the principal such 'reservoir'.

culture of the death instinct'.[34] Thus both the ego and the super-ego function as sources of psychical energy. The energy emanating from the ego is primarily libidinal, while that of the super-ego primarily aggressive. The super-ego directs its aggressive energy towards the ego, while the ego itself directs its psychical energy towards external objects.

What is the connection between the mechanisms constructing the ego and the super-ego and their being sources of psychical energy? Freud provides an answer in the case of the super-ego:

> The super-ego arises from an identification with the father taken as a model. Every such identification is in the nature of a desexualization or even a sublimation. It now seems as though when a transformation of this kind takes place, an instinctual defusion occurs at the same time. After sublimation the erotic component no longer has the power to bind the whole of the destructiveness that was combined with it, and this is released in the form of an inclination to aggression and destruction.[35]

It is therefore because the abandoned object-cathexes internalized within the super-ego are charged with psychical energy that it functions as a source of aggression. Since the ego itself is constructed also as a 'precipitate of abandoned object cathexes', we could generalize Freud's account to include the ego as well. It could be argued that the elements internalized within the ego are also invested with psychical energy, this time of an overall libidinal nature. Thus the super-ego and the ego can function as sources of psychical energy because they represent an organization of such energy, in the instinctual investment of the internalized elements.

The life/death drives distinction, indicating the always fused nature of psychical energy is relevant here. Usually the erotic binding of the energy directed to objects that are to be later internalized through identification is such that the aggressive impulses are of no particular importance. In this case these elements are internalized within the ego. If, however, the aggressive impulses are significant, the process of identification can introduce within the ego an important aggressive component which results in the formation or reinforcement of the super-ego. As a result, the energy emanating from the ego is never 'purely' libidinal nor is that of the super-ego 'purely' aggressive. It is rather energy of a fused nature with the libidinal or aggressive impulses predominating.[36] The determinants of the direction and the

34. Freud, *The Ego and the Id*, p. 394.
35. Ibid., p. 396.
36. Thus the ambivalence towards 'objects', which Freud emphasized, can be explained even in the case of psychical energy originating in the ego.

intensity of this energy can only be the construction of these agencies, i.e. the objects already internalized and their instinctual investment.

Thus Freud's second topography of the psyche provides what his theory of drives does not: an account of *structuring* of psychical energy within the agencies of the ego and the super-ego and a theorization of the mechanisms that this structuring operates through.

We turn now to the *type* of object-choices that can become, subsequently, internalized within the ego and super-ego. Freud, prior to the introduction of his second topography, discussed the type of objects internalized within the ego in relation to sexual drives and in relation to melancholia. In the first case the nature of objects that are eventually internalized is partially predetermined: initially the autoerotic objects of the oral and anal phases, alongside them a parental object-choice, and, after the latency period, the sexual object-choice of puberty. In the case of melancholia, Freud admits the possibility of identification with and incorporation of certain characteristics of the loved person which are not considered of a directly sexual nature and which are not predetermined.[37]

After the introduction of the second topography, however, Freud does not provide any specific account of the type of objects that can be internalized within the ego. He concentrates mostly on the super-ego, which, as the outcome of the 'complete' Oedipus complex, represents a double identification with both the father and the mother. For both identifications to exist simultaneously though, ('in some way united with each other'), it is necessarily implied that they are identifications not with 'complete' persons, or simply with the parent's sex, but with elements of behaviour related to this sex. Freud is to further enlarge on the 'contents' such identifications may consist of. Identifications are related not only to 'natural' characteristics related to the parent's sex, not only to 'natural' positions – father or mother – within the family, but related to social features as well, covering a variety of modalities, from patterns of behaviour to norms and rules: 'Is not only the personal qualities of these parents that is making itself felt, but also everything that had a determining effect on them themselves, the taste and standards of the social class in which they lived and the innate dispositions and traditions of the race from which they sprang.'[38] Thus the super-ego is presented as the potential vehicle through which a whole host of features of the most diverse nature and

---

37. S. Freud, 'Mourning and Melancholia' (1915), P.F.L. 11, Harmondsworth, 1984, p. 257.
38. Freud, 'An Outline of Psychoanalysis', p. 442.

including elements of a specifically *social* origin can be incorporated within the individual.

All the above types of possible identifications, in so far as they are limited to the super-ego, can only operate in a negative, aggressive way within the psyche. There seems to be no *a priori* reason, however, to deny the possibility of similar identifications operating in a positive way, i.e. of their being internalized within the ego. The identity of internalization and identification mechanisms in the two agencies indicates this possibility, as indeed do Freud's earlier remarks on melancholia. Yet Freud does not extend his account of the type of objects internalizable within the super-ego to the ego proper. A possible reason, in so far as objects of social origin are concerned, is that he considers civilization and society in general as operating primarily through a sense of guilt, i.e. primarily through the super-ego. His 'omission' to extend these elements to the ego itself could be, therefore, intentional and based on an axiomatic assumption that is unwarranted. However, there is nothing in the theorization of ego/super-ego construction mechanisms that would support this exclusion. In principle, therefore, we could extend the type of objects internalizable within the super-ego to the ego as well. In what follows we shall indicate the support such a view has from post-Freudian research.

As for the determinants of the instinctual investment of internalized elements regarding the type (aggressive/libidinal) and the intensity of this investment, Freud provides an answer in the case of the Oedipal phase and the creation of the super-ego. The strength of the aggression of the super-ego against the ego, the strength, in other words, of the super-ego itself, depends on the relationship of the child with the parents, the relation between the relative strength of the aggressive and libidinal components simultaneously directed towards the father and the strength of the libidinal ties with the mother.[39] Therefore the instinctual investment of the elements of the super-ego depends on the relational context of the family, i.e. on the child's relational position *vis-à-vis* his parents. Once again we could generalize these remarks to include the ego and consider that, in general, the child's relationship to the significant others is what determines the kind and intensity of instinctual investment of the elements internalized within both the ego and the super-ego.

---

39. In the case of boys. A similar account is provided for girls. (Cf. 'The Dissolution of the Oedipus Complex' (1924) and 'Some Psychical Consequences of the Anatomical Distinction between the Sexes' (1925) both in P.F.L. 7, Harmondsworth, 1977).

A number of theorists have contributed to an amplification and expansion of Freud's account of psychical agencies. The principal areas of concern of these contributions are the innate dynamic behind the emergence of these agencies, the mechanisms through which they are constructed and the type of internalizable objects.

The existence of an independent dynamic driving the formation of the ego, of a certain innate tendency of ego development operating from the very beginning, has been emphasized by a number of theorists, most notably the so-called 'ego-theorists' (H. Hartmann, E. Kris, D. Rapaport, among others). Hartmann, for example, insists that 'The ego may be more – and very likely is more – than a developmental by-product of the influence of reality on instinctual drives; it has a partly independent origin [. . .] we may speak of an autonomous factor in ego-development in the same way as we consider the instinctual drives autonomous agents of development.'[40]

Other analysts, while recognizing the existence of such a dynamic, stress that it does not operate autonomously within the developing infant, but that it has to be seen in relation to significant others, in the early stages primarily the mother. D. Winnicott, for example, while accepting that some form of ego exists from the very beginning ('there is no id before ego')[41], considers that this ego initially exists in an undifferentiated relationship with the mother. Only gradually can the infant conceive of itself as separate from the mother and from other 'objects', having passed through a stage of 'transitional' objects.[42] The 'maturational process' of the ego depends on a 'good enough mother' and a generally facilitating environment.

Through observation, M. Mahler and her collaborators have specified certain stages in the process of ego development as it gradually differentiates itself from the mother, a process they termed 'separation–individuation':

- the initial symbiotic phase (up to 5 months)
- the differentiation subphase (dawning awareness of separateness, awareness of separateness)
- the practising subphase (attention directed to new motor achievements, seemingly to the near exclusion of mother, 10 to 15 months)

40. H. Hartmann, 'Comments on the Psychoanalytic Theory of the Ego' (1952), in *Essays on Ego Psychology*, London, 1964, p. 119.
41. D.W. Winnicott, 'Ego Integration in Child Development' (1962) in *Collected Papers II* (*The Maturational Process and the Facilitating Environment*), London, 1965, p. 56.
42. D.W. Winnicott, 'Transitional Objects and Transitional Phenomena' (1951), in *Collected Papers I* (*Through Paediatrics to Psychoanalysis*), London, 1975, p. 229.

– the rapprochement subphase (renewed demand upon the mother but as separate and continued growth of autonomous ego apparatuses, 15 to 22 months)
– and, finally, consolidation of individuality and gradual attainment of libidinal object constancy (22 to 36 months).[43]

These phases towards individuation are seen as powered by 'the drive for and toward individuation [that] in the normal infant is an innate, powerful *given*, which, although it may be muted by protracted interference, does manifest itself all along the separation-individuation process.'[44]

Parallel to the affirmation of the independent dynamic of ego-development and the recognition of the importance of the significant environment for the manifestation of this dynamic, significant contributions have been made concerning the mechanisms of ego and super-ego construction, emphasizing mainly the importance of (external) object relations for the development of these agencies.[45]

M. Klein's pioneering work is such a case. She focusses on the early months and years of life and provides a detailed account of the mechanisms of object internalization and ego-construction. Stressing the anxiety facing the newborn, Klein introduces the notion of splitting of external objects into 'part-objects', 'good' or 'bad'. The 'good' part-objects are incorporated within the psyche through introjection while the 'bad' ones are neutralized through their projection to the 'outside' of the ego (this period has been termed the paranoid-schizoid position). Gradually, as the infant grows, 'the various aspects – loved and hated, good and bad – of the objects come close together, and these objects are now whole persons.'[46] The ego becomes more integrated and the mother and father can now be introjected as 'whole' persons (this is the infantile depressive position). Klein sees the life and death instincts operating from the very beginning as independent entities,

43. M. Mahler *et al.*, *The Psychological Birth of the Human Infant*, London, 1975, p. 260.
44. Ibid., p. 206, emphasis added. In this context, Lacan's emphasis on an independent dynamic in the emergence of the ego, a dynamic manifested in the mirror phase, is also relevant.
45. The innate dynamic of ego emergence and development has to be seen as operating alongside the mechanisms of ego-construction Freud and other theorists such as Klein proposed. The existence of an innate dynamic does not invalidate the importance the environment has for the make-up of the ego through the internalization of external objects. This is explicitly stressed by both Winnicott and Mahler, while even the ego-theorists indicate the importance of the environment, though in a more general way.
46. M. Klein, 'Some Theoretical Conclusions Regarding the Emotional Life of the Infant' (1952), in *Envy and Gratitude*, London, 1988, p. 72.

attached to the good or bad objects respectively. Along with the ego developing primarily through the introjection of 'good' objects, the super-ego is seen as having an equally early origin through the introjection of the 'bad' objects.

Klein's notions of part-objects, splitting, the importance of introjective and projective identification have gained wide acceptance. However, her assumption that life and death instincts are fully defined at the beginning of psychical development has been considered very inflexible, while the early origin of the super-ego has been a matter of debate. She has also been criticized for failing to theorize sufficiently the emergence of a primary ego on the grounds that 'the dialectic of good and bad, partial and whole, the introjected and the projected, is inconceivable without the first boundary of an ego – however rudimentary it might be – defining an inside and an outside.'[47]

As a possible alternative to the Kleinian model, R. Fairbairn proposed that the ego has to be considered as existing in a primary, undifferentiated form from the very start and that libido, instead of 'pleasure-seeking' has to be seen as 'object-seeking'. In accordance with Klein, he considers that the ego splits the 'figure of his mother into two objects – a satisfying ("good") one and an unsatisfying ("bad") one'[48] – but he adds that the ego internalizes the 'bad' object in an attempt to neutralize it, further splits this internalized object into two – an 'exciting' and a 'rejecting' object – and finally represses both objects along with parts of the ego that remain attached to them. Thus 'the basic endopsychic structure' includes the 'central' ego, the 'libidinal' ego (attached to the exciting object) and the 'internal saboteur' (attached to the rejecting object).[49] The role of the 'internal saboteur' is similar to that of the super-ego.

Fairbairn's intention is to remove any biologism from the psychoanalytic account of ego development and to stress the importance of (external) object relations for this development. It has to be noted, though, that the Freudian assertion of libido as pleasure-seeking does not, by itself, imply any biologism. Freud's theory of ego-construction implies precisely that the libido is 'object-seeking' both in the case of sexual drives and in the case of ego-libido. Similarly, Fairbairn's criticism of Klein's use of life and death instincts cannot be levelled at Freud. Klein considers the two categories of

47. Laplanche and Pontalis, *The Language of Psychoanalysis*, p. 81.
48. R.D. Fairbairn, 'A Synopsis of the Development of the Author's Views Regarding the Structure of the Personality' (1951), in *Psychoanalytic Studies of the Personality*, London, 1952, p. 172.
49. R.D. Fairbairn, 'Object Relationships and Dynamic Structure' (1946), in *Psychoanalytic Studies of the Personality*, p. 147.

drives as differentiated forces already there in the beginning and subsequently embodied in the agencies of the ego and the super-ego. In contrast, Freud's use of the life/death dualism is intended primarily to indicate the ambivalent and fused nature of psychical energy rather than to assign an independent status to these two forms of drives. As for the specific mechanisms Fairbairn proposes – a series of splittings within the ego – while they cannot be properly evaluated outside analytic practice itself, they introduce a divergence from the Freudian account not fully justified by Fairbairn's criticisms of Freud and Klein. Unlike Klein's theorizations, which can be easily appended to Freud's, Fairbairn's cannot.

A middle way between Klein and Fairbairn is presented by E. Jacobson. Jacobson accepts the Kleinian mechanisms of ego-construction, retains the emphasis on the early internalization of aggressive elements as precursors of the super-ego but proposes a more plastic conception of psychic energy: 'At the very beginning of life, the instinctual energy is still in an undifferentiated state; but from birth on it develops into two kinds of psychic drives with different qualities under the influence of external stimulations.'[50] Both the ego and the super-ego are seen as created out of a combination of libidinal, aggressive and neutralized forces, while the super-ego is considered as slowly emerging as a separate structure within the ego through the combination of earlier disconnected elements (an 'archaic imagery referring to castration fears, imagery relating to parental prohibitions and demands, and imagery derived from the child's narcissistic/moral-perfectionist strivings')[51]. Jacobson's synthesis incorporates most of the novel developments related to the dynamic and mechanisms of early ego-development in a scheme that does not depart much from Freud's own, while she avoids the most challengeable assertions of others.

Regarding the type of objects internalized within the ego – and the super-ego – the Kleinian school admits a certain immediate capacity of perception of objects related to 'the child's parents' bodies and to his own'[52] which can be split and internalized with no separation between the object and the still undeveloped ego, a separation that is only gradually effected. These early internalized elements should be considered, Jacobson remarks, as 'multiple, rapidly changing and not yet clearly distinguished part images of love objects and body part

---

50. E. Jacobson, *The Self and Object World*, London, 1964, p. 13.
51. Ibid., p. 119.
52. H. Segal, 'Notes on Symbol Formation' (1957), in *The Work of Hanna Segal*, New York, 1981, p. 51.

images [which] are formed and linked up with the memory traces of past pleasure–unpleasure experiences and become vested with libidinal and aggressive forces'.[53] As the child grows, the objects are felt as 'whole' and a separation between the ego and the objects is established.[54] Along with this separation, the growing exposure of the child to language and other symbolic systems and the increased capability of cognitive perception gradually expand the world of objects that can be internalized:

> As the child learns to walk and talk [. . .] the object imagery gradually extends to the surrounding animate and inanimate world. [As the latency period begins and] increasingly realistic preconscious representations of the animate and inanimate, concrete and abstract object world are formed, and can be stabilised by their firm and lasting cathexis with libidinal, aggressive and neutralized elements.[55]

Laplanche notes that such later identifications can be with 'character traits, or even with a particular flash of personality, which is quite localized in time or space and often caught in flight, as it were, precisely because of its artificial and bizarre character' or 'partial identifications with an act of speech, notably an interdiction' (mainly for super-ego identifications) or 'a type of identification referring explicitly to structure: an identification with the position of the other, which consequently presupposes an interpersonal interplay of relations and, as a rule, at least two other positions coinciding with the vestiges of a triangle: clearly, such would be the case for Oedipal identifications'.[56] And Erikson remarks that

> Children, at different stages of their development identify with those part aspects of people by which are most immediately affected, whether in reality or fantasy. These part aspects are favoured not because of their social acceptability (they often are everything but the parent's most adjusted attributes) but by the nature of infantile fantasy which only gradually gives way to a more realistic anticipation of social reality.[57]

At an even later stage there can be identifications with explicit social norms or rules, identifications which presuppose the ability to

53. Jacobson, *The Self and Object World*, p. 53.
54. 'When the depressive position has been reached, the main characteristic of object relations is that the object is felt as a whole object. In connection with this there is a greater degree of awareness of differentiation and of the separateness between the ego and the object.' (Segal, 'Notes on Symbol Formation', p. 55).
55. Jacobson, *The Self and Object World*, p. 53.
56. Laplanche, *Life and Death in Psychoanalysis*, p. 80.
57. E. Erikson, 'The Problem of Ego Identity' (1956) in *Identity and the Life Cycle*, New York, 1980, p. 121.

perceive them as such, an ability that only gradually appears. As Piaget's research has shown, for example, concepts such as 'native land', 'social justice' and rational, aesthetic or social ideals, do not acquire adequate affective value until the age of twelve or more.[58]

Thus the early, innate ability of the infant to recognize, however imperfectly, and incorporate by splitting bodily parts of himself and the parents, accompanied by the emergence of innate representatives in fantasies, contrasts with the later phase in which a certain cohesiveness of the ego and a conceptual/perceptual maturation allow a much greater range of objects to be perceived, instinctually cathected and internalized. It is at this stage that the mechanism of identification proper that Freud described can be said to operate. Coextensive with this second phase is the acquisition from the psyche of an externally originating, indeed social, corpus of 'psychical representatives' which replace the earlier, innate ones. Fundamentally necessary for such a transition is the existence of a symbolic (social) universe from which the child can borrow the means for the perception of 'objects'. The two processes – that of acquiring an 'external' symbolic universe and that of the transition to a wider world of objects cathected and internalized – have to be seen as gradually developing together, along with a certain maturation of the perceptual/cognitive apparatus which is necessary for both processes to evolve.[59] It is the interrelation of all these factors that allows the gradual build-up of the structures of the ego and super-ego: 'Cognitive development, affective development and the development of structures representing internalized object relations are intimately linked.'[60] And there is a growing complexity characterizing the possible internalized elements: from part-objects to whole objects to patterns of behaviour and elements of character to interpersonal relations to norms and ideas.

In all the above discussion no distinction was made between the objects that can be internalized within the ego and those within the super-ego. Indeed an important contribution of all these post-Freudian developments is the extension of the diverse nature of possible objects of internalization – including 'social' objects – to the ego. Thus Freud's limitation of certain (primarily social) elements to the super-ego can be seen as unjustified. Such elements can be considered as

58. J. Piaget and B. Inhelder, *The Psychology of the Child* (1966), London, 1969, p. 151.

59. J. Piaget and his school have produced a theory of the stages of development of the perceptual/cognitive apparatus. This theory, far from being opposed to the psychoanalytic one, actually complements it.

60. O. Kernberg, *Object Relations Theory and Clinical Psychoanalysis*, New York, 1976, p. 69.

operating both positively – through libidinal identifications within the ego – and negatively – through aggressive identifications – within the super-ego.

Regarding the dynamic aspect of the internalized elements, post-Freudian developments affirm that internalized objects are instinctually invested with either predominantly libidinal or predominantly aggressive energy already in the very early processes of introjection and projection. As for the determinants of the kind and strength of the instinctual investment of these internalized objects, it is confirmed that even in the early years it depends on the relationship of the child with significant others. At the beginning, this relationship cannot be properly called an interpersonal one, the ego not having developed enough. It is only gradually that the child begins to experience others as separate and to direct to them libidinal or aggressive impulses which influence the investment of elements s/he internalizes from these others. The case of the Oedipus complex is then only one stage in a series of similar processes.

Thus post-Freudian developments – which are and have to be seen as complementary – amplify and enrich Freud's account.[61] An innate dynamic of ego development (implicit in Freud's theorization) is explicitly theorized, while the determinant role significant others play in order for this dynamic to be manifested is affirmed. New mechanisms of object internalization (splitting of objects, projective and introjective identification of part-objects) at the early stages of ego- and super-ego- creation are introduced, complementing the central mechanism of identification that Freud proposed. The close connection of processes of identification with the internalization of socially originating psychical representatives and with cognitive/perceptual maturation is noted while the type of objects that can be internalized is more extensively theorized: from early relatively

61. We noted above the complementary nature of theories focussing on the innate dynamic of ego emergence and those clarifying mechanisms of ego and super-ego construction. Regarding the second group of theories, usually identified, in different combinations, as 'object-relations' ones, it has to be stressed that they do not present a 'non-biologistic' version of psychoanalysis as opposed to the Freudian version. This is the view expressed by H. Gunthrip, who opposes Freud and Klein to Fairbairn (*Personality Structure and Human Interaction*, London, 1961), and, more recently, by N. Chodorow ('Beyond Drive Theory: Object Relations and the Limits of Radical Individualism', *Theory and Society*, no. 14, 1985, p. 306). Apart from Balint's attribution of early libidinal object-choices to the relation with the mother (which removes the given nature of autoerotic object-choices that Freud postulated), the Freudian account is as free of biologism as any of those of the above authors. This is because Freud does not, at least since the introduction of his second topography, base his theorization of psychical structuring on (biologically predetermined) drives but rather on the agencies of the ego and the super-ego.

predetermined bodily parts/part-objects to whole objects, patterns of behaviour, elements of character and ideal elements. It is affirmed that such objects can be internalized equally within the ego and the super-ego, expanding Freud's account which limited the internalization of certain 'social' elements to the latter. Finally, it is explicitly recognized that the elements internalized are instinctually invested, even at the early stages, and that the kind and intensity of this investment depends on the relationship of the child to significant others. Thus a fuller picture of the emergence, dynamics and mechanisms of construction of the ego and super-ego is presented and it is confirmed that these agencies correspond to the most significant form of organization and structuring of psychical energy.

Structuring and Indeterminacy

The outline of the psychoanalytic theory of psychical structuring presented so far may give the impression that we refer to processes operating only during childhood and which produce fully delimited and definable psychical agencies. However, this is not the case. The structuring of the psyche is a process that continues throughout the individual's life while the agencies of the ego and the super-ego are neither fully definable nor homogeneous.

Psychoanalysts, Freud included, have traditionally paid little attention to post-Oedipal, adolescent or adult processes of psychical structuring relating to the ego or super-ego. Within analytic practice, emphasis on the early years may be justified, because most neuroses can be traced back to these years and thus successfully treated. Psychoses seem to require a return to even earlier formative stages of the ego. For analytic/clinical practice in general, therefore, the early years of life are the most significant. However, the mechanisms postulated in ego- and super-ego-construction are not inherently limited to the early years but appear to have a certain generality. It has to be accepted, obviously, that earlier identifications are more formative, because they create the basic structures of the ego and super-ego and consequently the impact of any later structuring on the economy of the psyche is relatively smaller. Also, as Jacobson remarks, 'after adolescence, ego development proceeds less and less along the lines of identification and grants increasing room to independent critical and self-critical judgement and to the individual, autonomous trends of the ego and its *Anlage*.'[62] This does not imply, however, that processes of identification cease to operate after

62. Jacobson, *The Self and Object World*, p. 194.

adolescence. Indeed, such processes have to be seen as continuing throughout life. Freud himself accounted for group ties by postulating the existence of 'partial identifications' based on the perception of a 'common quality shared with some other person who is not an object of the sexual instinct'.[63] These partial identifications, functioning in a positive way and employing libidinal impulses, provide the main mechanism of group ties.

Apart from Freud's remarks, however, psychoanalytic theory at present does not offer any theorization specifically oriented towards processes of – unconscious – psychical structuring in adulthood. We cannot, for example, judge the relative weight of processes of identification compared with the 'critical and self-critical judgement' of the ego. At the present state of knowledge, we can only assert that psychical structuring through internalization of external 'objects' within the ego and super-ego continues in adulthood, though we cannot assess its importance.

The inherent anthropomorphism in the notions of ego and super-ego may give the impression that these agencies are fully delimited and homogeneous. However, Freud repeatedly stresses that the ego and super-ego are never fully distinguishable from each other and from the id: 'The ego is not sharply separated from the id; its lower portion merges into it. [The super-ego] is a grade in the ego, a differentiation within the ego, a part of the ego.'[64]

Even within a single agency, we do not have a homogeneous and consistent structure. Freud recognizes 'contrary attitudes' existing within the ego,[65] while Hartmann considers that 'the many ego functions not only they have different strengths but they actually oppose each other'.[66] The lack of homogeneity extends to the type of objects internalized. Freud remarks, apropos of the ego-ideal, the precursor of the super-ego within which it was to be subsequently located, that 'each individual is a component part of numerous groups, he is bound by ties of identification in many directions, and he has built up his ego ideal upon the most various models.'[67] Certain writers did try to impose coherence on the diverse identifications of the ego, such as Erikson in his claim that in adolescence an integration of past identifications is effected: '[A fixed identity] is superordinated to any

63. S. Freud, *Group Psychology and the Analysis of the Ego* (1921), P.F.L. 12, Harmondsworth, 1985, p. 137.
64. Freud, *The Ego and the Id*, p. 367.
65. Freud, 'An Outline of Psychoanalysis', p. 440.
66. Hartmann, 'Comments on the Psychoanalytic Theory of the Ego', p. 139.
67. Freud, *Group Psychology and the Analysis of the Ego*, p. 161.

single identification with individuals of the past: it includes all significant identifications, but it also alters them in order to make a unique and a reasonable coherent whole of them.'[68] However, there is nothing in the psychoanalytic theorization of the ego implying that this is a necessary outcome. While a certain cohesion between different identifications is needed in order for them to coexist, their fusion into 'a unique and coherent whole' has to be seen as an ideal rather than as the norm. Indeed, the degree of closure of the ego may vary historically through more or less intense processes of individuation.

The ego and the super-ego are also not homogeneous from an instinctual/dynamic point of view. Although the distinction between the two agencies corresponds to the great dividing line within the psyche between libidinal and aggressive instinctual investment of internalized elements, neither is the ego ever purely libidinal nor the super-ego ever purely aggressive. Due to the always fused nature of the instinctual energy investing the internalized objects, any such object is also invested with a certain degree of the opposing kind of psychical energy.

Thus while the ego and super-ego *do* represent a structuring and organization of psychical energy, this structuring should not be taken as producing fully homogeneous and closed wholes. Rather the two agencies are composed of potentially or actually conflicting elements, conflicting impulses, and they may pursue contradicting functions. Moreover, they are never fully delimited and distinguishable from one another and from the id. It could be said that the ego and super-ego represent only lines of partial differentiation and organization, dynamic equilibria in flux in which conflicting, conflicting impulses coexist in a precarious balance. Since the self as a whole, the individual as such, is composed of these agencies and of the id, it is easy to see the deconstructing effect psychoanalytic theory has to any claim for the attribution of an 'essence' to the individual, or for considering the individual as a homogeneous, coherent entity. Although we have to accept the existence of a certain closure and cohesiveness within the psyche as a whole, we have to consider any such closure as representing a multiplicity of entities in dynamic equilibrium rather than a homogeneous single agency.

The theorization of the ego and super-ego as structured agencies within the psyche invariably evokes the question of the relation between this theory of psychical structuring – of the whole, that is, of the second topography – to the first topography, and specifically

68. Erikson, 'The Problem of Ego Identity', p. 121.

to the fundamental Freudian concept of the unconscious. In the second topography, the id is presented as 'open at its end to somatic influences [. . .] filled with energy reaching it from the instincts [. . .] striving to bring about the instinctual needs subject to the observance of the pleasure principle',[69] as 'a chaos [which] has no organisation',[70] and as following the specific modality previously attributed to the unconscious (primary process, timelessness). Thus the id could be easily identified with the unconscious entirely. Is it the case, then, that the ego and the super-ego fall wholly or primarily within consciousness? If so, given the important functions assumed by these agencies, the notion of the unconscious would become marginal while the specificity of its modality would be of no particular importance. However, the answer is in the negative. The ego and the super-ego straddle the conscious/unconscious dichotomy, operating at both levels.

Both agencies 'merge' with the id. Indeed of the super-ego Freud remarks that 'as heir to the Oedipus complex it has intimate relations with the id; it is more remote than the ego from the perceptual system.'[71] Moreover, the censorship of dreams attributed to the super-ego operates unconsciously. The same can be said of the sense of guilt in obsessional neurotics: 'We may say that the sufferer from compulsions and prohibitions behaves as if he were dominated by a sense of guilt, of which, however, he knows nothing, so that we must call it an unconscious sense of guilt.'[72] The super-ego, therefore, not only merges with the id, it also *functions* unconsciously (as well as consciously).

The case of the ego is more complicated. The ego is the agency that includes the conscious/rational functions of the organism: 'The ego can be seen as what may be called reason and common sense, in contrast to the id, which contains the passions.'[73] In contrast to the id, which has 'no organization', the ego is 'organization'.[74] In contrast to the unbound and freely mobile energy of the id, the ego represents bound energy.[75] While the id follows the 'pleasure' principle and the primary process, the ego is seen as functioning through the reality principle and as following the secondary process. However, the ego

69. Freud, *New Introductory Lectures on Psychoanalysis*, p. 106.

70. Ibid., p. 100.

71. Ibid., p. 111.

72. S. Freud, 'Obsessive Actions and Religious Practices' (1907), P.F.L. 13, Harmondsworth, 1985, p. 37.

73. Freud, *The Ego and the Id*, p. 364.

74. S. Freud, *Inhibitions, Symptoms and Anxiety* (1926), P.F.L. 10, Harmondsworth, 1979, p. 250.

75. Freud, 'An Outline of Psychoanalysis', p. 395.

does not cease to be also a 'part' of the id: '[T]he ego is not sharply separated from the id; its lower portion merges with the id.'[76] In his sketch of the 'mental personality' Freud presents graphically the ego as extending within the unconscious[77] and he recognizes that 'large portions of the ego, and particularly the super-ego, which cannot be denied the characteristics of preconsciousness, nonetheless remain for the most part unconscious in the phenomenological sense of the word.'[78]

But it is not only in the phenomenological sense that the ego can be considered unconscious. It also functions at an unconscious level, as in the case of defence mechanisms: 'We have come upon something in the ego itself which is also unconscious, which behaves exactly like the repressed – that is, which produces powerful effects without itself being conscious and which requires special work before it can be made conscious.'[79] These mechanisms 'are not just unconscious in the sense that the subject is ignorant of their motive and mechanism, but more profoundly so in that they present a compulsive, repetitive and unrealistic aspect which makes them comparable to the very repressed against which they are struggling'.[80] It has been argued also that, in certain cases, the ego follows the primary process.[81] Thus both the ego and the super-ego function unconsciously.

In addition, the mechanisms of construction of these agencies – identification and the other internalization processes – operate unconsciously. At the early stages of ego-construction there is no ego proper that could become 'conscious' of these mechanisms, but even in the case of later identifications, the process remains unconscious (even adult identifications of the type Freud describes in group-formation are unconscious). Moreover, the actual make-up, the configuration of the ego and the super-ego, i.e. the objects internalized and their instinctual investment, also remain unconscious and are never directly accessible to consciousness. This configuration can be deduced from endopsychic operation, from manifestations in consciousness as thoughts or affects (or from consequent manifestations in behaviour) but it cannot be approached in any direct or unmediated way. It remains firmly unconscious.

Thus parts of the ego – and the super-ego – merge with the id, operate at an unconscious level, and exhibit features (primary process,

76. Freud, *The Ego and the Id*, p. 367.
77. Freud, *New Introductory Lectures on Psychoanalysis*, p. 111.
78. Freud, 'An Outline of Psychoanalysis', p. 394.
79. Freud, *The Ego and the Id*, p. 356.
80. Laplanche and Pontalis, *The Language of Psychoanalysis*, p. 139.
81. Hartmann, 'Comments on the Psychoanalytic Theory of the Ego', p. 131.

source of psychical energy) that have been explicitly attributed to the unconscious in Freud's first topography. Moreover, the construction of the ego and super-ego is unconsciously produced and remains at an unconscious level, never directly approachable. It can be concluded, therefore, that the ego and super-ego are – also – unconscious. Hence a simple contrast cannot be sustained between the id as unconscious, referring to unbound energy, primary process, irrationality and passions and the ego as preconscious/conscious following the secondary process and being the embodiment of reason. The ego (and the super-ego) should be seen as straddling the previous dichotomy of conscious/unconscious and as existing in both these 'areas'. In its 'upper' regions the ego includes consciousness and rational thought while its 'lower' regions participate in the modality of the unconscious. The unconscious/conscious polarity is not replicated as the id/ego one but it exists *within* the ego. The ego has to be seen as covering the whole spectrum from consciousness to the unconscious, and the same, to a lesser degree, can be said for the super-ego.

But if this is so, the difference between the unconscious ego and the unconscious id can be nothing other than the difference between structured and unstructured unconscious respectively. A difference between bound and unbound energy does not refer only to consciousness and the unconscious respectively, but exists also *within* the level of the unconscious. The unconscious itself has to be regarded as structurable. It could be argued, therefore, that the second Freudian topography introduces the concept of structured psychical energy within the field defined as unconscious in the first topography. The 'construction' of the ego and the super-ego is 'the synthesis in the course of which free energy is transformed into bounded energy'.[82] The emergence of these agencies corresponds to a structuring of part of the undifferentiated instinctual energy of the id, without this structuring necessarily implying a change of level (from the unconscious to consciousness). As O. Kernberg remarks: 'The repressed portion of the id would possess an internal organization as well as specific structures composed of self-image, object-image and unacceptable impulse components [. . .] we would have to conclude that the repressed portion of the id is not pure id, but an ego id.'[83] Freud's ambivalence about the exact location of the ego can be seen as indicative of the difficulty he had in acknowledging the full implications his later phase of thinking had for the notion of the unconscious. And Lacan's famous remark 'the unconscious is

---

82. Freud, 'An Outline of Psychoanalysis', p. 395.
83. Kernberg, *Object Relations Theory and Clinical Psychoanalysis*, p. 43.

structured like a language' could be read with the emphasis on the 'structured' rather than on 'language'.

However, this structuring does not produce fully closed, fully homogeneous entities in either the objects internalized, the type of psychical energy investing these objects or the functions the agencies of the ego and super-ego pursue. Moreover, the ego and the super-ego are not fully distinguishable from the id and they are not fully differentiated from each other. The 'structuring' of the unconscious that these agencies represent is partial and precarious. This seems to be in accordance with the chaotic modality attributed to the id and the unconscious in general: even though it does admit a certain structuring, unconscious psychical energy is not amenable to a full organization, a full structuring, a complete 'binding'. It could be argued that it is *because* the ego and the super-ego are – also – unconscious that they are not fully closed and definable entities. Their unconscious parts have to be seen as lines of partial organization and structuring surrounded by and merging with the chaotic instinctual energy of the id from which they can never be fully distinguished.

Thus the psychoanalytic theorization of psychical structuring corresponding to Freud's second topography, is an affirmation of the structurable nature of the unconscious and of the specific nature of this structuring, and hence further advances the theorization of this fundamental concept. It is an extension and enrichment of the first topography rather than a substitute for it.

Given that the ego and super-ego are never fully delimited and that they function also on the level of the unconscious, it would be expected that the process of their construction through successive identifications would include points of indeterminacy. Indeed, this is the case.

The construction of the ego and super-ego depends on the internalization of elements from the significant environment. As the child grows, the type of objects internalized becomes more and more indeterminate, encompassing a growing variety of objects. However, even when the general type of possible internalizable objects is known – as in the early stages of ego-development – the actual choice of object and hence the configuration of the agencies cannot be deduced from its general type. This is even more the case in later years when there is an almost endless variety of possible types of internalizable elements. The history of object-choices internalized within the ego and super-ego, and hence the actual make-up of these agencies is not deducible in any mechanical way from the significant environment.

This indeterminacy holds, in a more pronounced way, for the

investment of the internalized objects with instinctual energy. The level of this investment as well as the degree of aggressive/libidinal elements it incorporates are influenced by the relationship of the child to the significant environment (the significant others). The instinctual investment of these elements is thus the result of a dynamic process of interaction. Even at early stages when the significant environment is limited to the mother and the type of object-choice is limited, the investment of these objects – as 'good' or 'bad' – and the intensity of this investment cannot be deduced from the mother's behaviour but is the outcome of the mother–infant relationship (as Mahler's study indicates). Freud's remarks on the severity of the super-ego are pertinent here: '[T]he original severity of the super-ego does not – or does not so much – represent the severity which one has experienced from it [the object], or which one attributes to it; the severity of the former seems to be independent of that of the latter.'[84] The strength of the super-ego is not, then, deducible from the environment of the child but is only *influenced* to an indeterminable degree by this environment.

The make-up, the specific configuration of the ego, regarding both the type of internalized objects and the type and level of instinctual investment, cannot be deduced in any mechanical way from the significant environment. Even when growing up in the same environment, every person remains unique because different 'objects' are internalized in different ways. This assertion is not invalidated by the parallel affirmation of an innate dynamic in the development of the ego, a dynamic that can be considered as including given stages in a fixed sequence (of the type Mahler or Kernberg propose). The fixed sequence regards only the necessary and gradual emergence of the ego and super-ego as agencies and its stages but not the actual objects internalized nor their psychical investment. The agencies of the ego and super-ego are the same for every individual and define the individual as a specific, separate entity. However, the configuration of these agencies is not universal but personal and it is this configuration that constitutes the individuality of a person.

Besides the indeterminacy arising from the impossibility of deciding which elements from a given environment will become important for the psyche, there is another, more radical, degree of indeterminacy. It stems from the fact that the ego and the super-ego are – also – unconscious and as such the structuring of the psychical energy they represent is always partial and incomplete, while, at the

---

84. S. Freud, *Civilization and Its Discontents* (1929), P.F.L. 12, Harmondsworth, 1985, p. 323.

same time, it can never be 'known' in any direct, unmediated or 'objective' way.

The ego and the super-ego are never fully closed, determinable or homogeneous entities. They contain diverging or even contradictory impulses and are surrounded by and merging with the chaotic instinctual energy of the id. The structuring of psychical energy these agencies refer to, because of the nature of the unconscious, can never be a full, complete or fully determinable one. Although this structuring does produce effects within the psyche, there can never be a strict causal account of these effects. Indeed the very postulation of the existence of the agencies of the ego and super-ego is only an attempt to partially theorize a process that remains, in its totality, non-theorizable.

Since the process of construction of the agencies of the ego and the super-ego is unconscious, and the configuration of these agencies remains unconscious, there is never any direct way of 'knowing' even these few effects that can be theorized. It can never be known, for example, *how* objects that have been internalized 'exist' within these agencies. Only after being manifested in consciousness as ideas, thoughts or affects can some of these objects become 'known'. But because the ego and super-ego represent dynamic equilibria in flux these manifestations are never unidimensional. Conflicting affects and ideas – which may also change over time – can stem from the same unconscious engraving. Besides, there is always a change of state when these elements become conscious, a change of state that is also never unidimensionally defined and which does not 'reflect' in any accurate way the unconscious transcription itself. Any manifestation of the unconscious content is always an interpretation of it. Yet these manifestations are all we have to deduce the existence of unconscious elements internalized within the ego and super-ego and indeed the existence of these agencies as such.

Thus the configuration of the endopsychic agencies of the ego and the super-ego can never be fully, conclusively or 'objectively' determined. The unconscious part of the ego and the super-ego represents an invisible area, the existence of which can be postulated from its effects on the level of consciousness but never be fully 'known', both because of the nature of any structuring of the unconscious and because the unconscious is never directly accessible. At this point psychoanalytic theorization reaches its limits. It pursues a theory of determinacy and a rational account of endopsychic agencies as far as it can. But it cannot fail to admit that the objects analyzed ultimately escape any full theorization; they are not fully analyzable in any coherent and rational way. And this is because they operate on just that level that escapes any fully rational account: the level of the unconscious. Hence, the theorization of this level of indeterminacy is a specific contribution of psychoanalytic theory, since it alone theorizes the modality of the unconscious.[85]

A radical level of indeterminacy has, therefore, to be accepted as *necessarily* characterizing the emergence of psychical agencies that correspond to a structuring of unconscious psychical energy. To assert the impossibility of full determination is another way of asserting the possibility of the emergence of the non-determined, of elements for which no causal line of emergence can ever be traced and which have to be considered as 'radically new'. *Radically new* images or representations can emerge within the psyche, despite the fact that both the initial origin of representations the psyche uses and the internalized objects within the ego and the super-ego are 'borrowed' from the environment. A *radical creativity* within the psyche can be admitted, corresponding to Castoriadis's 'radical imagination': 'The representative flux is, makes itself, as self alteration, the incessant emergence of the other in and through the positing of images or figures.'[86]

At this point the dynamic account of psychical structuring introduced by the second Freudian topography of the psyche is completed. The endopsychic agencies which are the result of this structuring, the ego and the super-ego, are far from fully delimited and homogeneous.

---

85. Lacan theorizes the indeterminacy associated with the level of the unconscious in a different way. He refers to 'orders', the imaginary and the symbolic, through which the psyche operates. For the symbolic order to become internalized, a certain breach in the imaginary order is required, a 'gap opened by a prematuration of the imaginary'. This gap signifies a lack – the *'manque-à-etre'* (J. Lacan, 'Remarque sur le rapport de D. Lagache' (1961), Écrits, Paris, 1966, p. 655) – traversing the imaginary and – presumably – the symbolic order and inhibiting any full closure of the psyche. However, for the psyche to require the assumption of a 'lack' to denote its openness, the implicit assumption is that it could otherwise be conceived as a closed entity that only the existence of this 'lack' prevents from being fully closed. The reference to 'orders' – the imaginary and the symbolic – also has an implied connotation of closed universes, which, in principle, could be seen as self-enclosed and self-sustainable, unless something external inhibits their closure. Finally, the 'I' (*Moi*) is also seen as though it could have been a closed, homogeneous entity if only the 'lack' had not existed. The 'lack' functions, therefore, as a kind of negative essence that inhibits the full closure of the psyche in all its levels. Thus Lacan's theorization retains a kind of metaphysics, even if in a negative form. On the contrary, Freud's account and its implications do not, nor do they need to: the unconscious is not originally, or even potentially, a closed entity. It is simply an entity that is never fully structurable. Hence, a certain necessary openness of the psyche is always implied.

86. C. Castoriadis, *The Imaginary Institution of Society*, Cambridge, 1987, p. 329.

They merge with the id and with each other, they contain contradictory elements and straddle the conscious/unconscious divide, representing also a structuring of unconscious psychical energy. Because of the nature of the unconscious, however, this structuring is never full, complete, or fully determinable. As a consequence, the process of ego and super-ego construction involves points of unavoidable indeterminacy, allowing the possibility of the emergence of the radically new, of the non-determined within the psyche.

We can now proceed to the central concern of the study, the question guiding the preceding account of psychoanalytic theory: the question of the relationship between the psychical and the social.

−11−

The Social Individual

The Psyche as Fundamentally Social

The psychoanalytic theorization of the psyche allows a detailed account of the ways in which the social environment influences the psyche, at both the levels of consciousness and the unconscious, to create a social individual.

To begin with, the social is at the origin of the representations the psyche uses. The primal, innate representatives which are relatively predetermined and refer to certain themes common to all individuals (Freud's primal phantasies, Jung's archetypes, Klein's representations of bodily parts, and so on), are gradually – and smoothly – replaced by others, sharing the same modality but originating outside the psyche. These externally acquired representatives are not predetermined in their content. They depend on and are intelligible only within the symbolic/meaningful universe in which the child becomes gradually enmeshed, the social universe of meanings and significations. This universe is the 'symbolic order' to which Lacan refers or the 'world of representations' of Castoriadis's. The represent-ations used by the psyche, therefore, both at the level of consciousness and at the level of the unconscious, are social.

However, in so far as social representations or symbols enter the unconscious, they are subjected to its specific modality and they necessitate a change of state to become conscious again. Within the unconscious, symbols or representations do not exist as systems amenable to full formalization, they have a non-logical, non-rational modality.

At the level of consciousness, the social-symbolic universe supports also the cognitive development of the psyche, operating through the conscious ego. Once cognitive maturation has reached a certain stage, explicit social values and norms can be internalized either at an unconscious, or at a conscious/preconscious level.

Concurrently with 'representations', the social environment is the source of objects of identification and internalization within the agencies of the ego and super-ego. In early phases of ego development the type of such objects is restricted and predetermined, referring mainly to child's and parents' bodily parts and functions, passing gradually from part-objects to whole objects and to whole persons. Even at these stages, the 'source' of these objects – the significant others and especially the mother – do not cease to be overdetermined as persons by social factors which, though not directly perceivable by the infant, have a certain influence on the features and objects the infant does conceive. As Mahler remarks (and it has to be remembered that these remarks are to be found within a work primarily oriented towards the affirmation of innate givens in ego development):

> Three variables involving the mother are of particular importance in shaping, promoting, or hindering the individual child's adaptability, drive, and ego development and the beginning structuralization of precursors of his super-ego: (1) The mother's personality structure. (2) The developmental process of her parental function. (3) The mother's conscious, but particularly unconscious, fantasy regarding the individual child.[1]

At a later stage, with the broadening of the type of objects internalized, character traits, behaviour patterns, interdictions and moral values, 'elements of class, race, nation', and, later, abstract concepts and ideologies are internalized. Most of these 'objects' of identification refer to greater social-structural wholes within which they become intelligible. Some of them, indeed, can only be described through the reference to such a whole. Even when the internalized objects are character traits, behaviour patterns and the like, seemingly 'personal' rather than 'social', these elements are themselves the result of, firstly, a similar process of socially influenced psychical structuring of the significant others and, secondly, of the current position and function of these others within social networks. To a significant extent, therefore, they are also social ones. Thus, although the internalized 'objects' may be transmitted through the individuals more close to the child – initially the parents, later other significant individuals – they refer not only to these individuals or only to the contexts within which the growing child encounters them, but to broader social contexts. Either directly or indirectly, these 'objects' are social.

As is the case with representations, the internalization of elements within the (unconscious) ego and super-ego does not imply a replication of them within the psyche, but the production of certain

---

1. M. Mahler *et al.*, *The Psychological Birth of the Human Infant*, London, 1975, p. 202.

bounded lines of instinctual energy, of a certain instinctual structuring, that somehow corresponds to these objects.[2]

The social environment influences also the instinctual investment of internalized objects. The objects internalized within the ego and super-ego are always invested with psychical energy, primarily libidinal in the case of the ego and primarily aggressive in the case of the super-ego. The intensity and type of psychical energy directed to cathected objects and, correspondingly, the strength and kind of instinctual investment of internalized elements (or of whole agencies as the ego and super-ego), depends on the relationship of the child with the significant others (a relationship that can be called 'interpersonal' only after the ego has developed to a certain degree of cohesiveness). Obviously, the form of both early and later such significant environments (the nuclear or extended family or its absence in the case of primitive societies, the modes of education and so on) are historically specific and socially determined. In addition, the psychical make-up of the persons who form these environments and enter into relationships with the child, a make-up that is bound to influence the relationship itself, is the result of these persons' own psychical development which has also been socially influenced. The dynamics of instinctual energy investing the objects internalized, therefore (and, at a larger scale, the agencies of ego and super-ego themselves), is also determined by social factors.

There are, therefore, three 'modes' of environmental (social) influence on the functioning, development and structuring of the individual psyche: the origin of representations the psyche uses, the 'objects' internalized within the ego and the super-ego, and the instinctual investment of these objects. All three operate in a simultaneous and meshed way and it is only for analytic purposes that we distinguish them. They refer to a deep, foundational, and mostly unconscious level of environmental influence on the psyche and reveal that the very constitution of the psyche is a function of elements and influences that can only be described as social. In its contents, dynamics and way of 'expression' the human psyche can only be understood through a reference to specific social contexts.

Alongside these deep and/or unconscious influences, the individual adapts to the social environment also in a conscious/rational way. This form of adaptation refers to specific ways in which a person

---

2. As T. Adorno remarks: 'If there is any truth in Freud's notion of the archaic and indeed "timeless" nature of the unconscious, the concrete social circumstances and motivations cannot enter it without been altered and "reduced"' ('Sociology and Psychology', *New Left Review*, no. 47, 1968, p. 80).

consciously and rationally orients himself with respect to the significant (social) environment. To do so, the individual needs a certain 'knowledge', a system of concepts and ideas that s/he can use to rationally conceive his/her situation, aims and means. The concepts and ideas are themselves a social/historical creation, the accumulation of past knowledge. In addition, the individual also needs a system of norms and values, specifically social, to evaluate aims and choose means to attain them. Thus in a conscious/rational adaptation the social is the objective environment itself while at the same time it provides the intellectual means by which the process can be accomplished. This form of adaptation has been theorized long before psychoanalysis.[3] Psychoanalytic theory simply offers the means to locate it alongside other social environmental influences.

The primary psychical agent effecting this adaptation can be recognized as the conscious/rational ego, a certain maturation of which is a prerequisite for such processes to operate. If they are to become fully operational, moreover, a sufficient cognitive maturation and ability to internalize norms, ideas and values is necessary. As Piaget's research has shown, such maturation emerges slowly and can be considered operational only in adolescence and adulthood. Thus the conscious/rational adaptation to the social environment is a relatively late phenomenon in the child's development. However, even before this kind of adaptation becomes significant, the individual is already socially 'adapted' through the processes of 'deep' structuring of the psyche, processes which continue to operate alongside rational/conscious adaptation ones in later years.

The increased weight and significance of processes of conscious/rational adaptation to the social environment and of critical/self-critical judgement in adolescence and adulthood should not be taken as indicating that unconscious identification processes and object internalization cease to operate. Little attention to such processes has been paid by psychoanalytic theory and practice since, in terms of psychical economy, the early influences are the most significant. However, the theorization of these mechanisms is particularly important when a theory of the social individual and his actions is sought.

For post-Oedipal stages, the correlation of the modes of unconscious social influence with theories of education is obvious. However, the connection between the two remains to be worked out. To cite only two examples: I. Illich remarks that the participation of

---

3. This is the traditional means-end scheme. Parsons in *The Structure of Social Action* offers the most elaborate theorization of this scheme.

a child in the everyday practice of the modern school, makes the child internalize and accept certain values, irrespective of the content of what is taught. Children come to know, more specifically, that 'everything can be measured, including their imagination, knowledge, values [. . .] and indeed, man himself.'[4] This internalization operates otherwise than through explicit transmission of knowledge. The values are incorporated within the very organizational order of the school of which the child is a member and whose practices s/he follows. Knowledge of these values is not conscious or cognitive, but we do not know how either mechanisms of identification or unconscious symbol internalization could be used to explain it.

In a similar vein, B. Bernstein elaborates a theory of 'codes' to account for class specific differences in communicative orientation. A 'code' is a 'regulative principle, tacitly accepted, which selects and organises relevant meanings, forms of realisation and evoking contexts'[5] and is created implicitly, through participation in 'classification and framing relationships' of the familial and educational environment. Bernstein's code is not simply cognitive, but a constituent element of the psyche, acquired unconsciously and having profound implications for the further development of the self. Once again, however, it is not easy to relate Bernstein's concepts to the psychoanalytic mechanisms of endopsychic structuring, though the existence of a close relationship is obvious. Work in the field of theorization of unconscious mechanisms accompanying education processes is needed to integrate theories of education with the mechanisms that psychoanalysis postulates.

Concerning adulthood, many authors have referred to operations of the social within the individual which function unconsciously – at least in the phenomenological sense – and which do seem to influence the structure of the psyche in a relatively permanent way (as it can be judged from subsequent behaviour or thought). A case in point is Foucault's reference to 'disciplines' as 'the methods which made possible the meticulous control of the operations of the body, which assured the constant subjection of its forces and imposed upon them a relation of docility–utility',[6] methods operating through 'meticulous control of activity in space and time'. His examples are the army, the

4. I. Illich, *Deschooling Society* (1971), Harmondsworth, 1976, p. 45.
5. B. Bernstein, 'Elaborated and Restricted Codes: Overview and Criticisms' in *The Structuring of Pedagogic Discourse* (vol. 4, *Class, Codes and Control*), London, 1990, p. 101.
6. M. Foucault, *Discipline and Punish* (1975), Harmondsworth, 1979, p. 137. Foucault notes also the analogy between these 'disciplines' and the capitalist organization of work in modern factories, an analogy stressed by Marx.

school, the hospital and the prison as they become organized at the end of the eighteenth century. Here is a series of techniques aimed at changing the individual's behaviour, techniques operating on the body and its activities without apparently passing through a cognitive operation. The only way these techniques could have an effect on behaviour would be if, in psychodynamic terms, they effected a certain structuring of the psyche. This structuring operates at an unconscious level, at least in the phenomenological/descriptive sense. However, the exact relationship between the function of these 'disciplines' and the processes of psychical structuring theorized by psychoanalysis remains to be specified. For example, can the function of the 'disciplines' be assimilated through the identification processes?

Althusser's theorization of ideology falls into the same category. For Althusser the participation of the subject in certain practices ('material practices governed by material rituals', just as Pascal's advice to the unfaithful: 'kneel down, move your lips in prayer, and you will believe')[7] has a certain effect on the individual, an effect manifested in the 'imaginary' sphere, creating the 'imaginary relationship of individuals to their real conditions of existence'.[8] While the 'imaginary relationship' is conscious, its mode of creation – through participation in certain practices – and its mode of function – being not directly assessed by rational thought – indicate unconscious processes. Only the end product of these processes is manifested in consciousness. Similarly, A. Sohn-Rethel has insisted that certain concepts of abstract thought (for example solipsism, abstract quantity, abstract time and space) have originated not in thought itself but in the realm of social practice and particularly in exchange through money in the market. He claims that 'the exchange abstraction is not thought, but it has the form of thought before it can be transformed to actual thought.'[9] S. Zizek notes that Sohn-Rethel's remark indicates precisely the level of the unconscious, as that 'form of thought whose ontological status is not that of thought'.[10] Zizek himself stresses the general importance of 'ideological fantasy' operating on the level of the unconscious.

Althusser's 'imaginary dimension' and Zizek's 'fantasy', like Foucault's 'disciplines', refer to a certain structuring, a certain influence of the unconscious through participation in social practices. This structuring may subsequently be manifested as conscious

7. L. Althusser, 'Ideology and Ideological State Apparatuses' (1970), in *Lenin and Philosophy*, London, 1977, p. 158.
8. Ibid., p. 153.
9. A. Sohn-Rethel, *Intellectual and Manual Labour*, London, 1978, p. 59.
10. S. Zizek, *The Sublime Object of Ideology*, London, 1989, p. 19.

thought. Though no specific indication of the actual endopsychic processes this structuring operates through is made, its existence at the level of the unconscious and its origin through participation in social practices are persuasively asserted.

These examples – among other possible ones – indicate that social influences on the level of the adult individual unconscious do exist. The unconscious of the adult is not only populated by infantile remnants but it is also an active layer of functioning of the mind into which the social environment can operate. No theorizations have been advanced about the mode of endopsychic operation of this structuring and its relation to the earlier modes, though the relevance of the participation in social practices has been indicated. Explicit and detailed links between the social influences these studies point out and the mechanisms that psychoanalysis theorizes remain to be elaborated (Freud's pioneering work on group identifications is one of the few studies that have addressed this question)[11]. However, there can be no doubt about the existence of these social influences operating on the unconscious of adults or about their importance from the point of view of a theory of both the individual psyche and the social.

To summarize, the social operates on the psyche in a variety of ways:

1. At a deep, fundamental level of psychic structuring referring mainly to early years. Three different, though interrelated, modes of this operation can be distinguished: the internalization of social representations and symbols, the internalization of 'objects' of identification and the instinctual investment of the latter.
2. In processes identical with or similar to the foregoing which continue, with diminishing importance, throughout the individual's life. These two cases refer primarily to an unconscious level, both in the 'phenomenological' and in the 'dynamic' sense.
3. In a cognitive/rational way both by determining the symbolic universe the individual has access to and by providing an 'objective' environment to which the individual consciously and rationally adapts.

---

11. The relevance of 'practice' does not vitiate the importance of other ways the social influences psychical structuring; Freud's 'partial identifications' is such a case. A question arises whether there can be a case of unconscious – and not cognitive – influence of systems of ideas/symbols operating alongside participation in practices. The questions R. Barthes raises in *Mythologies* ([1957], London, 1973, pp. 117ff) are an example.

Thus, while 'the crucial adaptation man has to make is to the social structure',[12] this 'adaptation' is multifaceted and complex. To ignore any of the ways in which the social influences the psyche, or to concentrate on only some of their constitutive modes, limits the view of both the individual and the social. At the same time it is obvious that the very constitution of the individual psyche – on both consciousness and the unconscious – is inconceivable without a social environment.[13]

Against Misinterpretations

It is necessary at this point to discuss a number of different interpretations of psychoanalytic theory on the interrelationship between the social and the psychical. Very few of Freud's followers and successors posed the question of the 'origin' of the elements 'discovered' within the psyche through analytic practice, being

12. H. Hartmann, *Ego Psychology and the Problem of Adaptation* (1938), New York, 1958, p. 31.
13. A note can be added here concerning the differences between human and animal psychical development psychoanalytic theory makes possible to present. Much within the human psyche have to be seen as operating on the same level as that of higher animals. Even though psychoanalysis is not directly concerned with them, the existence within the human psyche of relatively given, biologically constant instincts – mainly of a self preservative nature – has to be admitted. It is the type of instincts Freud initially presented as 'ego-instincts' in general, dropping this characterisation later, but never ceasing to accept their existence. Recent research has shown that such instincts have to be seen not any more as 'givens changed by the environment', but as 'organizations which, through learning, integrate various inborn patterns ("building blocks") into flexible overall plans' (O. Kernberg, *Object Relations Theory and Clinical Psychoanalysis*, New York, 1976, p. 86). They remain, however, biologically predetermined to a significant extent. On the other hand, a certain form of 'ego' and mechanisms of ego formation through identification and similar processes are likely to exist in higher mammals. We can recall, in this context, Lorenz's mechanism of 'imprinting' operating even in 'lower' animals (for example, K. Lorenz, *On Aggression*, London, 1976). The particularity of human psychical development lies not in the existence of an ego but rather in the type of objects internalized within this ego and in the plasticity and indeterminacy *vis-à-vis* nature the process of its development exhibits. Ego-development in humans has very few biologically predetermined constants, limited to the early years of life. As the child grows up, the importance of the social environment as the source of internalized objects and their instinctual investment becomes predominant. Within this environment the actual path of psychic development exhibits an extraordinary plasticity and indeterminacy. A great variety of objects can be internalized, a variety connected also with the cognitive and rational capabilities of the human mind. To these differences in ego-development the existence of a super-ego and superior cognitive abilities, both exclusive to the human psyche, have to be added. Thus, while we should speak of a continuum rather than of a sharp differentiation between the 'animal' and the 'human', there is a certain specificity that characterizes human psychical development.

content to take these elements as given and historically constant (and/ or taking the contexts these elements refer to – for example the family – as also given and not as socially and historically specific). Most often – with notable exceptions – it was not psychoanalysts but other theorists who tried to provide common ground between the psychoanalytic theory of the psyche and a theory of the social. Broadly speaking, such attempts can be divided to those which do not recognize the inescapably social nature of the human individual that psychoanalytic theory indicates – including Freud's own theory of civilization – and to those which, although recognizing the importance of the social for the functioning of the individual psyche, present a one-sided account of the way the social influences the individual.

One of psychoanalysis's most profound insights is that it is impossible to conceive the individual psyche without reference to social contexts. However, although this insight is necessarily derived from the psychoanalytic theorization of the psyche, it has not been articulated, or even accepted by most psychoanalysts, Freud included.

Freud asserts that 'sociology [. . .] dealing as it does with the behaviour of people in society, cannot be anything but applied psychology. Strictly speaking there are only two sciences: psychology, pure and applied, and natural science.'[14] He argues not only that the individual psyche is conceivable outside the social but, moreover, that the social ('civilization') is opposed to man's freedom, ascribing thus to a kind of Rousseaunesque romanticism for the pre-civilization state of nature when man was 'free' without burden:

> Every individual is virtually an enemy of civilization, though civilization is supposed to be an object of universal human interest[15] [. . .] The liberty of the individual is no gift of civilization. It was greater before there was any civilization, though then, it is true, it had for the most part no value, since the individual was scarcely in a position to defend it.[16]

For Freud the primary carrier of civilization is the super-ego, the role of which is equivalent to that of conscience and which is the origin of the 'sense of guilt': 'If civilization is a necessary course of development from the family to humanity as a whole then [. . .] there is inextricably bound up with it an increase of the sense of guilt [. . .]

14. S. Freud, *New Introductory Lectures on Psychoanalysis* (1933), Penguin/ Pelican Freud Library (P.F.L.) 2, Harmondsworth, 1973, p. 216.
15. S. Freud, *The Future of an Illusion* (1927), P.F.L. 12, Harmondsworth, 1985, p. 184.
16. S. Freud, *Civilization and Its Discontents* (1929), P.F.L. 15, Harmondsworth, 1985, p. 284.

the price we pay for our advance in civilization is a loss of happiness through the heightening of the sense of guilt.'[17]

To argue for the existence of a state of 'happiness' or 'freedom' prior to civilization, the possibility of a societal stage of development in which the super-ego does not exist as an individual psychical agency has to be postulated. As Freud has to admit, however, the super-ego does exist in primitive societies, though it is organized along totemic and not familial lines.[18] Thus he is forced to consider that the 'pre-civilization state of happiness' is not to be found in actual primitive societies but in a supposed 'primal horde' before the killing of the father/leader. The existence of such a 'primal horde' is definitely problematic, going against all available ethnographic or archaeological material. But even if we accept its existence, it would still be impossible, within Freud's own theorization of the psyche, to sustain the idea that the horde could consist of individuals without a psychic agency comparable to the super-ego.

This is because the mechanism Freud proposes for the emergence of the super-ego is based on the existence of aggressive impulses towards the father rather than on any actual deed.[19] Freud remarks that 'the mere hostile impulse against the father, the mere existence of a wishful fantasy of killing and devouring him, would have been enough to produce the moral reaction that created totemism and taboo.'[20] Such 'hostile impulses' always exist within the psyche and would have also to exist in the supposed primal horde, even before the 'killing of the father' which for Freud marks 'the beginning of so many things – of social organization, of moral restrictions and of religion'.[21] The development of an individual that did not involve a certain relationship to others is inconceivable. Equally inconceivable, given the existence of aggressive impulses within the psyche, is that any such relationship would not produce, at one stage or another, an aggressive agency crystallizing out of these impulses, even if this agency does not have the cohesiveness Freud attributes to the super-ego. The existence of a stage of primitive happiness, therefore, of no aggressive agency within the psyche, is not sustainable in the context of Freud's own theorizations. Post-Freudian developments further indicate the

17. Freud, *Civilization and Its Discontents*, pp. 326, 327.
18. S. Freud, *Totem and Taboo* (1913), P.F.L. 13, Harmondsworth, 1985.
19. The superego emerges, according to Freud, from the ambivalent attitude towards the father during the Oedipal phase: the identification with the father is accompanied by a diffusion of instincts and the internalization of the aggressive component within the super-ego.
20. Freud, *Totem and Taboo*, p. 222.
21. Ibid., p. 203.

unavoidability of the existence of an aggressive agency within the psyche, by affirming the early origin of super-ego components and the composite character of the super-ego – instead of seeing it solely as the result of the Oedipal phase.

If the possibility of a pre-civilization stage of happiness is excluded, what remains of Freud's thesis is that civilization does indeed function oppressively, i.e. that it operates only through the medium of the super-ego and that the advance in 'civilization' is marked by an increased 'sense of guilt'.

However, Freud nowhere actually offers an argument to support the thesis that only the super-ego carries elements of 'civilization'. He retains it axiomatically and, as we saw, at the cost of not specifying the type of ego-identifications which would have to be shown to be of a non-social nature. Yet, given the similarly of mechanisms of ego- and super-ego-construction, it is not consistent to consider socially relevant identifications as operating only 'prohibitively' through the super-ego and not also 'positively' through similar identifications within the ego itself. Indeed, post-Freudian research shows that the same kind of identifications operate in both the ego and the super-ego, though of course charged with different kinds of psychical energy. As for the severity of the super-ego, Freud himself remarks that there is no necessary connection between a specific pattern of upbringing and the 'sense of guilt' one feels: 'The original severity of the super-ego does not so much represent the severity which one has experienced from it [the object] or which one attributes to it [. . .] the severity of the former seems to be independent to that of the latter.'[22] C. Lasch has shown that modern day 'permissive' upbringing often results in a much more severe super-ego than the traditional authoritarian upbringing.[23] Thus there is no evidence that advance in civilization indeed produces and/or requires more 'guilt' or a stronger super-ego.

Freud's own attempt to retain a presocial or asocial individual, therefore, and to oppose him/her to civilization fails within the context of the theorization of the psyche he himself proposed – and which he does not repudiate to advance his argument on civilization. One could say that it is only his implicit – and axiomatic – adherence to a Rousseauesque/Romantic view that made him persist with his attachment to this thesis.

Interpretations of Freud of a much more rigid if questionable nature are even less capable to sustain a similar argument. At the extreme,

22. Freud, *Civilization and Its Discontents*, p. 323.
23. C. Lasch, *Heaven in a Heartless World: the Family Besieged*, New York, 1977; also *The Culture of Narcissism*, New York, 1979.

these are interpretations based on a primary and biological incompatibility of civilization and the development of libido. Such is one main thread of W. Reich's thought. The argument is that libido, seen as limited to the sexual function, needs to be liberated from the social constraints placed upon it in order for the individual to become truly emancipated. Such a view loses all of the complexity of Freud's theorization on both sexuality and civilization, reducing the individual to a biological creature, against which his/her social existence operates. The same can be said for biologistic interpretations of opposing aims that use Freud as a vehicle for the reduction of the social to the biological and affirm, through this reduction, the natural/ inalterable character of the social.

Equally misguided are approaches such as those of E. Fromm or K. Horney (labelled, along with others, as 'culturalists'). They attempt to reintroduce a kind of 'essence' of the individual, an 'essence' which becomes 'lost' or 'alienated' by modern society. However, the Freudian account stands in sharp contrast to any such 'essentialism' of the psyche. While the social criticism of these authors may be perfectly justifiable, its ontological basis postulates a kind of existentialist psychology from which the Freudian account is radically different. There is no way to determine, through a reference to the psyche's 'true being', a 'sane' from an 'non-sane' society.[24]

A similar criticism may be directed towards more sophisticated approaches advancing essentially the same argument. Such a case is H. Marcuse's interpretation of Freud. Marcuse does accept the socially constructed nature of the psyche but considers that, apart from unavoidable repression proper, there is also 'surplus repression' supporting and being instilled by social domination.[25] He considers Freud's account of the primal horde to be about actual domination by the father transformed into repression, i.e. to a suppression of the libidinal drive by the sons. Repression, supported by actual domination, has been a central feature of all civilizations, made necessary by scarcity. In modern society, however, due to technological advances brought about by this very domination, scarcity could be overcome and therefore neither domination nor repression are necessary. A 'repression-free' libido can be used for a 'transformation of sexuality into eros', for the 'erotization of the entire personality',[26] which could also bind the death instinct.

24. The reference is to E. Fromm, *The Sane Society*, London, 1956.
25. Marcuse uses 'repression' in a non-technical sense to indicate 'processes of restraint, constraint and suppression' (H. Marcuse, *Eros and Civilization* [1956], London, 1987, p. 8).
26. Ibid., p. 202.

Psyche and Society

Marcuse works with an implicit theoretical model of the psyche which is simplistic. He reduces the psyche to a simple instinctual drive – the libido – which is repressed by civilization but which can be set free once more for greater individual happiness and fulfilment. Moreover, he does not specify any endopsychic mechanism by which repression would operate (he does not offer, for example, any comments on the relationship of a strong super-ego to repression) nor any connecting process that would 'translate' domination on the level of society to repression on the level of the individual psyche. Therefore, while his social critique and Utopia may be perfectly acceptable,[27] their grounding on an interpretation of Freud's theorization of the psyche cannot be accepted.

To conclude: despite attempts by Freud and others to assert a fundamental opposition between the individual and the social – an opposition that would necessitate the existence of a somehow presocial individual – the very theorization of the psyche that psychoanalytic theory offers precludes such an opposition. On the contrary, it indicates that the social is unavoidably included within any individual psyche and that it cannot be, in any simple way, contrasted with it. Moreover, the criterion of greater individual happiness as the basis for a critique of society and the building of alternative Utopias has to be rejected. Once the necessity of some form of 'society' for the very construction of the human psyche has been asserted, it has also to be accepted that within *any* social order the possibility of some forms of happiness necessarily exist. An alternative society can offer alternative ways of libidinal satisfaction or can offer already existing ways to a greater number of people. There is no way, however, to judge whether this will produce 'happier' individuals in general and to base the critique or ideal on a higher level of happiness. There is no single measure of happiness which could provide an ultimate criterion. Freud himself remarks that 'happiness in the reduced sense in which we recognize it as possible, is a problem of the economics of the individual's libido. There is no golden rule which applies to everyone.'[28] Social critique and social Utopias can be rationally

27. It has been pointed out, however, that Marcuse's Utopia is essentially individualistic, involving only individual gratification (N. Chodorow, 'Beyond Drive Theory: Object Relations and the Limits of Radical Individualism', *Theory and Society*, no. 14, 1985, pp. 271–319). For the individualism that underpins Marcuse's work in general – as well as that of Horkheimer's – see P.B. Miller, *Domination and Power*, London, 1987.
28. Freud, *Civilization and Its Discontents*, p. 271.

– 178 –

defended and sought after, but not in the name of 'happiness' as such.[29]

However, a certain opposition between the individual psyche and the social does exist, though in a form quite different from that in which Freud presented it. It stems from the fact that the structuring of the unconscious is never full and never covers the entirety of the (unconscious) psychical energy. The id remains outside and beyond such a structuring, as 'the great reservoir of psychical energy'. Between the structured and unstructured parts of the unconscious a certain tension can be indicated, precisely the tension between the reality and the pleasure principle. Psychical energy as such can be considered as resisting any structuring. Freud's references to the unconscious (in his first topography) and to the id (in his second) indicate such a tension, though it is presented as one between the 'irrational' id and the 'rational' ego. It can be understood, though, as one between the structured unconscious and the unstructured one, as the resistance of the primary psychical energy to any structuring. This is not to say, of course, that an individual psychical apparatus can emerge without such a structuring.

Now, in so far as this structuring is socially influenced and the agencies of the ego and super-ego are (also) socially determined, there is a tension between the structured/social part of the psyche and the unstructured, 'chaotic' mass of psychical energy that is the id. As Castoriadis remarks, '[T]he institution of the social individual is the imposition on the psyche of an organization which is essentially heterogeneous with it.'[30] Freud's opposition between the psyche and civilization can be thus understood as indicating not that the psychical is not, also, social but as pointing out the tension, the 'opposition', between the structured and the unstructured parts of the psyche. This opposition exists not between the individual and 'civilization' but *within* the individual's psychical apparatus and in no way diminishes the inescapably social nature of the individual.

The necessarily social nature of the individual psyche does not invalidate also the fact that some features of social organization can be seen as corresponding to psychical needs, most often infantile. It is obvious that the social, being a precondition of psychical development, cannot be derived from a theorization of this

29. 'Happiness' in the context of the above discussion has to be seen as over and above a certain integration of the ego and super-ego that would allow a 'normal' functioning of the psyche. However fuzzy the line of differentiation between the 'normal' and 'in need of therapy' (let alone 'pathological'), cases regarded as needing analytic/clinical attention fall below this minimum requirement for an adequate function of the individual. Obviously the above argument does not refer to such cases.

30. C. Castoriadis, *The Imaginary Institution of Society*, Cambridge, 1987, p. 298.

development. However, since there are also instinctual needs inherent within the psyche – presumably biologically predetermined – certain aspects of social organization have to reflect these needs. Freud emphasizes, in this context, the persistence into adulthood of needs primarily related to early phases of psychic development and the correspondence to these needs of societal institutional features. Such is the case of religion: the animism and magic of primitive societies can be seen as reproducing, at a societal level, the infantile belief in the 'omnipotence of thoughts', which persists in the unconscious of the adult and is manifested in dreams. Indeed, religion at large can be seen as corresponding to the infantile psychological needs for protection, which are 'the oldest, strongest and most urgent wishes of mankind'.[31] Other authors have noted that the attitude to the monarch/king has many common features to that towards God. The monarch takes the place of (or is the earthly incarnation, or the representative of) God.[32] Thus aspects of the political organization of society can be seen as linked with early infantile needs as well.

The fact that these 'needs' are 'infantile', should not be taken as indicating that they correspond to an atavistic return to stages long passed in the individual's history. Freud repeatedly emphasizes that the early stages continue to function alongside later ones, the more so since they do so in the unconscious within which the linear notion of time does not hold. The importance of the psychical 'needs' to which social institutions respond and correspond should not be underestimated, nor should such needs be considered as being necessarily 'overcome' by societal development. It is most probable that some form of social institution would always have to take account, in one way or another, of these needs. However, the 'correspondence' of social institutions/features to psychical needs and processes does not imply that the former can be derived from the latter. The social institutions/formations to which the above refer show a considerable degree of variation and difference and represent only a small part of an overall society or social formation. The social as a whole is never reducible to such needs.

The recognition of the fundamental role the social plays in the very construction of the psyche, alongside any conscious/rational adaptation, is not enough. In so far as some of the modes in which the social operates on the psyche – principally on the level of the

---

31. Freud, *The Future of an Illusion*, p. 212.
32. For example, G. Deleuze and F. Guattari, *Anti-Oedipus* (1972), London, 1984. Also C. Lefort, 'The Image of the Body and Totalitarianism' (1979), in *The Political Forms of Modern Society*, Cambridge, 1986.

unconscious – are emphasized at the expense of others, an one-sided view of psychical social influences (and, indirectly, of the social), is presented.

One such case is the emphasis on the 'symbolic' that characterized structuralism and the writers influenced by it, an approach that can claim Lacan as its major proponent in psychoanalysis. The emphasis is on the social origin of the representations the psyche uses, while the role of the significant environment as a source of internalized objects and of their instinctual investment is sidelined. Such approaches need not take the 'structuralist' line that Lacan follows, namely the assertion of a formal approach to the structuring of the unconscious. Castoriadis, for example, stresses the open and indeterminate modality of these representations within the unconscious. Yet, though he acknowledges that the 'unconscious exists as an indissociably representative/affective/intentional flux' Castoriadis concentrates on 'representations' for all his references to the unconscious. Such approaches present the social in a one-sided way as well, solely as a system or universe of significations: Lacan identifies the symbolic with the social entirely, while for Castoriadis the social remains primarily a 'world of representations'.

The very conception of objects to be internalized necessitates 'symbols' and representations and hence the 'symbolic' or a 'world of representations'. However, the internalization of such objects corresponds also to a structuring of psychical energy through the agencies of the ego and super-ego, a structuring that has a permanence and produces effects. A preoccupation with the 'symbolic order' alone is blind to this dynamic aspect of structuring, and to corresponding social features.

On the other hand, more 'sociologically' oriented interpretations of psychoanalysis tend to focus exclusively to the influence the environment has on the structuring of the individual psyche. Such is the case in Parsons's appropriation of Freud on a general theoretical level and the more specific studies of N. Chodorow,[33] D. Dinnerstein[34] and C. Lasch[35] which concentrate on the influence of early environment on the dynamic make-up of the psyche. These studies neglect the importance of the universe of social representations, symbols and meanings which are also internalized within the psyche and which cannot be dissociated from the internalized objects. In

33. N. Chodorow, *The Reproduction of Mothering*, Los Angeles, 1978.

34. D. Dinnerstein, *The Rocking of the Cradle and the Ruling of the World*, London, 1976. Published in the United States as *The Mermaid and the Minotaur*.

35. C. Lasch, *Heaven in a Heartless World: the Family Besieged*; idem, *The Culture of Narcissism*; idem, *The Minimal Self*, London, 1985.

addition, they usually present a linear causal account of the ways the social determines the psyche, ignoring the points of indeterminacy pointed out here as necessarily existing within the process.

This is especially the case in Parsons. He limits the social influence on the early years of life to the production of a set of 'motivational forces' involved in 'the maintenance of, and alteration to, the structure of a social system'.[36] The symbolic/representational universe is seen as relevant only at the conscious/cognitive level. Moreover, for Parsons the unconscious remains a purely descriptive category. The creation of 'motivational forces' appropriate to the social system is considered straightforward, passing through no register with the specificity of the Freudian unconscious. Psychoanalysis is thus presented as one more theory of 'socialization'.

In general, there is no reason to give priority to one of the modes of social influence on the psyche. They are equally necessary for the functioning and structuring of the human psychical apparatus and cannot be distinguished other than in an analytic sense. Hence, only a reference to all three modes in equal measure and recognition of their linkage can offer a balanced account of the relationship between the psyche and the social.

Some of the theorizations that focus on the importance of the social environment, tend to assert also that social organizations, agencies, structures corresponding to earlier, more fundamental levels of psychical structuring are also more fundamental at a societal level. A common form of this argument is to say that the mode of familial organization, or the mode of the mothering process, can explain the organization of other spheres of social life (politics, for example). The arguments of certain feminist writers such as D. Dinnerstein and N. Chodorow,[37] fall within this category. They both consider mothering relations to determine the different character of the sexes and hence the whole of the gender divisions. In the case of Dinnerstein mothering relations determine also the attitude towards the physical environment and the very existence of political domination.

Even regarding the dynamics of the individual psyche, however, despite the great emphasis analytic practice places on the early developmental stages, there is no claim – in Freud or his followers – that these stages determine subsequent ones. Though the past history and configuration of the ego *influence* future object-choices, they do

---

36. T. Parsons, 'Psychoanalysis and the Social Structure' (1948), in *Essays in Sociological Theory*, New York, 1954, p. 340.

37. Dinnerstein, *The Rocking of the Cradle*; Chodorow, *The Reproduction of Mothering*.

not *determine* them. And although earlier object-choices and environmental influences play a more important role in the economy of the psyche than later ones, it cannot be said that the latter are determined by the former. The points of indeterminacy we identified within the process of ego- and super-ego-construction apply both to the external environment and to the influence of the existing ego and super-ego at any moment. If the early structuring of the psyche cannot be regarded as determining the future development of the psyche as such, even less can social agencies or institutions corresponding to these early years be considered to reflect or be reflected on the whole of society. One could reasonably argue that the more entrenched social functions/features are, the more they would be reflected also on the structures/institutions influencing the early years of life. But even if this assertion is accepted (which requires evidence), complex social phenomena such as politics, domination, the relation of sexes or the relation to nature cannot be considered to be necessarily reflected or, even less, to be determined by the modes/institutions/features of early societal influence on the psyche.

The Specificity of the Individual

The fact that the individual is inescapably and profoundly socially influenced, should not be taken as implying that the individual can be 'dissolved' within this influence. This is both because the social environment operates in conjunction with other factors, and because the social determination as such is never full or complete.

   The social influences on the psyche are limited, at the level of the unconscious, to the internalization of representations and to the construction of the ego and super-ego and, at the level of consciousness, to the internalization of symbolic systems, 'knowledge' and norms. These influences represent only part of the factors determining psychical development. The emergence of the ego and super-ego is supported by a certain internal – and biologically given – dynamic which gradually creates these agencies. The recognition of the existence of such a dynamic has been implicit in Freud and was explicitly theorized by a number of researchers (Hartmann and the ego-psychologists, Mahler and her collaborators and Kernberg). This dynamic produces the individual and assures a certain closure of the 'self' as a whole. This closure is never complete and does not imply either fully homogeneous structures/agencies (the ego and super-ego) or lack of internal conflict within these agencies. The ego and the super-ego never form fully coherent wholes. Yet a certain integration does exist, and a certain dynamic pointing towards such an integration is in operation. The emergence and relative closure of the agencies of the ego and super-ego, therefore, is not a function of the social environment.

In addition, the agencies of the ego and super-ego are not the only forms of organization of psychical energy. The development of sexual drives that Freud theorizes is another case, so are biologically determined instinctual modes influencing behaviour which Freud considers includes among 'self-preservative' instincts. Psychoanalysis does not theorize these instincts and their development but does not deny their existence either. Thus the social determination of the psyche concerns part only of its total organization and development. Finally, the psyche also contains the id, a reservoir of 'free' and unbound psychical energy which can never be totally bound. Any structuring, therefore, of psychical energy on the level of the unconscious is partial with respect to the total psychical energy.

Even the actual social influences on the psyche, because of the indeterminate nature of any structuring of psychical energy, always remain *influences* and never *determinations*.

A first degree of indeterminacy is implied in the impossibility of predefining the 'objects' that are to be cathected/internalized out of the available objects within the significant social environment. In a similar way the intensity and type of instinctual investment of these objects cannot be deduced in any mechanical way from the social environment. Consequently, the configuration and instinctual dynamics of the ego and super-ego cannot be predefined, even if all the details of the significant environments at all times were given. The same environment can produce different structural effects in different individuals according to the choices the psychical apparatus may make. If this is true for the early, semibiological stages of ego-development, it is even more so for the stage of adolescence or adulthood when no prediction about the direction of further structuring can be made.

In addition to this first degree of indeterminacy, in so far as the internalization of objects, significations and their instinctual investment operate within the unconscious, a further, more fundamental level of indeterminacy can be discerned. The construction of the endopsychic agencies of the ego and super-ego refers only to a partial and incomplete structuring of unconscious psychical energy. This structuring, because of the mode of being of the unconscious, corresponds not to fully delimited agencies but to the emergence of lines of relatively structured psychical energy, never fully discernible from the unstructured mass of the id. The structuring can be approached only through its manifestations on the level of consciousness or by becoming conscious through analytic practice. But any such 'becoming conscious' involves a change of state, an interpretation, which is never unidimensional nor can it lead back in a definite way to the unconscious itself. Moreover, the *same* unconscious content, because of its being a line of relative and not absolute structuring of psychical energy, can produce disparate or even conflicting thoughts, affects or ideas. Thus, even if we somehow knew the actual objects cathected and internalized – and their instinctual investment – it would be impossible to know their actual effect on the psyche, their mode of existence within the ego or super-ego, or the ways in which they may be manifested in consciousness. No strict line of causality can be drawn for the impact the social environment has on the psyche, at least in so far as we refer to the unconscious. Only a certain insight into the importance of environmental influences for the construction of the psyche is possible – and this is what sustains the field of socio-psychological investigation. But a fully causal theory of the social construction of the human psyche has to be ruled out.

The impossibility of postulating any full determination implies also that the emergence of radically new elements in the psyche is always possible. Such elements originate within and because of the modality of the unconscious but become manifested (as ideas or affects) on the level of consciousness. The psyche, though influenced in a fundamental way by the social environment, retains thus the possibility of the emergence of the radically new.

Finally we have to add the indeterminacy that the existence of the conscious/rational ego implies, because of the relative autonomy of this level of the ego. The rational processes of thought are conditioned by the unconscious ego and the id in so far as motivational forces guiding logical and rational operations are concerned. The system of concepts and ideas that rational thought requires, as also the norms and values guiding action are socially determined. However, the multiplicity of possible motivations coming directly from the id and the possibility to have multiple and even conflicting motivations coming from the unconscious ego and super-ego (because of their lack of homogeneity) allow a range of possible directions of motivation. Moreover, in so far as the individual 'adapts' to the environment in a conscious/rational manner, the result of this adaptation is also indeterminate, since there are usually a number of alternative ways to rationally or instrumentally adapt to the same environment, even given the same 'knowledge' and 'norms' or values. Thus the conscious/rational ego – and consequently the individual – retains a certain autonomy regarding any instrumental adaptation to a given social environment.

The combined effect of instrumental autonomy and of the possibility of the emergence of the radically new within the psyche is a higher degree of autonomy open to the conscious/rational ego: it is that theorized by Castoriadis as 'autonomy' in the strict sense, putting oneself and the social into question and bringing forward novel forms, ideas, actions. Castoriadis observes that this possibility would not exist 'if ensemblist-identitary logic totally exhausted what exists'. To interpret this assertion: no possibility of such autonomy would exist if the underlying social influences on the psyche were determining it fully. It is only because the influences of the social at the level of the unconscious entail points of indeterminacy, and particularly the radical indeterminacy due to the nature of the unconscious, that 'autonomy' in this sense is really possible. Only if the possibility of the emergence of the non-determined, the radically new, within the psyche is affirmed, can such a level of autonomy be asserted. The conscious/rational ego, therefore, further to adapting instrumentally to the social environment, can become the vehicle through which the 'radical imagination' orients action and thought. However, this level of autonomy is potential rather than actual, its emergence being – as Castoriadis remarks – a historically specific event.

The presence of biologically given constants in the processes of psychical development; the points of indeterminacy necessarily existing within the social influence on the psyche, particularly regarding the impossibility of advancing any fully causal theory of unconscious structuring; and the relative autonomy of the conscious/rational ego (usually of an instrumental but potentially a more radical nature), all indicate that though the psychoanalytic theorization of the psyche asserts the profoundly social nature of the individual psyche, it never implies any full determination of the individual by the social. We do not have one more variant of a socialization theory in which the individuals appear as perfect clones of 'roles' or structural positions. While these roles and positions do influence the individual at a fundamental level of psychical development and operation, the precise outcome of this influence remains indeterminable. The social is a prerequisite for the development of the individual psyche. The individual psyche, however, can never be reduced to the social.

Society and Psyche

An Open Theory of Social Reproduction

The elaboration of a theory of the ways the social influences the psyche, within the broader framework of the psychoanalytic theory of the psyche provides, at the same time, an account of social reproduction through the individual.

The sum of determinations/influences on the psyche is manifested both as products of consciousness and as action or behaviour. Thoughts, ideas or affects originate in an unknown form in the unconscious, either within the agencies of the ego and the super-ego or within the id. They may, consequently, present themselves as such in consciousness or they may, as motivations, induce or influence a certain behaviour or a course of action on the part of the individual. In the latter case they can operate in tandem with the conscious ego, but it is also possible that the ego can contradict their dictates. The conscious ego, itself using a stock of knowledge and systems of norms and values, may carry out motivations coming from the unconscious or it may be able to resist such impulses and influence behaviour counter to internal motivational pressure.

The social environment is the origin of the significations the psyche uses and of the 'objects' internalized within the ego and the super-ego while it influences the instinctual investment of these objects. It also provides the symbolic universe and the systems of norms and values the conscious ego uses to orient action. Social influences – conscious and unconscious – can be thus manifested either as products of consciousness (thoughts, ideas, concepts) or directly at the level of individual action, or, more usually, in a combined way. Such action and thoughts, albeit individual ones, are directed towards a social milieu within which they become meaningful or, indeed, intelligible. Individual thoughts, concepts, ideas, acquire significance only when they feed back to the stream of social thought, language, knowledge. As for individual action it is almost always executed within a social framework. Thus both products of consciousness and the action/ behaviour of the individual sustain and reproduce a social environment that had been a necessary precondition for their emergence. We have here, therefore, the outline of a theory of social reproduction at its most elementary level, the level of the individual. Based of Freud's diagram of the psyche[1] we could attempt an illustration of the process, frozen at a moment in time:

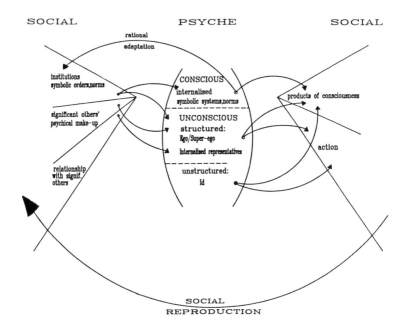

Figure 3

This model of social reproduction is a comprehensive one. It outlines the different modes in which the social influences the psyche, specifies the psychical levels – conscious/unconscious – these modes operate on and presents how the social influences are manifested at the level of thought and action.

The model corresponds closely to the requirements posed by 'theories of structuration'. Being much more detailed than Giddens's – while avoiding any relapse to individualism – it can be seen as

---

1. S. Freud, *The Ego and the Id* (1923), Penguin/Pelican Freud Library (P.F.L.) 11, Harmondsworth, 1984, p. 363; also idem, *New Introductory Lectures on Psychoanalysis* (1933), P.F.L. 2, Harmondsworth, 1973, p. 111.

providing a theorization for what Bourdieu's generic notion of habitus stands for. The structuring of the unconscious through the construction of the agencies of the ego and the super-ego and the manifestation of this structuring in social practice correspond closely to the 'structured dispositions' of the habitus, 'embodied' rather than known, constructed through growing up in a given environment and manifested in social practice without necessarily becoming conscious. At the same time, the role of socially originating 'representatives' internalized within the psyche to which Bourdieu does not refer, is highlighted. Evidently, the model draws from Castoriadis, expanding his account to include not only the internalization of 'social imaginary significations' but also socially originating objects internalized within the ego and super-ego and the socially influenced instinctual investment of these objects. Correspondingly, the manifestation of these social influences is not limited to the (re)production of social imaginary significations but includes also direct (motivational) determinants of social action and practice. Thus both the role of representations and that of practice are given due recognition.

The real importance of this model of social reproduction, however, lies in that it theorizes the existence of points of indeterminacy necessarily present within the process. While a social environment is absolutely necessary for the development of the psyche, there are elements in the psychical make-up of the individual which cannot be traced back to a social influence: impulses coming from the id, biologically determined instinctual modes of behaviour, the internal dynamic and closure of the ego. These factors, however, are in general determinable (excepting perhaps the case of certain id impulses). They constitute a biologically given background upon which social historical variations may be engraved. The points of indeterminacy we refer to concern specifically social environmental influences and they include:

1. The impossibility to derive from the social environment, in a mechanical way, the actual 'objects' that will be internalized in the process of ego- and super-ego-construction, as well as their instinctual investment. It is impossible to predict the actual configuration and psychical dynamic of the ego and super-ego even if we knew the significant environment at all times of a person's life.
2. The radical indeterminacy implied by the construction of the endopsychic agencies of the ego and super-ego at the level of the unconscious. The structuring of unconscious psychical energy that these agencies represent remains always partial and incomplete. Moreover, it can be approached only through its manifestations on the level of consciousness and/or action. But these manifestations,

involving a change of state, an 'interpretation', are never unidimensional nor can they lead back in a definite way to the unconscious itself. Thus no fully causal theory of social determinations at the level of the unconscious can be advanced. As a consequence, the radically new, the non-determined can always emerge at that level and become manifest through the conscious ego.

3. The limited autonomy the conscious/rational ego has in instrumentally adapting to the social environment, despite using socially originating symbolic systems, knowledge and norms and being influenced by the unconscious ego and id.

4. The possibility of a higher level of autonomy, concerning a conscious project of questioning the very determinations of the self and the social and aiming at social or individual transformation. This level of autonomy can exist only because the modality of the unconscious does not allow any full and final determinations to operate. It is always potentially present, though its actualization remains historically specific.

The above points ensure that no strict line of causality between the social environment influencing the individual and the individual's actions or thoughts can be established. Thus the reproduction of the social through the psyche cannot be seen as subject to strict causal influences and no full theory of this reproduction can be presented – even potentially or ultimately. An 'openness' and indeterminacy is necessarily and unavoidably inherent in this reproduction. To put it differently, the emergence of 'something new', of something that cannot be deduced from existing determinations of the psyche always exists.

Thus a way to conceptualize the social as 'open' in a dynamic sense is presented, locating this 'openness' in the necessary and unavoidable points of indeterminacy inherent in the reproduction of the social through the individual psyche. This way provides an alternative to either a reduction of the social to ideas as Laclau and Mouffe seem to effect, or to the postulation of a transcendental level behind and beyond the positivity of social phenomena as Castoriadis's theorization may be taken to imply.[2] Castoriadis's argument of an

---

2. The proposed theorization provides an alternative also to attempts to transpose a Lacanian theorization of the 'openness' and indeterminacy of the unconscious directly on the level of the social. S. Zizek, for example, affirms that the 'symbolic order' itself is open due to the operation of the Lacanian 'lack': 'The most radical dimension of Lacanian theory lies [. . .] in realising that the [. . .] symbolic order itself is also barré, crossed-out, by a fundamental impossibility, structured around an impossible/traumatic kernel, around a central lack' (S. Zizek, *The Sublime Object*

identity in modality between the (individual) unconscious and the 'magma of social imaginary significations' is extended, introducing a causal link: it is primarily *because* the social is reproduced through the unconscious that it is open and indeterminate.

At the same time an overall structural orientation is retained. The theorization of indeterminacy presented is fully congruent with a structural conception of the social on the lines of a differential definition of structure. The social 'elements' that influence the psyche belong to different social structural wholes, which are in turn reproduced through the manifestation of these influences as products of consciousness or action. These structural wholes, however, are never fully closed, fully definable ones as structural/objectivist theories assume. The unavoidable indeterminacy introduced by their reproduction through the psyche implies that alterity is inherent in their reproduction, in other words that novel elements, not predeterminable, can always appear within them.

Thus, while the outlined theorization of social reproduction affirms as strongly as structuration theories the irreducibility of the individual to the social, it rejects any *a priori* subjectivism and avoids a relapse to individualism. The synthesis sought of the aims of structuration theories and the theorization of the social as 'open' proves to be indeed fruitful, avoiding the shortfalls of the respective theories and providing a more fully worked out alternative to the structural/objectivist approaches we started from.

The Unconscious Dimension of the Social

The structuring of unconscious psychical energy depends, to a significant extent, on social factors. The representations the unconscious uses, the 'objects' internalized in the process of ego- and super-ego-construction, the instinctual investment of these objects, are all social in origin or socially determined. In turn these social determinants lie behind the manifestations of the unconscious content on the level of consciousness or action, manifestations which are also

---

of Ideology, London, 1989, p. 122). Zizek transposes to the level of the social, without offering any connecting mechanism, a concept that is already essentialist in nature in the way Lacan uses it for the level of the unconscious (see note 85, chapter 10, p. 164). One can only assume that this 'lack' operates at a transcendental level, behind and beyond the positivity of social phenomena. If in Castoriadis such a transcendentalism is a possible interpretation, in Zizek it is unavoidable. However, to assert the 'openness' of the social, as that of the psyche, the postulation of a 'lack' is not necessary. The reproduction of the social through the individual necessarily introduces such an openness and at many levels, including the radical indeterminacy stemming from the unconscious.

socially relevant. The unconscious is, therefore, an important level of social reproduction through the psyche. And although not all the factors of indeterminacy inherent in this reproduction are related to the unconscious, the most significant ones, including the possibility of the emergence of the 'radically new', are. Thus the affirmation of the importance the unconscious has in social reproduction, along with its characteristic modality psychoanalytic theory alone theorizes, are pivotal for the theorization of the social as open and indeterminate. To a significant extent it is *because* the social is reproduced through the level of the individual unconscious and *because* the unconscious has the characteristic modality psychoanalytic theory attributes to it that the social can be said to be open and indeterminate.

The unconscious, however, is not only a level of the psyche through which social structural wholes are reproduced. It is also *part* of such structures to the extent that it includes socially originating and socially relevant elements. The elements of a social structure internalized within the psyche and reproducing this structure through individual action and thought are a significant constituent of the structure as such. And since there are such elements internalized at the level of the unconscious, the unconscious itself becomes a level of the social, a level on which the social not only is reproduced, but it also 'exists'. The (individual) unconscious is not external to the social but a necessary and important dimension of it. Therefore, any definition of the social has to take into account the elements internalized and existing within the unconscious of the individuals comprising society. We can use the term the *unconscious dimension of the social* to indicate both the sum of such elements/influences and the dynamic role the unconscious plays in social reproduction. Since the psyche cannot develop without a social environment and socially originating internalized elements and since the unconscious plays a central role in social reproduction, the unconscious dimension is always present in the social matrix.

The recognition of the existence of an unconscious dimension of the social is important in that it allows a conceptualization of a level of social meaning not reducible to either nature/biology or to consciousness. Traditionally, the only way to conceptualize 'meaning' has been conscious meaning: ideas, thoughts, conscious representations, and products of consciousness in general. The 'non-meaningful' could be attributed to 'nature' or to 'biology' and analyzed in the manner of the natural sciences. The psychoanalytic theorization of the psyche, however, introduced the level of the unconscious as always 'represented' – using, moreover, socially originating representatives – communicating with consciousness –

and even determining certain aspects of it – and yet not reducible to consciousness or to biologically given instincts. The level of the unconscious is always and inescapably 'meaningful'. Moreover, since the unconscious uses socially originating representatives to manifest itself and refers to socially influenced or determined structured forms of psychical energy, this 'meaning' is social. Hence the unconscious dimension of the social corresponds also to a social dimension of meaning.

The existence of a dimension of the social meaningful but not coextensive with consciousness has been identified by many theorists in the past though never fully theorized. Marx indicates the existence of such a level in his notion of a 'material' level of the social, specifically human and connected to social action, not reducible to consciousness or biology/nature and determining the 'forms of consciousness'. Similarly, Durkheim's 'social life' capable of generating concepts and (theoretical) categories without being reducible to them or Pareto's 'residues' which determine what people think and which are intelligible at a social level, indicate such a level of the social. The affirmation of the existence of an unconscious dimension of the social allows us to present a theory of this level without accepting either Marx's essentialist framework or a 'positivist' epistemology. In the same way, Weber's 'traditional' and 'affective' action can be seen as 'meaningful' and yet as not necessarily reducible to deviations of rational action. Finally, the theorization of a socially structured dimension of meaning different from rational/conceptual thought and yet partially accessible to it provides the background upon which could be based a non subjectivist interpretive procedure of the type Dilthey, Husserl and Mead all indicate.

Among more contemporary theorists the postulation of an unconscious dimension of the social offers a way of locating Althusser's 'imaginary' field within which ideology functions, while rejecting the reducibility of this field to the ultimate objectivity of the underlying structure of production. Similarly, the 'meaningfulness' of the social to which Laclau and Mouffe refer can be accepted without necessarily reducing the social to the level of ideas; the unconscious dimension of the social provides an alternative register for this 'meaning', always underlying action and thought but never coextensive with consciousness. The connection Laclau and Mouffe introduce between the 'meaningfulness' of the social and its 'openness' can be thus more satisfactorily theorized.

The unconscious dimension of the social includes Castoriadis's 'magma of social imaginary significations' but it is a broader term, comprising also the structuring of unconscious psychical energy that underlies equally social action/behaviour and consciousness. Indeed, in some authors (Marx, Durkheim and Mead) the social level of 'meaning' that is not reducible to nature or consciousness is specifically associated with social practice. Similarly, Bourdieu claimed that social practice has a specific modality irreducible to the 'formal operations' of rational thought, without however providing a satisfactory theory of this modality. The theorization of an unconscious dimension of the social allows the elaboration of a theory of social practice as meaningful and yet as not reducible to the level of ideas, as will be argued more extensively below.

The theorization of an unconscious dimension as a level of 'existence' of the social also establishes, in addition to the 'dynamic openness' inherent in social reproduction, another type of indeterminacy and 'openness' – a 'static' one. It is never possible to directly approach the (individual) unconscious and hence to know as what the social elements internalized at this level exist. These elements – unconscious representatives or structuring of psychical energy within the agencies of the ego and super-ego – can become known only through their manifestation at the level of consciousness. However, such manifestations are never unidimensional. Variable thoughts, ideas, or actions, possibly in conflict with each other, may originate in the same unconscious content. Moreover, these elements do not represent a transposition of this content in consciousness, merely a manifestation of it. Thus, though we can approximate the unconscious context, there are many possible approximations, all equally valid, many interpretations, none of which can be considered privileged. Therefore, the social elements internalized within and shaping the individual unconscious are never directly approachable and never fully knowable as such.

Moreover, since the unconscious is a level of individual psychical operation, even when this level is approached, as for example in the context of analytic practice, the social nature of internalized objects or influences is not always apparent. The interpretation of individual thoughts and affects with the aim of reaching the underlying unconscious content rarely allows the localization and identification of social elements as such. The unconscious dimension of the social is equally not directly observable on the level of concrete social phenomena. Observable social phenomena – whether ideas, concepts, social rules, norms and values or social action and practice – are always manifestations of the unconscious dimension of the social, derivatives of this level. Therefore it is only by a combination of individual observation and social analysis that the social elements that have an effect on the unconscious and are reproduced through it can be identified and their significance for the social as a whole deduced. Even then, the exact way in which these elements 'exist' can never be fully known.

The recognition of the unconscious dimension of the social, therefore, introduces a relatively opaque level of the social, the existence of which we can derive in a complex way from individual and social analysis but which always remains beyond any full identification. The knowledge of this level always remains partial and incomplete. An 'openness' in our knowledge of the social, the result of the impossibility to fully assimilate a level of existence of the social to the modality of concepts and ideas has therefore to be admitted alongside the dynamic indeterminacy the reproduction of the social through this level implies. However, this 'openness' does not justify the postulation of any transcendental level. The unconscious is a 'positive' level of psychical operation, despite being never directly observable.

It has to be stressed that the unconscious dimension of the social, although always present, does not substitute the conscious dimension of the social more traditionally analysed; it constitutes only a necessary supplement. It provides a theoretical framework to account for the non-conscious, non-rational but also potentially immensely creative aspects of social life. While this is of crucial theoretical importance, it does not exhaust the theorization of the social. The level of the unconscious itself is not exclusively social; social determinations on the unconscious are just one level of influences among many. More importantly, the social operates to a great extent at the level of consciousness. Social functions or structures may exist wholly at the level of consciousness and others wholly at the level of the unconscious or, more usually, at both levels. To indicate at which level different social structural wholes operate, specific studies are necessary, studies which are outside the scope of the present work.

Returning to Social Theory

The presentation of a theory of social reproduction through the psyche and the affirmation of the existence of an 'unconscious dimension of the social' allow the theorization of the social as open and indeterminate in both a dynamic sense – related to its reproduction – and a static one – related to the mode of being of its 'unconscious dimension'. In this way the elaboration of a theoretical alternative to structural/objectivist approaches is completed. The break with these theories inaugurated by Laclau and Mouffe and by Castoriadis is taken a step further and a kind of synthesis between the latter theorists and 'structuration' theorists is effected.

The impasses structural/objectivist approaches face concerning the questions of agency and history can now, to a great extent, be overcome. Castoriadis has already presented an extensive theorization of autonomy and outlined the theoretical principles underlying a genuinely non-deterministic theory of history. We can now further expand his theorization. At the same time we can present elements towards a theory of social practice as a level with its own specificity, building upon Bourdieu's programmatic statements and establishing the connection between an open theory of the social and a theory of practice. Finally, we can indicate the consequences the theorization of an 'unconscious dimension of the social' has for social knowledge, i.e. for the epistemology of social sciences.

The autonomy of the social individual: The real dilemma facing social theory concerning the question of agency is how to avoid both a regression into individualism and the assertion of a full and complete determination of the individual by the social. While individualistic theories are untenable as a whole – as the psychoanalytic theorization of the psyche forcefully confirms – they do point out the undeniable existence of levels of autonomy in individual actors, not least in processes of 'micro' encounters and small-scale interaction. Moreover, at least the possibility of a higher degree of autonomy, underpinning intentional socially transformative action – political action in a broad sense – has also to be accepted, especially within theorizations – such as the Marxist one – which include an emancipatory project. However, structural approaches to the study of the social – including Marxism – have not been able to reconcile the social determination of the individual with the affirmation of the possibility of either a low-level ('micro') or a high-level ('macro') autonomy. Indeed, in so far as the social is conceptualized as fully closed and fully definable structural wholes, determining also the individual, not even the possibility of coexistence of contradicting or conflicting determinations operating on the same individual can be affirmed.

The preceding theorization of the formation of a social individual allows the elaboration of a middle way between the two extremes. The deep, fundamental role of social environmental influences for the construction of the psyche – both at the level of consciousness and at the level of the unconscious – is conclusively argued, and the continuity of these processes throughout the individual's life is indicated. However, this is qualified:

The social influences on the construction of the psyche are not the only ones, existing alongside biological determinations in the form of given instinctual modes and of the innate tendency for the development of endopsychic agencies. The central insight of 'sociobiological' approaches (that the individual is also biologically determined) can thus be accepted while rejecting their extreme claims of the total reducibility of the social to the biological.

Regarding the specifically *social* construction of the individual, this construction does not produce unidimensional or homogeneous individuals given the eclectic and arbitrary choice of objects internalized within the agencies of the ego and super-ego and of their instinctual investment. The modality of the unconscious allows the coexistence of diverging or even conflicting elements within the psyche. Thus the fiction of a homogeneous individuality common to structural theories of a Parsonian kind can be safely left behind.

Moreover, there are levels of autonomy always potentially open to the individual. A first level of autonomy, which we can term 'instru-mental', refers to the conscious ego's adaptation to a given social environment. Although the motivations influencing such adaptation (through their influence on conscious thought and action) come largely from an unconscious level socially shaped, the lack of homogeneity in the unconscious ego and super-ego ensures that such motivations can be diverse or even conflicting. In addition, there are also motivations not necessarily socially influenced, while the conscious ego may act counter to any unconscious motivations. Even when we can consider the ego as acting in a strictly rational/instrumental way, using socially originating systems of norms and systems of knowledge, there is always a range of alternative courses of action and thought to respond and adapt to the same social environment. Thus a social actor is never reducible to mechanistic and passive behaviour. S/He is always in a position to set aims, choose means to attain them, deploy strategies, exhibit, in short, all the characteristics the traditional means-end model attributes to the individual. The level of always present active agency emphasized by theorists of ('micro') interaction, as well as by Giddens and Bourdieu (and which Castoriadis does not specifically address) can be thus satisfactorily theorized.

Above and beyond 'instrumental' autonomy, there is a higher level of autonomy open to the individual, the one theorized by Castoriadis as autonomy in the strict sense. It refers to the possibility of putting oneself and the social into question with the explicit purpose of introducing novel forms, ideas, actions. The possibility of the emergence of the radically new, of the non-determined within the psyche — due to the specific modality of the unconscious — can be expressed through the conscious/rational ego and become a conscious program of social and individual transformation. The conscious ego can become thus the vehicle through which 'radical imagination' orients action and thought. This higher level of autonomy is a necessary prerequisite if intentional socially transformative action (political action in a broad and non trivial sense) is to be initiated and it can exist only because the modality of the unconscious does not allow any full and final determinations to operate. This autonomy can now be theorized independently and in addition to the level of 'instrumental' autonomy. While the latter is always present, the higher level of autonomy is potential rather than actual, requiring a suitable social environment to be manifested and is thus historically specific. Even this autonomy, however, is bounded. It can never lead to a fully transparent individuality (or, correlatively, to a self-transparent society), because neither the unconscious can be eliminated nor can the totality of social values, beliefs, norms be questioned. The psyche as a whole, as also the social will always remain something 'more' than we can reflexively know, understand or consciously create.

Thus, alongside the fundamentally social nature of the human individual, different levels of autonomy and active agency can be theorized, including both the self-reflexivity of an instrumental kind that 'micro' sociology indicates and the higher level of autonomy Castoriadis theorizes and which provides the foundation for a non-reductionist theorization of politics in the broadest sense. These levels of autonomy correspond to the points of indeterminacy social reproduction through the individual psyche necessarily includes and are a direct consequence of the theorization of this reproduction.

A middle road between individualism and strict holism can indeed be traced, allowing the incorporation of elements from both sides without swinging too far towards either and indicating that a satisfactory answer to the question of agency is possible within social theory. The affirmation of a certain activeness and autonomy of the individual can be made simultaneously with the acceptance of a social determination of the individual. While it is impossible to conceive of the individual psyche outside social contexts, it is equally impossible to conceive of the individual as simply the reflection of the social, or as the empty locus of social-structural wholes. The 'self' is such a reflection and such a locus; but it is also much more than that, exhibiting different levels of autonomy. The individual cannot be dissolved within the social; nor can the social, however, ever be surmounted by a sovereign individuality.

The emergence of the new in history: The theorization of history has been inextricably interwoven with the theorization of the social in its modern sense. History emerged as the field where the internal dynamic attributable to society was manifested. The discovery of the guiding principle behind this dynamic was the major preoccupation of nineteenth century theorists, inclined to present history as progressive development, necessary evolution, inescapable progress. Society was seen as the subject of history in a path of continuous evolution – and not only by theorists within the idealist tradition. Self-proclaimed positivists – from Comte to Mill to Durkheim – also adhered to a more or less explicit version of evolutionism. This has not lost its appeal in later times, as Parsons's later work reveals. Later, another view of history gradually emerged, rejecting evolutionism but still retaining the overall assumption of history as predetermined. The existence of transhistorical categories necessarily present in human societies but not necessarily developing in an evolutive sense was postulated. Elements of this view can be found in Marx or Weber – still intermingled with a progressive notion of history – but it is in Pareto that it is presented as such before resurfacing as the 'structuralist combinatory' (cf. Lévi-Strauss). In both cases historical becoming is predetermined from the start either as given possibilities of development or as given elements of possible combinations.

If any transhistorical constant or essence is to be rejected – as in Althusser's programmatic statements – the question of how is the social to be conceptualized emerges. If society is seen as fully closed and determinable structural wholes, there is no 'outside' to force a change. Hence these structures either remain diachronically the same – which is untenable – or they already contain the seeds of their alteration in the form of predeterminations, introducing once again transhistorical principles or constants. If one is to retain the anti-essentialist position along with a structural conception of the social, what is needed is to assert that social-structural wholes are 'open', in the sense that they are not predetermined and thus, while no strict line of causality can be established, alterations can occur. This is the principal unifying line behind the theorizations of Derrida, Laclau and Mouffe, and Castoriadis. Castoriadis in particular elaborates how such an approach introduces a non-deterministic theory of history, enabling the emergence 'of radical otherness, non-trivial novelty, of the absolutely new'.

While Castoriadis focusses on the principles behind a non-deterministic theory of history, the preceding theorization of the processes of social reproduction through the psyche and of the unavoidable points of indeterminacy inherent in these processes provides a more detailed theorization of historical 'openness' and indeterminacy. Moreover, the localization of the points of indeterminacy allows a few remarks on how the emergence of the new actually occurs.

An obvious source of historical change is the high level of autonomy social agents can potentially exhibit, putting themselves and the social into question and specifically aiming to induce social transformation of a radical nature. Once the possibility of this level of autonomy has been affirmed, it can indeed be seen at the origin of the emergence of the 'radically new'. Obviously, action of this type will have, at some point, to acquire a collective nature but its origin remains the individual's ability to initiate such a project. However, such action is relatively rare in the context of known history. Castoriadis indicates the few historical cases when autonomy in this sense could be said to exist as a societal possibility and the limited number of individuals it concerned even then. In the same vein, P. Anderson remarks that 'public goals [. . .] in their overwhelming majority have not aimed to transform social relations as such [. . .] collective projects which have sought to render their initiators authors of their collective mode of existence, in a conscious programme aimed at creating or remodelling whole social structures are relatively recent.'[3] Therefore individual and collective action specifically and intentionally aimed at radical social transformation, although important, cannot be considered the primary source of historical change.

The instrumental/rational adaptation of the individual to the social environment can also be a source of historical change, though on a smaller scale. Such adaptation implies a certain degree of indeterminacy, in the sense that its final outcome and its consequences for the social as a whole cannot be predetermined. The introduction of novel elements is therefore always a possibility. (It is to this case that the common reference to 'unintended consequences of action' mostly applies.)

Apart from the two cases above, the preceding analysis indicates that a third possibility, of an even more radical potential in the long run, is always present. This is the possibility of introducing new elements inherent in *any* action initiated by a social individual. Since every social action, individual or collective, never implies a mechanical reproduction of the social but necessarily includes points of indeterminacy, it can potentially introduce new and not previously determined elements within social-structural wholes in the course of routinely reproducing them. Of course, these elements are rarely noticed as such and their significance only gradually becomes apparent. The mechanism described, however, provides a fundamental principle assuring the continuous and necessary emergence of the

3. P. Anderson, *Arguments within English Marxism*, London, 1980, p. 20.

radically new, of the non-determined in history. The 'openness' and 'indeterminacy' of history can thus be traced back to the seemingly insignificant and at the time relatively unnoticed novel elements introduced in the course of non reflexive, everyday behaviour as well as to human action specifically aimed at social transformation or to the unintended consequences of instrumental adaptation to the social environment. The combined effect is the amazing diversity and plurality of human societal forms, a diversity that is impossible to reduce to given predeterminations or to adaptation to the natural environment.

Thus a theory supporting the always present possibility of the emergence of the new in history – whether social forms, structures, institutions or discourses – can be presented, against any claims of full determinism. It can be convincingly argued now that the outcome of social reproduction is never fully determined and therefore the emergence of novel elements within structural wholes is always possible.

It has to be stressed, however, that this theory refers only to the *possibility* and the *mechanisms* of the emergence of the new. Whether novel elements emerging can survive historically and/or become significant is another question altogether. Why certain structural entities retain permanence while others do not is probably a function of existing and antecedent conditions and seems amenable to causal analysis, specific in each case and requiring a specific inquiry. Similarly, the recognition of the always present possibility of change does not imply anything about the rate of such change, which can vary significantly and which is also a function of other, exogenous factors. What is outlined here is simply a number of fundamental principles and basic mechanisms supporting the affirmation of the 'openness' of history and hence the impossibility of any general theory of history.

Towards a theory of social practice: The very existence of a science of the social is conditional on the possibility of theorizing social practice and its 'meaning'. An obvious way is to reduce practice to the conscious meaning associated with it in the form of ideas and thoughts participating actors have. Correlatively, action that appears not to be guided by explicit, conscious meaning is considered as 'meaningless', guided perhaps by intentions or motives of a pure (psycho)dynamic nature. In this way the social is reduced to either ideas or nature, with all the drawbacks such a reductionism entails.

However, it is possible to theorize social practice as a level of the social with its own specificity, not necessarily reducible to that of conscious ideas or thoughts. This possibility has been indicated many times in the history of social thought. Most of the theorists we identified as indicating the existence of a social level irreducible to both nature and consciousness – a level we theorized as the unconscious dimension of the social – had, in fact, the realm of practice in mind. Marx's 'material level', the 'material intercourse of man' (and 'production') refer primarily to social practice. Durkheim has social practice in mind when he refers to 'social life' producing the conceptual ideas of a given society (mentioning 'rites' as an example) as also Pareto when referring to 'residues'. Weber's types of action refer to practice, while Mead similarly considers the 'primary social meaning' to be 'present in the social act'. However, it was only on the assumption of an essentialist framework (as with Marx or Weber) or of an *a priori* epistemological position (as with Durkheim or Pareto) that the irreducibility of practice could be grounded. Among contemporary theorists, Bourdieu explicitly addresses the question of practice, asserting its specific modality, different from 'reflective explications' and irreducible to 'formal operations'. He also connects this modality, the 'logic of practice', with the 'structured dispositions' of the habitus which reproduce it without necessarily passing through consciousness. However, Bourdieu ultimately reduces the 'logic of practice' to an imperfect variant of formal/discursive operations.

The recognition of an unconscious dimension of the social as a positive level of social functioning and existence provides an alternative framework for a theory of social practice. Practice can be now theorized as *one* level of the manifestation of the unconscious dimension of the social, alongside the level of consciousness and conceptual thought.

The social elements internalized within the unconscious and its socially influenced structuring underlie both products of consciousness and individual social action. At the same time any structuring of the unconscious always carries 'meaning' which is also social in origin (because both the origin of psychical representatives is social and the structuring of unconscious psychical energy is a function of social influences). This meaning is behind the explicit meaning expressed in the form of conceptual language in thoughts or ideas but it is also carried by any 'motivation' or intention stemming from the unconscious. And since such motivations and intentions can directly influence practice (without necessarily passing through consciousness), any action, quite independently or even in contradiction of any conscious and explicit meaning associated with it, always carries another dimension of (social) meaning, referring back to the unconscious. It follows that a specific dimension of social meaning can be considered proper to the level of social practice. This level of meaning refers directly to the unconscious dimension of the social and should be distinguished from identifiable conscious ideas or norms associated with and possibly guiding practice. They both form part of the overall process of action and practice but no necessary accordance between them can be assumed.[4]

Moreover, participation in social practices also *produces* effects at the level of the unconscious, not only during childhood but throughout the individual's life. Interaction with significant others provides objects of identification and plays a determinant role for the instinctual investment of internalized objects during the development of the ego and super-ego. Participation in social practices in adulthood can also be seen as producing changes within the psyche of a permanent and unconscious kind (on the model of Foucault's 'disciplines', Althusser's 'material practices' and Sohn-Rethel's 'social exchange'). The fact that these 'changes' can be manifested later in conscious thought (as 'ideology' or 'knowledge') confirms that they imply a certain transmission of 'meaning'. Social practice can thus be both the source of a meaningful structuring of the unconscious of the individuals participating, and itself the outcome of (always meaningful) unconscious motivations and intentions.

In this way a theoretical basis for a 'theory of practice' is provided. The classical theorists' emphasis on practice can be admitted while at the same time supplemented with a more general theoretical framework. A proper theorization of Bourdieu's 'logic of practice' can be also provided, connecting the meaning and the logic of practice with the unconscious and its mode of being. The connection between practice and habitus is that between practice and the social structuring of the unconscious. At the same time the specific modality Bourdieu attributes to the level of practice is extended to include the whole of the unconscious dimension of the social. Indeed the possibility of theorizing the level of meaning specific to practice and the consequent possibility of analysing this meaning independently of conscious ideas participating actors have, is one of the most significant contributions the theorization of the unconscious dimension of the social allows.

It has to stressed that the above provide only basic theoretical

---

4. The theorization of practice and its specificity is possible only if the whole range of factors influencing the structuring of the unconscious and the diverse forms of possible manifestations of these influences is acknowledged. If such influences are limited to the effect of the 'symbolic' (as in Lacan) or to the acquisition of 'representations' (as in Castoriadis), the connection between the structuring of the unconscious and the specificity of social practice cannot be recognized. Regarding the question of practice, the importance of a comprehensive theorization of the social construction of the unconscious and its advantages over one-sided accounts become obvious.

principles towards a non reductive theory of social practice. Further elaboration of the theoretical ground and the application of these principles to specific social analyses remains to be done. We can only note that the level of meaning proper to practice, since it refers back to the unconscious, has to be approached in the same way as the unconscious in general, i.e. through a hermeneutic procedure making this meaning explicit and conceptual without ever being final or definite.

Two possible ways of approaching this meaning could be indicated. The first is the possibility of interpreting *individual* social action based on motivations underpinning behaviour and deducing the social shaping of such motivations. This is of value both for analysing routine social reproduction on the level of the individual and for the analysis of large scale social movements. The second concerns the possibility to identify the 'meaning' inherent in social structures or institutions which is produced or reproduced through the practices such structures or institutions entail, independently of explicit ideas or ideologies supporting these institutions. The 'meaning' of organizations such as the school, the church, the state, the economy, or the firm can thus be analysed on the one hand with respect to explicit discourses associated with these organizations, and on the other with respect to the 'meaning' inherent in the practices they include. The two levels of meaning may complement each other or they may contradict each other.[5] This second way of approaching the meaning of social practice is a specifically *social* enquiry and does not include any analysis of individual motivations. The unconscious origin of this meaning provides simply guidelines as to its mode of being. In both cases, however, the meaning inherent in practice can only be approximated, through an interpretation that can be never final or complete.

On the nature of social knowledge: The preceding enquiry focussed almost exclusively on questions related to the way the social is, to its mode of being, rather than on epistemological questions. However, because 'ontological' and epistemological questions are always interwoven, within the arguments advanced there are also implications for a theory of social knowledge, to which we shall briefly refer.

The social can be successfully analysed only if we recognize that it is multifaceted and has a plurality of 'dimensions'. Such 'dimensions' can be postulated, for analytic purposes, as operating behind the objects social scientific enquiry encounters as immediate

5. Some of the most interesting analyses of the social arise when such contradictions exist. A classic example is Marx's emphasis on the distorted way the economic function of society is reflected on the level of ideology.

data – concrete actions and 'products of consciousness'. There is a natural/biological dimension referring to biologically given, and hence constant, determinants of social action, as also to the limitations imposed to society by its natural environment. There is an instrumental/rational dimension referring to actions guided solely by rational considerations of the conscious ego, including an instrumental adaptation to both the natural and social environment. There is also the dimension on which the present study has focussed, the unconscious dimension of the social, referring to social reproduction through and existence within the unconscious of the individuals and conditioned by the specific mode of being of the unconscious. The list is not conclusive, simply indicative. Moreover, different 'dimensions' may be distinguished from an analytic point of view, but they rarely operate independently; most often social processes are the combined outcome of many dimensions and causes.

Once the multifacity of the social is recognized, the postulation of a single mode of knowledge specific and exclusive to the study of the social cannot be sustained. Many different ways of getting to know what the social is and how it functions are possible and indeed necessary. The natural environment of a society, for instance, poses limits and has implications which can be fully analysed and described in the manner of natural sciences. The biological determinants inherent in the human being, presumed constant for the time scale of social scientific enquiry (short-term compared with the longer time span of biological changes) can also be considered subject to strict causal inferences. Thus an identity with the methods of natural science may be possible for specific dimensions of the social.

If we focus exclusively on social processes, however, any such identity becomes impossible. To describe instrumental/rational action, different rational choice or means-end models can be used, rendering intelligible the mechanisms of such action. However, no causal laws can be inferred, no prediction is possible. While the principles guiding such action can be adequately described, its outcome remains indeterminate. Only a limited similarity to the methods of natural sciences can be recognized in this case.

Even this similarity disappears when we seek to theorize the unconscious dimension of the social. This dimension, consisting of social elements internalized within and shaping the individual unconscious, is doubly inaccessible. Any internalized elements and any configuration of the unconscious are only deducible through manifestations in consciousness and action. Such deductions, however, can never be final or definite, they are always interpretations depending on the interpretational context. In addition, in order to identify those elements that are also social, a previous knowledge of the social contexts within which they emerge and within which they are intelligible is required. Thus the identification of elements pertaining to the unconscious dimension of the social requires a combination of individual and social analysis, with all the added qualifications any knowledge of the unconscious implies.

The type of approach proper to this dimension – as to the unconscious in general – is hermeneutic. It has, however, to be distinguished from a hermeneutics approximating 'first order' concepts to higher order ones. What is involved here is interpreting a level radically different from and not reducible to conceptual thought (though accessible to it). In so far as the unconscious content is concerned, even 'first order' concepts are already an interpretation. Any knowledge of the unconscious dimension of the social implies and necessitates a *radical* hermeneutics, a hermeneutics involving a passage from one type of modality (the unconscious) to another (conscious rational thought). Indeed, the theorization of this dimension as a level of the social that is meaningful and yet different in kind from conceptual thought provides the necessary difference of levels that a truly hermeneutic procedure necessitates. And since the elements internalized within the unconscious are intelligible and meaningful only within social structural wholes, it is a structural rather than a subjectivist hermeneutics we refer to.

Thus the unconscious dimension of the social provides the ontological basis that was lacking in traditional structural hermeneutics. At the same time, the necessity of a hermeneutic procedure is extended to include social practice alongside the different forms of social representing, the unconscious dimension underlying both of them. To the hermeneutics of ideas, of the 'text' that has been the traditional focus of hermeneutics, a hermeneutics of social practice can be added.[6]

However, the hermeneutic approach is of value only for a 'static' knowledge of the unconscious dimension of the social. The role this dimension plays in social reproduction through the psyche remains to a significant extent not theorizable. While the mechanisms of structuring of unconscious psychical energy can be identified, the outcome of the reproduction is indeterminate. Indeed, the possibility always exists that radically new elements – that were not present in

6. Gadamer considers that a foundation for hermeneutics can be found in the 'openness' inherent in language. Since behind this 'openness' lies the modality of the unconscious, we can reconfirm Gadamer's radical historicity of social knowledge while providing a more comprehensive theoretical basis and extending it to cover the realm of practice as well.

the preceding state not even potentially – may emerge. No principle or mechanism behind this possibility can be identified apart from the specific mode of being of the unconscious.

The affirmation of the existence of an unconscious dimension of the social, therefore, has important epistemological implications. It precludes any full or 'objective' knowledge of the social as a whole – since it can never be fully or definitely known. In order to theorize the social we can refer to logically constructed systems of concepts but we cannot assume an identity between this theoretical model and its 'object'. We cannot, in Bourdieu's words, substitute the 'reality of the model for the model of the reality'. Vico's *verum et factum convertuntur* ('truth and human deeds/facts are interchangeable') applies only partially to the social world. Similarly, the points of indeterminacy inherent in social reproduction through the psyche imply the impossibility of ever fully determining the historical trajectory. No laws, no overall pattern, no evolutionary principles can claim to describe historical development, our knowledge of which can never be complete. A hermeneutic procedure can offer insights into the working and mode of being of the unconscious dimension, but this knowledge remains always limited and partial.

Conclusion

This study may be provisional in terms of a complete theory, but the main defining lines of a theorization of the social–psyche interface have been drawn and some important theoretical consequences have been highlighted – to briefly recapitulate:

The analysis of the psyche offered in part 3 – drawing from a certain interpretation of psychoanalytic theory and inspired by Castoriadis's work[1] – allows a very precise localization of the social influences on the development of the psyche as well as the determination of the level (conscious/unconscious) these influences operate on. The social environment operates both on: (i) a deep unconscious level, providing the representations the psyche uses, the objects that become internalized in the process of construction of the agencies of the ego and super-ego and influencing the level and type of instinctual investment of these objects; and (ii) on the level of consciousness, providing the cognitive systems of concepts, symbols and norms conscious thought uses, as well as the objective environment to which the individual can rationally adapt.

Since these social determinations are manifested, in turn, as products of consciousness or guide (social) action, we have in the above the main lines of a theorization of social reproduction on its most elementary level, i.e. through the individual psyche. A comprehensive theory of 'structuration' can be thus presented (stressing the importance of both representations and social action/ practice), advancing along the path Giddens and Bourdieu are seen as indicating in part 2 but avoiding any relapse to individualism (as with Giddens) and going beyond the use of generic concepts (as in the case of Bourdieu).

Throughout the processes of this reproduction the role of the (individual) unconscious remains central and constitutes a level at which the social not only is reproduced but also 'exists'. The central

1. Far from being at best parallel and at worst incommensurable, psychoanalytic and social theory are shown to be of crucial importance to one another in so far as a general theorization of the social and of the psyche is concerned. Of course, they retain their independence in areas of enquiry specific to each. For example, the specific importance psychoanalytic theory has for the analytic practice from which it originates remains outside the interests of social theory.

role of the unconscious continues, moreover, for the whole of an individual's life. The presence of an 'unconscious dimension of the social' can therefore be justifiably asserted, providing a theorization of a level of the social that is 'meaningful' (since the unconscious is always so) and yet not reducible to consciousness or 'nature' (since the unconscious has its own specific, and irreducible, modality).

As pointed out in part 1, the existence and importance of such a level of the social has been repeatedly indicated in the history of social thought (Marx's 'material level', later Durkheim's 'social life', Pareto's 'residues', Dilthey, Husserl and Mead's socially-structured and yet not ideal dimension of meaning, Althusser's 'imaginary', being just a few examples). Theorizing this dimension in relation to the unconscious provides both a more developed account and avoids its being reduced to other social levels or instances.

More importantly, the recognition of the existence of the unconscious dimension of the social and the theory of social reproduction presented allow an alternative theorization of a necessary 'openness' and indeterminacy of the social. Inherent within the processes of social reproduction through the psyche are unavoidable points of indeterminacy. While the individual is inconceivable as an entity outside a social environment, s/he is not reducible to such an environment. Other influences, besides social ones, are present in determining the structure and make-up of the psyche. Moreover, social influences as such incorporate points of indeterminacy. These are due to the instrumental autonomy of the conscious/rational ego, to the impossibility to predefine the actual choice and instinctual investment of internalizable objects, and finally to the radical indeterminacy implied by social reproduction through the level of the unconscious. The specific modality of the unconscious precludes any fully causal theory of its structuring and introduces the possibility of the emergence of the radically new, of the non-determined within the psyche. Consequently, the outcome of social reproduction through the psyche can never be fully determined. To this dynamic indeterminacy it has to be added the 'openness' implied by the impossibility to ever fully know how social elements internalized within the unconscious exist.

Thus a theorization of the social as 'open', a central concern of the tradition of thought exemplified in part 2 by Derrida, Laclau and Mouffe and, in a more developed way, by Castoriadis, can be derived from a theory of social reproduction through the psyche. No reduction of the social to the realm of ideas (as a probable interpretation of Laclau and Mouffe's work might suggest) is necessary, nor is the postulation of a transcendental level behind and beyond the positivity of the social (as Castoriadis's 'magma of social imaginary significations' may be taken to imply). Therefore the synthesis between the theorization of the social as 'open' and the direction theories of structuration indicate is indeed possible and fruitful, avoiding individual shortcomings while retaining their essential insights.

This synthesis constitutes, at the same time, a fully worked-out alternative to the structural/objectivist theories of the social which were a starting point for the present study. An overall structural framework is retained, but social-structural wholes are not seen as closed or as fully determinable but rather as inherently open. The questions of history and agency which were problematic for such approaches can now be more fruitfully addressed.

The points of indeterminacy within the processes of reproduction indicate that the emergence of the new in history can be theorized as necessarily and always inherent in social reproduction without any reference to teleological or otherwise deterministic models and without necessarily implying intentional action specifically aimed at social transformation. Precisely because of this indeterminacy, the autonomy of the individual – and hence of any collectivity – can be also affirmed, despite the deep and foundational role of social determinations/influences. Moreover, levels of autonomy can be discerned: a 'low' level of instrumental autonomy due to the conscious/rational ego as well as a 'high' level manifested necessarily through the conscious ego but due to the radical indeterminacy social reproduction through the unconscious implies. Thus the hypothesis advanced with respect to Marx's work in chapter 1 and taken up again in chapter 2 for a number of other authors can be seen to be justified: the theorization of a level of the social not reducible to either nature or consciousness is indeed central in overcoming the problems the questions of individual autonomy and historical change pose, such a level referring to the central role of the unconscious in processes of social reproduction.

At the same time a theorization of the specificity of social practice can be offered. Social practice, due to its being a locus of possible direct manifestations of unconscious determinants and due to the always 'meaningful' nature of the unconscious, can be theorized as always meaningful alongside and irrespective of conscious meanings associated with it. The level of practice can therefore be considered as having a specificity and effectivity distinct from that of discourse and ideas while always retaining a social 'meaning'. The foundation for a 'theory of practice' for which Bourdieu indicates the need and which is hinted at in the writings of many classical theorists is thus laid.

Conclusion

Finally, the acknowledgement of the existence of an unconscious dimension of the social allows certain inferences to be drawn regarding the mode of social knowledge. The unconscious dimension, underlying social phenomena but never directly accessible or unidimensional in its manifestations, implies the impossibility of any full, final or objective knowledge of the social in toto and introduces the necessity – and the theoretical foundation – for a radical hermeneutic approach.

The theoretical elements proposed provide thus a way out of traditional impasses and outline a possible alternative approach. The objectives drawn up in part 1 of the study regarding the questions of agency, history and social knowledge seem to have been largely met (along with the questions the theorization of social practice poses), while the hypotheses advanced prove to be fruitful. A model of social reproduction through the individual psyche is outlined and the existence and significance of an 'unconscious dimension of the social' is argued. On the way, the possibility of a synthesis between structuration theories and approaches advancing an open theory of the social is effected and the crucial significance of a specific interpretation of psychoanalytic theory is established. Of course, the above constitute only tentative steps on a path still largely unexplored, the general direction of which, however, has paradoxically been indicated long ago.

Bibliography

Adorno, T., 'Sociology and Psychology', *New Left Review*, no. 47, 1968

Althusser, L., 'Contradiction and Overdetermination' (1962), and 'Marxism and Humanism' (1965), in *For Marx*, Harmondsworth, 1969

——, 'Eléments d'autocritique' (1974), in *Essays in Self-Criticism*, London, 1976

——, 'Lenin and Philosophy' (1968), 'Lenin before Hegel' (1969), 'Ideology and Ideological State Apparatuses' (1970), and 'Freud and Lacan' (1969), in *Lenin and Philosophy*, London, 1977

——, 'The Object of Capital' (1968), and 'From Capital to Marx's Philosophy' (1968), in L. Althusser and E. Balibar, *Reading Capital*, London, 1970

Amin, S., *Accumulation on a World Scale*, Sussex, 1974

Anderson, P., *Arguments within English Marxism*, London, 1980

Archer, M., 'Morphogenesis vs. Structuration', *British Journal of Sociology*, vol. 33, no. 4, 1982

Balibar, E., 'The Basic Concepts of Historical Materialism', in L. Althusser and E. Balibar, *Reading Capital*, London, 1970

——, 'Sur la dialectique historique', in *Cinq études du matérialisme historique*, Paris, 1974

Balint, M., 'Critical Notes on the Theory of Pregenital Organisations of the Libido' (1935), and 'Early Developmental Stages of the Ego. Primary Object-love' (1937), in *Primary Love and Psychoanalytic Technique*, London, 1952

Barthes, R., *Mythologies* (1957), London, 1973

Baudrillard, J., *The Mirror of Production* (1968), St. Luis, 1975

Bernstein, B., 'Elaborated and Restricted Codes: Overview and Criticisms', in *The Structuring of Pedagogic Discourse*, vol. 4 of *Class, Codes and Control*, London, 1992

Bhaskar, R., *The Possibility of Naturalism*, London, 1989

Blumer, H., 'Society as Symbolic Interaction', in A.M. Rose (ed.), *Human Behaviour and Social Processes*, London, 1962

Bourdieu, P., *Distinction: A Social Critique of the Judgement of Taste* (1979), London, 1984

———, *The Logic of Practice* (1980), Cambridge, 1990
———, *Homo Academicus* (1984), Cambridge, 1988
———, *Outline of a Theory of Practice*, Cambridge, 1977
———, 'The Social Space and the Genesis of Groups', *Theory and Society*, vol. 14, no. 6, 1985
Bourdieu, P. and Passeron, J.C., *Reproduction in Education, Society and Culture* (1970), London, 1977
Buckley, W., *Sociology and Modern Systems Theory*, New Jersey, 1967
Castoriadis, C., 'Fait et à faire', in G. Busino *et al.*, *Autonomie et autotransformation de la société: La philosophie militante de C. Castoriadis*, Genève, 1989
———, *The Imaginary Institution of Society* (1975), Cambridge, 1987
———, 'Modern Science and Philosophical Interrogation' (1973), and 'Value, Equality, Justice, Politics: From Marx to Aristotle and from Aristotle to Ourselves' (1975), in *Crossroads in the Labyrinth*, Brighton, 1984
———, 'Power, Politics, Autonomy' (1988), in *Philosophy, Politics, Autonomy*, Oxford, 1990
———, 'Psychanalyse et politique' (1987), in *Le monde morcelé*, Paris, 1990
———, 'Le régime social de la Russie' (1978), 'La logique des magmas et la question de l'autonomie' (1981), and 'Institution de la société et religion' (1982), in *Domaines de l'homme*, Paris, 1986
———, 'The State of the Subject Today' (1986), translation in *Thesis Eleven*, no. 24, 1989
Chodorow, N., 'Beyond Drive Theory: Object Relations and the Limits of Radical Individualism', *Theory and Society*, no. 14, 1985
———, *The Reproduction of Mothering*, Los Angeles, 1978
Chomsky, N., *Language and Mind*, New York, 1972
Cohen, G.A., *K. Marx's Theory of History: a Defence*, Oxford, 1978
Collins, R., 'Interaction Ritual Chains, Power and Property: the Micro-Macro Connection as an Empirically Based Theoretical Problem', in J. Alexander (ed.), *The Micro-Macro Link*, Berkeley, 1987
———, 'On the Micro-foundations of Macro-sociology', *American Journal of Sociology*, vol. 86, 1981
Comte, A., *Physique sociale* (lessons 46–60 of *Cours de philosophie positive* (1830–42), Paris, 1975
Cutler, A., Hindess, B., Hirst, P. and Hussain, A., *Marx's Capital and Capitalism Today*, 2 vols, London, 1977
Deleuze, G. and Guatari, F., *Anti-Oedipus* (1972), London, 1984
Derrida, J., 'The Ends of Man' (1968), and 'Différance' (1968), in *Margins of Philosophy*, Brighton, 1982
———, '"Genesis and Structure" and Phenomenology' (1959),

'Structure, Sign and Play in the Discourse of the Human Sciences' (1966), and 'Freud and the Scene of Writing' (1966), in *Writing and Difference*, London, 1978

——, *Of Grammatology* (1967), Baltimore, 1976

——, *Positions* (1972), London, 1987

Dews, P., *Logics of Disintegration*, London, 1987

Dickson, D., *Alternative Technology and the Politics of Technical Change*, London, 1974

Dilthey, W., *Selected Writings*, H. Rickman (ed.), Cambridge, 1976

DiMaggio, P., 'Review Essay on P. Bourdieu', *American Journal of Sociology*, vol. 84, no. 6, 1979

Dinnerstein, D., *The Rocking of the Cradle and the Ruling of the World*, London, 1976 (Published in the United States as *The Mermaid and the Minotaur*)

Durkheim, E., *The Division of Labour in Society* (1893), London, 1984

——, *Elementary Forms of Religious Life* (1912), London, 1961

——, *The Rules of Sociological Method* (1901), London, 1982

——, 'Individual and Collective Representations' (1898), in E. Durkheim, *Sociology and Philosophy*, London, 1953

Elliot, A., *Social Theory and Psychoanalysis in Transition*, London, 1992

Elster, J., *Making Sense of Marx*, Cambridge, 1985

——, *Nuts and Bolts for the Social Sciences*, Cambridge, 1989

Erikson, E., 'The Problem of Ego Identity' (1956), in *Identity and the Life Cycle*, New York, 1980

Fairbairn, R.D., 'Object Relationships and Dynamic Structure' (1946), and 'A Synopsis of the Development of the Author's Views Regarding the Structure of the Personality' (1951), in *Psychoanalytic Studies of the Personality*, London, 1952

Foucault, M., *The Archaeology of Knowledge* (1969), London, 1972

——, *Discipline and Punish* (1975), Harmondsworth, 1979

——, 'What Is an Author?' and 'What Is Enlightenment?' in P. Rabinow (ed.), *The Foucault Reader*, Harmondsworth, 1986

——, *The Order of Things* (1966), London, 1974

Freud, S., *Beyond the Pleasure Principle* (1920), Penguin/Pelican Freud Library (P.F.L.) 11, Harmondsworth, 1984. The edition used for Freud's works is the Penguin/Pelican Freud Library (P.F.L.) in fifteen volumes which is a reprint of the Standard Edition in paperback form.

——, *Civilization and Its Discontents* (1929), P.F.L. 12, Harmondsworth, 1985

——, *The Ego and the Id* (1923), P.F.L. 11, Harmondsworth, 1984

——, 'The Dissolution of the Oedipus Complex' (1924), and 'Some

Psychical Consequences of the Anatomical Distinction Between the Sexes' (1925), in P.F.L. 7, Harmondsworth, 1977

——, *The Future of an Illusion* (1927), P.F.L. 12, Harmondsworth, 1985

——, *Group Psychology and the Analysis of the Ego* (1921), P.F.L. 12, Harmondsworth, 1985

——, *Inhibitions, Symptoms and Anxiety* (1926), P.F.L. 10, Harmondsworth, 1979

——, 'Instincts and Their Vicissitudes' (1915), P.F.L. 11, Harmondsworth, 1984

——, *The Interpretation of Dreams* (1900), Penguin/Pelican Freud Library (P.F.L.) 4, Harmondsworth, 1976.

——, 'Mourning and Melancholia' (1915), P.F.L. 11, Harmondsworth, 1984

——, *New Introductory Lectures on Psychoanalysis* (1933), P.F.L. 2, Harmondsworth, 1973

——, 'Obsessive Actions and Religious Practices' (1907), P.F.L. 13, Harmondsworth, 1985

——, 'On Narcissism: An Introduction' (1914), P.F.L. 11, Harmondsworth, 1984

——, 'An Outline of Psychoanalysis' (1938), P.F.L. 15, Harmondsworth, 1986

——, 'Repression' (1915), P.F.L. 11, Harmondsworth, 1984

——, *Three Essays on the Theory of Sexuality* (1905), P.F.L. 7, Harmondsworth, 1977

——, *Totem and Taboo* (1913), P.F.L. 13, Harmondsworth, 1985

——, 'The Unconscious' (1915), P.F.L. 11, Harmondsworth, 1984

Fromm, E., *The Sane Society*, London, 1956

Gadamer, H.G., *Truth and Method*, London, 1979

Gane, M., 'Giddens and the Crisis of Social Theory', *Economy and Society*, vol. 12, no. 3, 1983

Garfinkel, H., 'What Is Ethnomethodology?'(1967), in *Studies in Ethnomethodology* (1968), Cambridge, 1984

Geras, N., 'Post Marxism?', *New Left Review*, no. 163, 1987

Gashe, R., *The Tain of the Mirror*, Cambridge, 1986

Giddens, A., *Central Problems in Social Theory*, London, 1979

——, *The Constitution of Society*, Cambridge, 1984

——, *The Nation-state and Violence*, Cambridge, 1985

——, *New Rules of Sociological Method*, London, 1976

——, *Profiles and Critiques in Social Theory*, London, 1982

——, *Studies in Social and Political Theory*, London, 1979

Glucksmann, A., 'A Ventriloquist Structuralism' (1967), *New Left Review*, no. 72, 1972

Godelier, M., *The Mental and the Material* (1984), London, 1986

Goffman, E., *The Presentation of Self in Everyday Life*, New York, 1959

Goldmann, L., 'Structuralisme, marxisme, existentialisme', *Praxis*, no. 8, 1966

Gunthrip, H., *Personality Structure and Human Interaction*, London, 1961

Habermas, J., *The Philosophical Discourse of Modernity* (1985), Cambridge, 1990

———, *The Theory of Communicative Action* (1981), 2 vols, Cambridge, 1987

Hartman, H., 'Comments on the Psychoanalytic Theory of the Ego' (1952), in *Essays on Ego Psychology*, London, 1964

———, *Ego Psychology and the Problem of Adaptation* (1938), New York, 1958

Hindess, B. and Hirst, P., *Pre-Capitalist Modes of Production*, London, 1975

Honneth, A., 'The Fragmented World of Symbolic Forms: Reflections on P. Bourdieu's Sociology of Culture', *Theory, Culture and Society*, vol. 3, no. 3, 1986

Hunter, A., 'Post-Marxism and the New Social Movements', *Theory and Society*, no. 17, 1988

Husserl, E., *Cartesian Meditations* (1931), Dordrecht, 1960

———, *The Crisis of European Sciences and Transcendental Phenomenology* (1954), Evanston, 1970

Illich, I., *Deschooling Society* (1971), Harmondsworth, 1976

Jacobson, E., *The Self and Object World*, London, 1964

Jenkins, R., 'Pierre Bourdieu and the Reproduction of Determinism', *Sociology*, vol. 31, 1982

Jung, C.G., 'Instinct and the Unconscious' (1919), and 'On the Nature of the Psyche' (1947), in *Collected Works*, vol. 8, London, 1960

———, 'Archetypes of the Collective Unconscious' (1954), in *Collected Works*, vol. 9, Part 1, London, 1959

Kernberg, O., *Object Relations Theory and Clinical Psychoanalysis*, New York, 1976

Klein, M., 'The Importance of Symbol-Formation in the Development of the Ego' (1930), in M. Klein, *Love, Guilt and Reparation: Works 1921–1945*, London, 1988

———, 'Some Theoretical Conclusions Regarding the Emotional Life of the Infant' (1952), in M. Klein, *Envy and Gratitude: Works 1946–1963*, London, 1988

Lacan, J., 'Aggressivity in Psychoanalysis' (1948), 'The Function and Field of Speech and Language in Psychoanalysis' (1953), 'On a

Question Preliminary to Any Possible Treatment of Psychosis'
(1958), and 'The Direction of Treatment and the Principles of Its
Power' (1958), in *Ecrits: A Selection*, London, 1977
——, 'Remarque sur le rapport de D. Lagache' (1961), in *Ecrits*, Paris,
1966
Laclau, E., 'New Reflections on the Revolution of Our Time', in *New
Reflections on the Revolution of Our Time*, London, 1990
——, *Politics and Ideology in Marxist Theory*, London, 1977
Laclau, E. and Mouffe, C., *Hegemony and Socialist Strategy*, London,
1985
——, 'Post Marxism without Apologies', *New Left Review*, no. 166,
1987
Laplanche, J., *Life and Death in Psychoanalysis* (1970), Baltimore,
1977
——, *New Foundations for Psychoanalysis*, Oxford, 1989
Laplanche, J. and Leclaire, S., 'The Unconscious: A Psychoanalytic
Study' (1961), *Yale French Studies*, no. 48, 1972
Laplanche, J. and Pontalis, J.B., 'Fantasy and the Origins of
Sexuality', *The International Journal of Psychoanalysis*, vol. 49,
1968
——, *The Language of Psychoanalysis* (1967), London, 1988
Lasch, C., *The Culture of Narcissism*, New York, 1979
——, *Heaven in a Heartless World: the Family Besieged*, New York,
1977.
——, *The Minimal Self*, London, 1985
Leach, E., *Lévi-Strauss*, London, 1970
Lefort, C., 'The Image of the Body and Totalitarianism' (1979), and
'The Logic of Totalitarianism' (1980), in *The Political Forms of
Modern Society*, Cambridge, 1986
Lévi-Strauss, C., *The Elementary Structures of Kinship* (1949),
Boston, 1969
——, 'Introduction to the Work of M. Mauss', in M. Mauss, *Sociologie
et anthropologie*, Paris, 1950
——, *Myth and Meaning*, London, 1978
——, 'Structural Analysis in Linguistics and Anthropology' (1945),
'Language and the Analysis of Social Laws' (1951), and 'Social
Structure' (1952), in *Structural Anthropology I*, London, 1968
Lorenz, K., *On Aggression*, London, 1976
Luhmann, N., 'The Differentiation of Society' (1977), in *The
Differentiation of Society*, New York, 1982
Lukacs, G., 'Class Consciousness' (1920), in *History and Class
Consciousness*, London, 1971
Mahler, M. *et al.*, *The Psychological Birth of the Human Infant*,

London, 1975

Marcuse, H., *Eros and Civilisation* (1956), London, 1987

Marx, K., ——, *Capital* (1867), 3 vols, Lawrence and Wishart, London, 1954. See volume 1 in the Penguin edition (Harmondsworth, 1976) for the unpublished chapter.

——, Preface to 'A contribution to a critique of political economy' (1859), in K. Marx and F. Engels, *Selected Works*, 2 vols, vol. 1, London, 1953

——, 'General Introduction to Grundrisse' (1857), appendix to *The German Ideology*, C.J. Arthur (ed.), London, 1974

——, *Grundrisse* (1858), D. Mclellan (ed.), London, 1980

——, 'On the Jewish Question' (1843), and *Economic and Philosophic Manuscripts of 1844*, in K. Marx and F. Engels, *Collected Works*, vol. 3, London, 1975

Marx, K. and Engels, F., *The German Ideology* (1846), C.J. Arthur (ed.), London, 1974

Mead, G.H., *Mind, Self and Society*, C. Morris (ed.), Chicago, 1962

Merton, R., 'Manifest and Latent Functions' (1948), in *Social Theory and Social Structure*, Glencoe, 1963

Mill, J.S., *A System of Logic* (1843), London, 1967

Miller, P.B., *Domination and Power*, London, 1987

Mouzelis, N., *Back to Sociological Theory*, London, 1991

——, 'Marxism or Post-Marxism?', *New Left Review*, no. 167, 1988

Pareto, V., *The Mind and Society: A Treatise on General Sociology* (1916), 2 vols, New York, 1963

Parsons, T., 'A Paradigm of the Human Condition', in *Action Theory and the Human Condition*, New York, 1978

——, 'Psychoanalysis and the Social Structure' (1948), in *Essays in Sociological Theory*, New York, 1954

——, *The Social System*, London, 1951

——, 'Some Problems of General Theory in Sociology' (1970), in *Social Systems and the Evolution of Action Theory*, New York, 1977

——, *The Structure of Social Action* (1937), New York, 1968

——, 'Superego and the Theory of Social Systems' (1952), and 'Social Structure and the Development of Personality' (1958), in *Social Structure and Personality*, London, 1964

Parsons, T., Bales, R. *et al.*, *Family, Socialisation and Interaction Process*, London, 1956

Parsons, T. *et al.*, 'Some Fundamental Categories in the Theory of Action', in T. Parsons and E. Shills (eds), *Towards a General Theory of Action* (1951), New York, 1962

——, *Working Papers in the Theory of Action*, New York, 1953

Passineti, L., *Lectures on the Theory of Production*, London, 1977

Piaget, J. and Inhelder, B., *The Psychology of the Child* (1966), London, 1969

Rawls, J., *A Theory of Justice*, Oxford, 1972

Ricœur, P., *Freud and Philosophy*, New Haven, 1970

——, 'Image and Language in Psychoanalysis' (1976), in J. Smith (ed.) *Psychoanalysis and Language: Psychiatry and the Humanities*, vol. 3, New Haven, 1978

——, 'Structure and Hermeneutics' (1963), and 'Structure, Word, Event' (1967), in *The Conflict of Interpretations*, Evanston, 1974

Roemer, J., *A General Theory of Exploitation and Class*, Cambridge, 1982

——, (ed.), *Analytical Marxism*, Cambridge, 1986

Rousseau, J.-J., 'Discourse on the Origin of Inequality' (1755), and 'Social Contract' (1762), in *The Social Contract*, London, 1973

——, *Emile: or, On Education*, New York, 1979

Ryan, M., *Marxism and Deconstruction*, Baltimore, 1982

Saussure, F. de, *Course in General Linguistics* (1916), London, 1974

Savage, S., *The Theories of T. Parsons*, London, 1981

Segal, H., 'Notes on Symbol Formation' (1957), in *The Work of Hanna Segal*, New York, 1981

Shutz, A., 'Common-Sense and Scientific Interpretation of Human Action' (1953), in *Collected Papers I*, The Hague, 1962

——, *The Phenomenology of the Social World* (1932), London, 1972

——, 'Some Structures of the Life-World', in *Collected Papers III*, The Hague, 1970

Schutz, A. and Parsons, T., *The Correspondence of A. Schutz and T. Parsons*, R.H. Grathoff (ed.), Bloomington, 1978

Smith, A., *An Inquiry into the Nature and Causes of the Wealth of Nations* (1784), Indianapolis, 1976

Sohn-Rethel, A., *Intellectual and Manual Labour*, London, 1978

Spencer, H., *First Principles* (1862), in H. Spencer, *Structure, Function and Evolution*, S. Adreski (ed.), London, 1971

——, *Principles of Sociology*, vol. 1 (1876), S. Adreski (ed.), London, 1969.

Thompson, E.P., 'The Poverty of Theory', in *The Poverty of Theory and Other Essays*, London, 1978

Thompson, J., *Studies in the Theory of Ideology*, Cambridge, 1984

Timpanaro, S., *On Materialism*, London, 1975

Vico, G., *The New Science* (1744), Ithaca, 1948

Watkins, J., 'Ideal Types and Historical Explanation' (1952), 'Historical Explanation in the Social Sciences' (1957), and 'Methodological Individualism: a Reply' (1955), in J. O'Neil (ed.), *Modes of Individualism and Collectivism*, London, 1973

Weber, M., *Economy and Society*, Berkeley, 1978
Whyte, L., *The Unconscious before Freud*, London, 1962
Williams, R., *Keywords*, London, 1988
Winnicot, D.W., 'Ego Integration in Child development' (1962), in *Collected Papers II (The Maturational Process and the Facilitating Environment)*, London, 1965
——, 'Transitional Objects and Transitional Phenomena' (1951), in *Collected Papers I (Through Paediatrics to Psychoanalysis)*, London, 1975
Wood, E.M., *The Retreat from Class*, London, 1986
Zizek, S., 'Beyond Discourse Analysis' (1987), in E. Laclau, *New Reflections on the Revolution of Our Time*
——, *The Sublime Object of Ideology*, London, 1989

Index

adulthood 155–7, 170–3, 180
  rational adaptation in adolescence and
    adulthood 169–70
Althusser, Louis 47, 55, 58–65, 66
  ideology 64
  imaginary field ideology 68, 171, 193
  material practices 203
  rejection of transhistoricity 58–65
  science-ideology as theoreticism 62–3
  society as structural wholes 199
  structural causality 60–1
Anderson, Perry 200
Aristotle
  Politics 24
Austin, John 105
autonomy 1
  affirmation of possibility 114–16
  Althusser 63–4
  Bourdieu 91–2
  Castoriadis 113–14
  Giddens stresses 77
  and history 2, 200
  indeterminacy 195–6
  instrumental 197
  Laclau and Mouffe 106
  levels of 119–20, 190, 210
  model of social reproduction 190
  political not civil 18
  radical imagination 197–8
  social reproduction theory 196–8, 210

Balibar, Etienne 59–60
Baudrillard, Jean 21
behaviourism 29
Bernstein, B. 170
Bourdieu, Pierre 82–92
  active agency 197
  changed view of concept of the social
    25
  habitus 82–4, 86–8, 90–1, 189, 203
  identity 83–5
  kinship 85–6
  logic of practice 82, 88–91, 121, 194,
    196, 202, 203
  open theory of the social 196
  transcending subjectivism 91–2

Braudel, Ferdinand 58

Cantor, Georg 109
Capital (Marx) 11–15, 17, 21, 59, 60–1
capitalism 117
Castoriadis, Cornelius 68, 108–21, 195–
  6, 199
  autonomy 186, 196
  ensemblist-identitary logic 108–11
  history 196
  influence on social reproduction
    theory 208
  labour as a substance/essence 14
  modality of magmas 117–21
  openness of the social 93, 118–21
  opposition between individual and
    social 113, 179
  originary phantasmatization 131–2
  radical imagination 164
  social imaginary significations 110–13,
    116, 117–21, 121, 189, 190–1, 193
  social representation and social doing
    109–11, 118, 166
Chodorow, N. 181, 182
Chomsky, Noam 71
Christianity 24
civil society 18
class structure 25–6
Comte, Auguste 29, 199
  three stages of human mind 34–5
consciousness
  cognition 169
  communication with unconscious
    134–7
  forms of 9
  Husserl's ego cogito 38
  instrumental/rational dimension 205
  Marx on 20–2, 22
  practical 75–6, 80–1
  rational adaptation in adolescence and
    adulthood 169–70
  social reproduction theory 208
  social-symbolic universe 166
  and thought as rational 20
Course in General Linguistics (Saussure)
  55

– 221 –

Index

Index

Index

structural/functional approach 54
structural objectivism 66–7
The Structure of Social Action 41, 51–2, 55
transhistoricism 67
voluntarist theory of action 50
Pascal, Blaise 171
The Phenomenology of the Social World (Schutz) 41
philosophy
  ancient concept of society 23, 24
  Enlightenment 18, 19, 24–5
Piaget, Jean 153, 169
politics 10–11
  features of monarch/king and God 180
  Giddens on nation-state 78–9
  modern polity versus monarch 18
Politics (Aristotle) 24
positivism 27–34, 199
post-structuralism 68
production
  Althusser on Marx 58–61, 64
  determines social whole 14–15
  ideas 7–10
  Marx's analysis in *Capital* 21
  organization 8–10
  pure economic exploitation 16
  structured whole of capitalism 11–12, 20
psyche *see also* unconscious
  adulthood 155–7, 159
  Castoriadis 111–13, 116, 119
  ego and super-ego never a coherent whole 183–4
  environmental influences 168–70, 196–7
  Freud's theory 51–2, 143–8
  indeterminacy 161–5
  instincts and drives 138–43
  irreducible to social 186
  later theories of ego development 148–53
  psychoanalytic theory 174
  representations 181–2
  social needs of 179–80
  structured wholes 157–61, 191
  structuring 155–61
psychoanalytic theory 68 *see also* psyche; unconscious
  Castoriadis 111–13, 116
  Freud's followers on civilization and drives 177–8
  levels of autonomy 196
  psychoanalysis as socialization 182
  reaches limits at unconscious 163–4

representatives 127–9
  and social theory 1
psychology
  experimental 29

rationalism 20, 47–50, 66, 67
Reich, Wilhelm 177
religion 180
representations 127–9, 166–7, 192–3
  Freud 132–6
  symbols 181–2
Ricardo, David 11, 26
Ricoeur, Paul 71, 128
roles
  Bourdieu 85
  expectation 51–2
  sex roles 182
Rousseau, Jean-Jacques
  social contract 11
  society as a burden 24

Sartre, Jean-Paul 86
de Saussure, Ferdinand
  Course in General Linguistics 55
  definition of structure 57–8
  differential notion of structure 62
Schutz, Alfred 38, 39–42, 80
  ideal types 39–40, 41
  lifeworld 40–2, 45
set theory 109, 110
Smith, Adam 11, 25–6, 34
social reproduction theory
  autonomy 190, 196–8, 210
  determinism 200–1
  environmental influences 196–7
  hermeneutics 206–7
  history 198–201
  indeterminacy 189–91
  model of 187–91
  openness 190–1, 200–1, 209–10
  processes 208–10
  social practice 201–4, 210
  unconscious 210–11
social structure
  determined by production 14–15
  openness 2–3
  political and legal superstructure 10–11
  social power versus political power 18
  unconscious 2–3
The Social System (Parsons) 53
society and the social
  as a burden 24
  holistic study within positivism 31–4
  individual and 24, 71–2, 178–9

– 225 –